The Princeton Review®

Cracking the AP® PSYCHOLOGY Exam

2013 Edition

The Staff of The Princeton Review
Updated by Laura Talamo

PrincetonReview.com

Random House, Inc. New York

The Princeton Review, Inc.
111 Speen Street, Suite 550
Framingham, MA 01701
E-mail: editorialsupport@review.com

ISBN: 978-0-307-94517-4
ISSN: 1546-9093

Editor: Meave Shelton
Production Editor: Kristen Harding

Printed in the United States of America on
partially recycled paper.

10 9 8 7 6 5 4 3 2 1

2013 Edition

Editorial

Robert Franek, Senior VP, Publisher
Laura Braswell, Senior Editor
Selena Coppock, Senior Editor
Calvin Cato, Editor
Meave Shelton, Editor

Production

Michael Pavese, Publishing Director
Kathy Carter, Project Editor
Michelle Krapf, Editor
Michael Mazzei, Editor
Michael Breslosky, Associate Editor
Stephanie Tantum, Associate Editor
Kristen Harding, Associate Editor
Vince Bonavoglia, Artist
Danielle Joyce, Graphic Designer

Random House Publishing Team

Tom Russell, Publisher
Nicole Benhabib, Publishing Director
Ellen L. Reed, Production Manager
Alison Stoltzfus, Managing Editor

ACKNOWLEDGMENTS

The staff of The Princeton Review would like to give special thanks to Daniel McNickle for his excellent
work on the latest revision of this book.

CONTENTS

Part III: The Princeton Review AP Psychology Practice Tests   229

Introduction

WHAT IS THE PRINCETON REVIEW?

The Princeton Review is an international test-preparation company with branches in all major U.S. cities and several abroad. In 1981, John Katzman started teaching an SAT prep course in his parents' living room. Within five years, The Princeton Review had become the largest SAT prep program in the country.

Our phenomenal success in improving students' scores on standardized tests is due to a simple, innovative, and radically effective philosophy: Study the test, not just what the test claims to test. This approach has led to the development of techniques for taking standardized tests based on the principles the test writers themselves use to write the tests.

The Princeton Review has found that its methods work not just for cracking the SAT, but for any standardized test. We've already successfully applied our system to the GMAT, LSAT, MCAT, and GRE, to name just a few. Obviously, you need to be well versed in psychology to do well on the AP Psychology Exam, but you should remember that any standardized test is partly a measure of your ability to think like the people who write standardized tests. This book will help you brush up on your AP Psychology and prepare for the exam using our time-tested principle: Crack the system based on how the test is created.

We also offer books and online services that cover an enormous variety of education and career-related topics. If you're interested, check out our website at PrincetonReview.com.

HOW CAN WE HELP?

This book will help you beat the AP Psychology Exam by providing you with

- a complete yet compact review of the concepts tested on the exam

- the strategies you need to crack the test and score your best

- practice tests to help you master your AP strategy

COMPACT REVIEW

Your AP course work most likely covers lots of important concepts. With a whole year's worth of material, how can you tell what to study for the AP exam? We eliminate the guesswork for you, because in this book we provide a thorough yet concise review of all the topics tested on the AP Psych Exam. You see, when a teacher puts a course together, the goal is to help you learn and understand as much psychology as possible. Therefore, a good teacher will supplement the basics of the course with contemporary examples and other interesting illustrations to make the course more relevant. Although this is arguably the best way to teach a subject, it is not the best way to prepare for a standardized exam.

This book, unlike your course in school, has been put together strictly for the purpose of AP Psychology Exam preparation: We focus only on the topics you need to know to do well on the AP Psych Exam.

STRATEGIES

As you work through the first few chapters in this book, you will learn specific strategies about how to do better on this test. We're not saying that you can't do well on this exam if you don't know the difference between Pavlov's dog and Lassie, but we will teach you strategies that will stretch (and sometimes even go beyond) your knowledge of psychology to help you score points.

PRACTICE TESTS

This book also contains two full-length practice tests that are extremely close—both in format and question type—to the actual AP Psychology Exam. Work through these tests and use the explanations that are provided to learn why each of the answer choices is right or wrong. If you ace these practice tests, you can feel pretty confident that you'll do well on the real thing in May. So, let's get cracking!

PART I

Cracking the System

1

About the AP
Psychology Exam

THE SMART TESTER

Taking a standardized exam introduces a whole new dimension of testing that is not present in a regular, teacher-generated exam. The process of developing an AP test is led by a committee (designated by the College Board) that works closely with test development specialists at Educational Testing Service (ETS). Now, you might say to yourself, "ETS? You mean the SAT people?" Yup—they have their hand in this test, too. So, unlike your teacher's exams, this test has all the expertise (aka the traps) of major standardized exams.

The good news is that we know how to dissect the AP Psych Exam. The Princeton Review has been cracking open standardized tests for years. So you have the experts at your service. This book will teach you how to approach each question to avoid careless errors, and how to handle issues such as time pressure and guessing. You'll even learn techniques to help crack a question about which you know only a smidgen of information. In short, working through this book will turn you into a smarter tester.

Smart-Tester Strategies

There are several things the smart tester knows about taking a standardized exam. Here's an overview.

Know Your Exam

Smart testers never go blindly into an exam. They first learn all they can about the test. So, smart tester, here's what you need to know.

Structure of the Exam

The AP Psychology Exam is divided into two sections with the following time allotments:

→ Section I—multiple-choice

100 questions . . . . 70 minutes

→ Section II—free-response

2 essay questions . . . . 50 minutes

All AP exams are administered during the second week of May. The exams, which cost $87 each, are administered by schools and are given either in the morning (beginning by 8:00 or 9:00 A.M.) or the afternoon (beginning by 12:00 P.M.). Call the College Board at (866) 630-9305, go to its website (www.collegeboard.com), or check with your guidance counselor to find out when your AP Psychology Exam will be administered and to answer any questions about accommodations for special needs, late testing, grade recipients, scheduling more than one AP test, etc. You should begin your registration process no later than early March. Grades can be accessed by phone in early July.

Section I

As you already know, Section I of the AP Psychology Exam contains 100 multiple-choice questions. You have 70 minutes to complete the section, and your Section I score counts for approximately two-thirds of your overall AP Psychology grade.

If you did a double-take when you saw that you are given only 70 minutes to do 100 questions, take a deep breath. Although having less than a minute per question poses a definite challenge, knowing certain techniques will make this severe time constraint seem much less daunting.

What Do They Want to Know?

The multiple-choice questions in Section I cover the fourteen main areas of psychology taught in most AP courses.

- History (2–4%)

- Methods and Approaches (6–8%)

- Biological Bases of Behavior (8–10%)

- Sensation and Perception (7–9%)

- States of Consciousness (2–4%)

- Learning (7–9%)

- Cognition (8–10%)

- Motivation and Emotion (7–9%)

- Developmental Psychology (7–9%)

- Personality (6–8%)

- Testing and Individual Differences (5–7%)

- Abnormal Psychology (7–9%)

- Treatment of Psychological Disorders (5–7%)

- Social Psychology (7–9%)

Notice that we have divided the review portion of this book into exactly those chapters for your convenience. Again, by focusing strictly on psychology as it's tested by the AP exam, we'll teach you what you need to know to make the grade.

Section II

Section II of the AP Psychology Exam consists of two free-response questions (aka essays). They each count for the same percentage of your grade and you must answer both. Section II counts for approximately one-third of your AP Psychology grade.

You have 50 minutes to complete BOTH essays—again, take a deep breath. Chapter 3 will teach you strategies so that you can be a smart essay writer. Plus, you will have several opportunities to practice writing essays before exam day. Use your tools and your practice tests to master this portion of your AP test. When the time comes, you will have all the tools you need to create high-scoring essays in a limited period of time.

Order of Difficulty

Why is it that whenever you take a multiple-choice test, you start out feeling as though you are doing well but then the questions grow increasingly difficult until you can't do them anymore? Is it you? Or is it the test?

It most certainly is not you. Most standardized tests, including Section I of the AP Psychology Exam, are arranged in a rough order of difficulty—in other words, the questions start out easy, and become progressively harder. We'll discuss this in more detail in Chapter 2.

Efficiently and Effectively

To score your personal best on the AP Psych Exam, you need to work efficiently and effectively. Working efficiently means working at a comfortable, directed pace—not fast, not too slow. Working effectively means getting as many questions right as you can and *not* losing points because of careless errors. As you practice the strategies for Section I of the exam, you will develop your own pace. You need to determine what working efficiently and effectively means for *you* so that you can score your personal best. Don't worry about what the kid sitting next to you is doing—take your own test and do the best you can.

But If I Don't Finish...

Lots of people think that they must answer every question to do well on an exam. Although that might be true on a school test, it is not true on a standardized test like the multiple-choice section of the AP Psychology Exam. We'll go into more detail about this issue in the next chapter, but for now just remember to slow down, be more accurate, and raise your score.

Process of Elimination

On Section I, four out of every five answer choices you read will be wrong. That's a lot of wrong answers to wade through. Instead of reading each question and trying to find the right answer from a sea of wrong choices, you may need to use Process of Elimination (POE). In other words, you need to get rid of wrong answer choices and choose from what's left. Look at the following example:

1. Of the following words, which is Norwegian?
   (A) Mommy
   (B) Daddy
   (C) Dog
   (D) Cat
   (E) Takk

Now, maybe you know a little Norwegian, and maybe you don't. Either way, did you have any trouble answering this question? Of course not. You were easily able to eliminate (A) through (D) because they are English, not Norwegian, making (E) the only plausible answer. Even though this example is over-simplified, the basic principle holds true: It often is easier to eliminate what is wrong than to find what is right. Use POE, and you will dramatically increase your score (see Chapter 2 for all the details of how to use this powerful technique).

Should I Guess?

Beginning with the May 2011 exam, AP exams in all subjects will no longer include a "guessing penalty" of –1/4 of a point for every incorrect answer. Instead, students will be assessed only on the total number of correct questions. A lot of AP materials, even those you receive in your AP class, may not include this information. It is really important to remember that if you are running out of time, you need to fill in all the bubbles before the time for the multiple-choice section is up. Even if you do not plan to spend a lot of time on every question, and even if you have no idea what the correct answer is, you need to fill something in.

PRACTICE TESTS

Even the College Board agrees that the single most effective way to prepare for a test like this one is to take practice exams. Doing some trial runs prior to the actual test will reduce your anxiety, bolster your confidence, and help you identify the areas that you need to work on. It will also help you overcome obstacles such as time constraints and question difficulty. This book includes two full AP Psychology practice tests, plus answers and explanations for your review. In addition, we strongly encourage you to order the 2007 *AP Psychology Released Exam* booklet from the College Board. These booklets provide the only available copies of real AP Psychology Exams that include the multiple-choice section of the test. For more help with the free-response section, you should check out **www.collegeboard.com**, where you can access the actual free-response questions and scoring guides from the past few years.

HOW TO DO WELL

How can you achieve your personal best score on the AP Psychology Exam? You've already taken the first step by purchasing this book. All the tools you need are in the pages of this book: AP Psychology review, smart-tester multiple-choice strategies, smart-tester essay strategies, drills, and practice tests. Work through the book, review your class notes and textbook, and you will be on your way to getting a great score.

JUST DO IT

At the end of this chapter you will find worksheets to help you plan out your study schedule. It is essential that you set aside some time at regular intervals to study for the AP Psych Exam.

We know that you have a lot going on: school work, activities, maybe jobs. However, the AP Psych Exam needs to make the priority list for a short, but critical, period of time. Think of it this way—if you do well on your AP Psychology Exam, you'll have the potential to:

1. Begin college with course credits already under your belt

2. Place out of this course in college

3. Save tuition money by not taking an introductory psych course

If you make the best use of your study time now, you'll see big rewards later on.

You Know More Than You Think You Do

Too often students are scared off by a question simply because they cannot spew out the textbook version of the answer. Do not underestimate your knowledge. In Section I of the test, all the textbook answers are given to you as answer choices—you just need to find the right one. Stretch your knowledge using the techniques, and you will be amazed at how much psychology you know!

USE IT LIKE IT IS

The best way to work through this book is to do it in order, a chapter at a time. You will be learning cumulatively as you go through the book, so it's best not to skip around too much.

Throughout the book, you'll also find Test Breaks: multiple-choice strategy drills at the end of a subject-review chapter. You need to practice your strategies continually to make them second nature—these drills will help you do just that.

OTHER PRACTICE

We also recommend that you use one of the two practice tests in this book as a "drill test." Go to Practice Test 1 intermittently and practice some of the strategies you have learned. Do a "timed drill" of ten easy questions, then ten medium questions. Or, after completing a subject-review chapter, go to the test and find all the questions related to that subject.

Note: Do not attempt to do any of the multiple-choice questions before you have completed Chapter 2. You will be wasting your time by doing questions before you know how to approach them. If you do use Practice Test 1 as a drill test, be sure to order a released exam from the College Board so that you will have two full practice tests to take under timed conditions. See the Practice Test section for guidelines on how to take timed exams effectively.

BUT I ONLY HAVE TWO WEEKS!

Attention, crammers: Practice every day!

So your exam is in two weeks and you thought you'd better start reviewing. Although this is not the best way to do it, here is the "Crammer's Review" method of prep.

- Order the 2007 *AP Psychology Released Exam* from the College Board and have it rush delivered to you.

- Flip to the end of each subject-review chapter and take the review quiz.

- Based on your performance, review the necessary psychology material in each chapter.

- Work through Chapters 2 and 3 thoroughly.

- Take the Test Breaks.

- Do short, timed intervals and other drills on Practice Test 1.

- Take Practice Test 2 and the 2007 exam; time yourself.

THE BOTTOM LINE

How will you do well on the AP Psychology Exam? Familiarize yourself with the test, review AP Psychology, learn smart-testing strategies, and take some practice tests. Set up a realistic practice plan for yourself and stick to it. Good luck!

2

Cracking the
Multiple-Choice Section

In this chapter we'll review some of the tips we talked about in Chapter 1, and get into a lot more detail. Section I of the AP Psychology Exam contains 100 multiple-choice questions that cover fourteen main areas of psychology (see Chapter 1 for a detailed list). You have 70 minutes to complete this section, and it counts for roughly two-thirds of your overall score. This time limit gives you less than one minute to answer each question. You might ask: "How can I possibly do well on this test when I have only about 42 seconds to answer each question?"

The answer: You do *not* need to work through all of the questions to do well on Section I of the AP Psychology Exam. In fact, smart testers often do not try to attempt every question and risk careless errors. Instead, smart testers choose which questions to tackle and which questions to simply guess on. "How do I choose?" you ask. To answer that question, let's take a closer look at the way the test is set up.

ORDER OF DIFFICULTY

If you have looked at any practice AP tests or taken tests like the SAT, you may have noticed that each time you begin a multiple-choice section, you find the questions manageable or even easy. But after a while, the test seems to become more difficult. Finally, near the end of the test, you may feel overwhelmed, as though you don't know any of the answers. Lots of students attribute this phenomenon to time pressure or exhaustion. But there's something else going on.

Many multiple-choice tests, including the AP Psychology Exam, have test questions arranged in a rough order of difficulty. In other words, the first part of the test contains mostly easy questions, the middle of the test contains questions of medium difficulty, and the last third of the exam contains primarily difficult questions. Now, why would a testing company set up a test in order of difficulty? Think about it: The company is trying to assess the psychology knowledge of thousands of students. If they placed all the hard questions at the beginning of the test or stuck them in intermittently, lots of students with pretty good, but not great, psychology knowledge would get stuck on the early questions and never get to the questions they could answer. They would lose time, have trouble building momentum, and generally get bogged down. The results would show two groups—a high-scoring group (the students who know almost all of the material and can answer almost all of the questions) and a low-scoring group (everyone else)—as opposed to a nice bell curve (where most students score somewhere around the middle).

EASY ONES FIRST, PLEASE

When a test is arranged in order of difficulty, everyone starts out answering easy questions. As students work through the test, they will hit a point at which they begin to have trouble. Companies that write standardized tests assert that this stumbling point shows where a student's knowledge of a subject pretty much ends. Although this is open to debate, arranging a test in order of difficulty does create a more nearly fair test for everyone.

SO WHAT?

How does all this information help you? If the easiest questions are at the beginning of the exam, followed by questions of medium difficulty, and then the tough stuff, what is the point of rushing through the first questions to get to the questions you can't answer? Easy questions are worth just as much as difficult questions. Therefore, to score well on Section I, you need to slow down and get as many of the easy and medium questions right as you can.

How to Score Your Personal Best on Section I

- Get all easy questions right

- Get most medium questions right

- Do the right thing on hard questions*

*See "Do The Right Thing" later in this chapter.

AP SCORING

We know that there is no guessing penalty anymore, but let's explore that using a hypothetical situation. Let's say you end up blindly guessing on 15 questions. Random selection suggests that you will get 3 of these 15 correct, which means you just earned 1 point. Because no points are deducted for wrong answers, the 4 wrong answers simply receive 0 points. If you are going to guess without any POE, don't waste time trying to wonder what the best letter is. Just pick your letter of the day and move on.

While blindly guessing should gain you a point here and there, using POE in conjunction with guessing increases your odds of getting questions right. Let's say on the 15 questions discussed above, you are able to narrow them all down to 3 choices through POE. Now, random selection suggests that you will get 5 questions right. So, you picked up 2 more points on hard questions through POE rather than random guessing.

While 5 points won't get you to your goal score, you won't be guessing (whether blindly or with POE) on the entire test. The point is that even blindly guessing should get you a point here and there, and thoughtful guessing based on POE is an important strategy when you are faced with a hard question.

One More Time

Let's say you get a Section I score of 66. If you do well on your essays, let's say 20 out of 25 each, you will get an AP grade of 5.

You get the picture. In other words, you can do extremely well on the AP Psych Exam even if you end up merely guessing on some multiple-choice test questions. In fact, you will do a lot better overall by not rushing through Section I and avoiding a lot of careless errors.

You do *not* need to work through all of the questions to do well on Section I of the AP Psychology Exam.

No One Will Ever Know

Raw scores are not reported to you, your school, or your colleges. Only the final score, ranging from 1 to 5, is reported. In other words, no one will ever know that you got an AP Psych Grade of 5 (extremely well qualified), but only got 75 percent of Section I questions correct and rocked the essays. It's the final grade that matters here, so take the test the smart way.

SMART-TESTER STRATEGIES

Let's move on to strategies for how to approach multiple-choice questions. Your own knowledge of psychology will be the key to doing well, but certain strategies will help you stretch your psych knowledge and crack the trickier questions. Once you've mastered some of the smart-tester strategies, we'll talk about how you can develop your personal approach to Section I.

SMART-TESTER STRATEGY #1: ASK IT LIKE IT IS

How often have you zipped through a question and picked the obvious answer, only to find that you misread the question? The most important thing you can do to increase your score on Section I is to make sure you understand what you are being asked.

After you read a question, take a second to make sure you understand it. Put the question in your own words or circle the key words in the question. Taking this first step will eliminate the possibility of your answering the wrong thing. Try the following example:

1. A person's refusal to accept an accurate diagnosis of a spouse's mental illness demonstrates the use of which of the following defense mechanisms?

How would you ask this question in your own words?

When someone doesn't want to accept really bad news, they are in...

Now the answer should be obvious: *denial*. By stating this question in everyday language, the answer pops out at you. Try another example:

19. The failure of bystanders to respond to a stranger's cries for help is sometimes explained as an instance of

How would you ask the question?

Why don't people do anything when someone is yelling, "help"?

In the case of question 19, you may not know the answer off the top of your head, but clarifying the question makes you better prepared to deal with the answer choices.

Let's look at one more:

22. The dependent variable in the experiment above is

In this case, you don't need to put the question into your own words. However, you want to make sure you look for the right thing when you hit the answer choices. Therefore, circle the key words *dependent variable* before you head to the answer choices.

Ask It Like It Is Drill

For each of the following questions, circle or underline the key words in the question. Then, if appropriate, jot down in your own words exactly what is being asked. Answers are on page 204.

3. Angie is a scientist who is interested in the physical basis of psychological phenomena such as motivation, emotion, and stress. She is called a(n)

10. One of the primary tools of the school of structuralism was

18. Binocular cues provide important cues for depth perception because

35. Constance is presented with a list of words. When asked to recall the words, she remembers only the words from the beginning and the end of the list. This phenomenon demonstrates which of the following types of effect?

47. The recognition-by-components theory asserts that we categorize objects by breaking them down into their component parts and then

56. Veronica is competing in a regional gymnastics competition. As she waits for her turn on the mat, she ignores the sounds of the crowd and instead mentally reviews her routine. Veronica is managing an anxiety-producing situation by employing

70. Which of the following was true of Stanley Milgram's studies of obedience?

88. In their discussions of the process of development, the advocates of the importance of nurture in the nature-nurture controversy emphasize which of the following?

Question Numbering

Whenever you start a question, check out the question number. It will tell you approximately how hard the question is (easy: 1–33ish; medium: 34–66ish; difficult: 67–100ish). We've numbered *all* the questions in this book (including drill questions) to reflect their approximate difficulty.

SMART-TESTER STRATEGY #2:
ANSWER BEFORE YOU ANSWER

Once you've translated the question, you go to the answer choices, right? *Stop right there...* Do you really think it's that easy? Of course not, or everyone would get all the questions right. You need to do a little work before you get mired down in the answer choices.

Beware of the Answer Choices

Answer choices are not our friends. In fact, think about what it takes for a test writer to develop five answer choices for each question. First, she needs to write the correct answer, making sure it is accurate but not too obvious. Then, she has to put in at least one or two close second choices. Finally, she needs to fill in the remaining choices and move on to the next question.

When taking a standardized test, most students read the question and then read each answer choice. What they fail to realize is that the answer choices are riddled with tricks, traps, and distracters designed to bump them off course.

Enter: The Smart Tester

Unlike your less savvy compatriots, you are a smart tester. You know that if you have an idea of the answer before you read the answer choices, you won't be tempted to pick something that is way off base. You also know that, because four of the five choices you read are wrong, it's best to assume that an answer is wrong until proven right.

After you translate the question into your own words, answer it *in your own words*. Now, that may mean actually knowing the exact answer (as in the case of *denial*), or it may mean putting yourself in the right ballpark before looking at the answer choices. Sometimes, it's actually helpful to cover the answer choices and make up your own answer. Then look at the choices and see which comes closest to your original thought. Let's look at one of the questions from your last drill:

3. Angie is a scientist who is interested in the physical basis of psychological phenomena such as motivation, emotion, and stress. She is called a(n)

First, how would you ask this question in your own words? Okay, now maybe you know the answer to this question, and maybe you don't. No problem. You can still answer the question before you look at the answer choices. If you can't spit out Angie's correct title immediately, answer the question by saying:

Angie is called a person who is into the physical basis of psychology.

With your answer in mind, look at each answer choice.

(A) psychologist
(B) anthropologist
(C) physical therapist
(D) paleontologist
(E) biopsychologist

Now, use your answer to find the credited response:

(A) Is a *psychologist* a person who's into the physical basis of psychology? No, this person is into more than just the physical basis.

(B) Is an *anthropologist* a person who's into the physical basis of psychology? No, an anthropologist is into cultures.

(C) Is a *physical therapist* a person who's into the physical basis of psychology? No, this person is not into the psychology part.

(D) Is a *paleontologist* a person who's into the physical basis of psychology? No idea what this person is.

(E) Is a *biopsychologist* a person who's into the physical basis of psychology? Yes.

Question Types

Although many of the questions on Section I ask you for factual information, about 30 percent of the questions are application questions—questions that ask you to use your knowledge of psychology to address a given situation. Application questions are no problem as long as you understand the question first. Just be sure to *Ask It Like It Is!*

Your answer? (E) *biopsychologist*. By answering the question before reading the answer choices, you were able to avoid getting tripped up in the first three answer choices. Plus, you realized the answer had to be (E) *biopsychologist* without necessarily knowing anything about (D) *paleontologist* (a paleontologist studies fossils, by the way).

SMART-TESTER STRATEGY #3:
PROCESS OF ELIMINATION (POE)

You have just learned your next big strategy: Process of Elimination (POE for short). Every time you answer a question you will use POE, which means getting rid of (eliminating) wrong answer choices and then choosing from what you have left. Why does it make sense always to answer questions this way? Because four of the five answer choices you read for each question are wrong. In other words, most of the answers you read on the test are wrong. It sometimes is much easier to identify two or three wrong answers on each question than it is to concentrate on finding the one right answer each time. By getting rid of two or three wrong answer choices on each question, you have substantially increased your accuracy and your guessing power.

Let's try another example:

> 97. Which of the following is an example of metacognition?

Ask It Like It Is: Circle *metacognition*, then define it:

Understanding cognitive (thought) processes.

Answer Before You Answer:

Find an example of people understanding how they think and learn.

Now, use POE to get rid of wrong answers:

> (A) Recognizing the faces of new in-laws after seeing them only in pictures
> (B) Memorizing 100 words from the dictionary
> (C) Understanding the role of various parts of the brain in perception
> (D) Accurately completing the logic in a deductive reasoning problem
> (E) Knowing the effectiveness of different strategies for learning statistical formulas

(A) Is *recognizing the faces* of people the same as understanding how one thinks and learns? No. Cross off this answer choice. Every time you decide an answer is not the one you want, cross it off.

(B) Is *memorizing* something the same as understanding how one thinks and learns? No. Cross it off.

(C)   Is *understanding the role of various parts of the brain in perception* the same as understanding how one thinks and learns? Not sure? Keep it and read the rest.

(D)   Is *accurately completing* a logic problem the same as understanding how one thinks and learns? No. Cross it off.

(E)   Is *knowing the effectiveness of different strategies for learning* the same as understanding how one thinks and learns? Sounds pretty close.

By using POE, you were able to easily narrow your choices down to (C) or (E). Once you have it down to two, compare your choices. Which one is closer to the answer you came up with? In this case, the answer is (E). *Understanding the role of various parts of the brain in perception* is still only knowledge of fact, not of mental processes. Notice the word *understanding* was used in (C), and not by coincidence. But, by using POE, you were able to escape the trap and answer the question correctly. By the way, did you notice that this was a question number 97? (Remember: questions are arranged from least to most difficult, making highest-numbered questions the hardest.) Only about 20 percent of test takers would answer this question correctly.

Meta What?

Okay, so POE is a great strategy, but what if you don't know what the key term in a question actually means? You have two choices: If this is a very hard question, which it was, you can simply skip it and come back to it if you have time. However, don't underestimate your knowledge. You may not be able to cough up the dictionary definition of metacognition, but pull the word apart: If you have spent more than a week in AP Psych class, you know that cognition has something to do with thinking. Then decide how you have heard the prefix *meta* used. How about metaphysics? So there's physics and metaphysics, and there's thinking (cognition) and meta-thinking (metacognition). It's probably some higher level of thinking. Although this rough definition may not get you to the exact answer, it will help you cross off some answer choices that will, in turn, help you make an intelligent guess.

> **Smart-Tester Strategy Review**
>
> **Strategy #1:** Ask It Like It Is: Read the question and put it into your own words.
>
> **Strategy #2:** Answer Before You Answer: Come up with your own answer to the question (exact or ballpark).
>
> **Strategy #3:** Process of Elimination (POE): Cross off each answer that is not close to yours. Pick the best match.

More on POE

Now let's say you read a question and don't know the answer. All is not lost. You can use your brain, the information in the question, and POE to get to the answer (or at least to a fifty-fifty chance of guessing the right answer). Look at the following example:

74. Which of the following best supports the assertion that intelligence is at least in part inherited?

(A) Pairs of fraternal twins have a greater correlation of IQ score than do other pairs of siblings.

(B) Pairs of twins reared together have a greater correlation of IQ score than do pairs of twins reared apart.

(C) Pairs of identical twins have a greater correlation of IQ score than do pairs of fraternal twins.

(D) Adopted children and their adoptive parents have a correlation of IQ score that is greater than zero.

(E) Adopted children and their adoptive parents have a greater correlation of IQ score than do the same children and their biological parents.

Did you read the answer choices for question 74 before you answered on your own? Don't forget, wrong answers are designed to confuse, not to assist. Be sure to follow your smart strategy and *not* look at the answer choices too soon. First, let's do smart strategies for question 74.

Ask It Like It Is: Circle the words *intelligence* and *inherited*. Then restate the question:

Which of the answers says genetics affects smarts?

Answer Before You Answer: If you answered, I don't know, no problem. Simply use what you do know and POE.

Use POE for each answer choice:

(A) Does the fact that *pairs of fraternal twins have a greater correlation of IQ score than do other pairs of siblings* indicate genetics affects smarts? Careful—are fraternal twins any different genetically from other sibling pairs? If you are unsure, leave this choice and go on.

(B) Does the fact that *pairs of twins reared together have a greater correlation of IQ score than do pairs of twins reared apart* indicate genetics affects smarts? No, it indicates the opposite because it implies that the nongenetic factors are more significant. Cross it off.

(C) Does the fact that *pairs of identical twins have a greater correlation of IQ score than do pairs of fraternal twins* indicate genetics affects smarts? Yes. Identical twins come from one egg, while fraternal twins come from two, making fraternal twins genetically less similar. Keep this answer choice and read on.

(D) Does the fact that *adopted children and their adoptive parents have a correlation of IQ score that is greater than zero* indicate genetics affects smarts? No, it indicates the opposite—nurture over nature. Cross this choice off.

(E) Does the fact that *adopted children and their adoptive parents have a greater correlation of IQ score than do the same children and their biological parents* indicate genetics affects smarts? No, it also indicates nurture over nature. Cross it off.

You've at least narrowed it down to two choices without even really knowing the answer—that's pretty cool. Now look at the two choices you have not crossed off. (C) very clearly shows genetics affects smarts, while (A) may or may not. What's your best guess? You got it: (C).

HOW LONG IS 70 MINUTES?

Right about now you are probably thinking, "Nice idea, and I'll probably finish about ten questions in seventy minutes following this strategy." Even though you don't need to work through every question on the test to do well, you do need to work efficiently and effectively.

As you know, rushing through the test and getting easy questions wrong is a bad idea. But how slow is too slow? After all, this is a timed test, and you do need to complete a significant number of the questions to do well.

WORK EFFICIENTLY AND EFFECTIVELY

The best way for you to determine your own personal pace is to work efficiently (don't dawdle) and effectively (get right what you do answer). In other words, although you don't want to rush through and make careless errors, you don't want to spend all day on one question. Work at a pace that allows you to get questions right without dragging your heels. If you find yourself lingering for too long over a question, make a decision and move on. However, if you are doing some good effective work on a question and have narrowed it down to two choices, don't lose the point because you "need to get to the next question."

Let's take a closer look at order of difficulty to help you with this idea of working efficiently and effectively.

Your Personal Pace

It is imperative that you choose a pace that is efficient and effective *for you*. It doesn't matter if your best friend can complete the entire section in 30 minutes. You need to work at a pace that will allow you to do as many questions as you can while maintaining accuracy. Set your own personal pace, and you will do your personal best.

QUESTION DIFFICULTY, REDUX

> ### Easy Questions
>
> - Tend to come early in the test
>
> - *Always* ask about something you know

Even if you're on question number three, if you don't know anything about the subject of the question, it won't be easy for you. Conversely, a question on the last third of the test may be tricky, but if you know the topic well it won't be that hard for you.

How can you score your personal best? Use your smart strategies efficiently and effectively.

Easy Questions Drill

On easy questions, you will be able to accomplish these steps rapidly. Most short, easy questions will take very little time from start to finish. Try this drill, working quickly but carefully. Before you begin, jot down your start time. Once you have finished, note your end time and check your answers for accuracy. Remember, the goal is to be efficient (work rapidly) and effective (work accurately).

Start Time: _____

1. Sigmund Freud is thought of as the originator of which of the following perspectives of psychology?

   (A) Biological
   (B) Psychoanalytic
   (C) Behavioral
   (D) Humanistic
   (E) Cognitive

2. A person who is attempting to overcome a heroin addiction is experiencing hallucinations, tremors, and other side effects. These painful experiences associated with the termination of an addiction are known as

   (A) denial
   (B) transduction
   (C) withdrawal
   (D) transference
   (E) psychosis

3. After several trials during which a dog is given a specific type of food each time a light is lit, there is evidence of conditioning if the dog salivates when

   (A) the food is presented and the light is not lit
   (B) the light is lit and the food is not present
   (C) the food and the light occur simultaneously
   (D) a different kind of food is presented
   (E) a tone is sounded when the food is presented

4. The basic unit of the nervous system is called the

    (A) soma
    (B) axon
    (C) cell
    (D) neuron
    (E) synapse

5. Which of the following methods of research is central to the behaviorist perspective?

    (A) Inferential statistics
    (B) Naturalistic observation
    (C) Surveying
    (D) Case study
    (E) Experimentation

End Time:_____

Right:_____

Turn to page 205 to check your answers. How did you do? Remember, if you finished in two minutes but missed even one question, you were working too fast. Don't throw away points on the easy questions.

By the Way...

The more psychology you have under your belt, the easier this test will be. The strategies you are learning here are designed to make the most of the psychology knowledge you possess—to keep you from missing answers to questions that you should be getting right. The strategies will also help you stretch your knowledge so you can answer questions about topics you only sort of know. However, although they will help you make smart guesses, the strategies won't make a question on a completely unfamiliar topic easy.

Medium Questions Drill

You will spend most of your test time on the medium questions. These are the questions that you will know, or sort-of know, but will need to answer very carefully so you don't lose points to tricks and traps. Try the next five questions as you did on the previous drill, working more slowly but still efficiently and effectively.

Start Time: _____

33. The primary drives of hunger and thirst are, for the most part, regulated by which of the following?

    (A) The medulla oblongata
    (B) The thalamus
    (C) The hypothalamus
    (D) The kidneys
    (E) The adrenal glands

34. Imposing order on individual details in order to view them as part of a whole is a basic principle of which of the following types of psychologists?

(A) Behaviorist
(B) Psychodynamic
(C) Humanistic
(D) Gestalt
(E) Cognitive socialist

35. To determine the number of students in the school who own personal computers, a school bookstore decides to survey the members of the introductory computer science class. A problem with this study is that

(A) the survey may not elicit the information the store is looking for
(B) the store is not surveying a representative sample of students
(C) the survey is being constructed without a hypothesis
(D) it is unclear as to whether the bookstore will be able to establish causation
(E) the survey is being given during school hours

36. When an individual looks through the window in the morning, the two regions of the cortex that are stimulated are

(A) the temporal lobes and the occipital lobes
(B) the parietal lobes and the frontal lobes
(C) the frontal lobes and the temporal lobes
(D) the temporal lobes and the parietal lobes
(E) the occipital lobes and the parietal lobes

37. Which of the following statements is true of behaviorism?

(A) It holds that most behaviors are the result of unconscious motives that come into conflict.
(B) It focuses on the development of the cognitive self in regards to behavior.
(C) It holds that development is largely a product of learning.
(D) It emphasizes the role of nature over the impact of nurture.
(E) It was developed to replace the cognitive and humanistic perspectives.

End Time:_____

Right:_____

Turn to pages 206–207 to check how you did this time. If you missed a question, no big deal (all the questions in the above two drills are about topics covered in the first two psych-review chapters of this book, so you'll have a chance to review them if you had trouble). If you missed more than one question and were finished in less than five minutes, you were working too fast. Slow the pace and pick up the accuracy.

Long Questions

You may have noticed on the medium drill that some questions have much longer answer choices than others. In the earlier sections of the test, you will have a *long-answer* question about every seven or so questions. Near the later part of the test, a long-answer question will occur more frequently. Throwing in questions with long-answer choices is one of the ways a test writer can make a question more difficult and more time-consuming.

To Skip or Not to Skip

Imagine yourself taking Section I. You're cruising along through the easy section, feelin' fine. Suddenly, you hit a speed bump. Question 10, a question that should be easy, seems much harder than you would expect. Keep in mind that no order of difficulty is perfect for each individual, especially on an exam that is testing each individual's knowledge of a particular subject. Chances are this particular question is either a misplaced difficult question or it's about a topic you don't happen to know very well. In any case, does it make sense for you suddenly to spend several minutes on question 10 when there are 90 questions to go, many of which will be easier for you than this one? Of course not. Remember, this is your test—you should take it in the order that is best for you.

Are We There Yet?—The Toughest Third

How about those tough questions? Should you just skip all of them? Of course not. You should work efficiently and effectively through the easy and medium portions of the test, making sure that you've gotten as many points as you can from those sections. With your remaining time, you should work your way smartly through the most challenging questions.

Once you pass question 70, you can be pretty sure that you have entered the most difficult third of the test. Even without looking at the question number, you can often tell when you've hit the difficult third because suddenly every question requires a lot more brain power than before. How can you get the most points out of this portion of the test?

Do the Right Thing

As we've mentioned, a question is difficult not only if it appears in the tough section of the test, but also if it is about a topic with which you are unfamiliar. Conversely, if you know a particular topic well, a question about it that happens to appear in the difficult portion of the test need not be difficult. Therefore, once you pass question 70, *Do the Right Thing!* This means, you should read each question to see first if you are familiar with the topic. If you are, go for it. If it sounds like Greek, skip it (draw a box around it so you can come back to it if you have time).

If you are familiar with the topic of a question, proceed as usual but with caution. Remember, this question was placed late in the test because it is somehow more difficult than the rest. Be sure to use your Smart-Tester Strategies: Ask It Like It Is, Answer Before You Answer, and POE. If you get it down to two choices and don't know which one is correct, make a smart guess and move on. You have a fifty-fifty chance of guessing correctly, so you are a lot better off than when you started.

Smart Guessing = Common Sense

Sometimes you will be familiar with the topic of a question, but not enough to answer the question. In addition to using your usual strategy, you can also use your common sense, and the information you do have, to use POE and then take a smart guess. Look at the following example:

> 87. Which of the following most accurately lists the stages of the Hans Seyle's general adaptation syndrome?
>
> (A) Shock, anger, self-control
> (B) Appraisal, stress response, coping
> (C) Alarm, resistance, exhaustion
> (D) Anxiety, fighting, adapting
> (E) Attack, flight, defense

Now, let's assume you have no idea what Hans Seyle's general adaptation syndrome is. You can still follow the smart strategy and use your common sense to get close to the answer.

Ask It Like It Is: Circle *general adaptation syndrome*. Think about what that term might mean:

It has something to do with adapting, and it's a syndrome, which often means something negative.

Answer Before You Answer: Stages of adaptation that seem to characterize a kind of syndrome.

Use POE:

(A) Are *shock, anger, and self-control* stages of adaptation that characterize a kind of syndrome? No, a syndrome would not end up in self-control. Cross it off.

(B) Are *appraisal, stress response, and coping* stages of adaptation that characterize a kind of syndrome? No, they seem much more normal and positive. Cross it off.

(C) Are *alarm, resistance,* and *exhaustion* stages of adaptation that characterize a kind of syndrome? This is the most feasible choice so far. Keep it and read on.

(D) Are *anxiety, fighting, and adapting* stages of adaptation that characterize a kind of syndrome? Again, a syndrome would not have a last stage of adapting. Cross it off.

(E) Are *attack, flight, and defense* stages of adaptation that characterize a kind of syndrome? This one also has negative attributes that could constitute a syndrome.

Keeping It Clean

Of course, the more psychology you know, the easier all the questions will be. Using common sense and POE will help you out not only when you are unsure of the material, but also when you know the material and want to avoid careless errors and trap answers.

You are left with (C) or (E). Take a guess and remember that you have narrowed your choices down to a fifty-fifty shot on a question about which you had no clue. The correct answer, by the way, is (C). Given that the name of the syndrome is the "general adaptation syndrome" and not the "best way to cause a fight" syndrome, (C) is your smarter guess.

Here's another example of how your common sense can help you eliminate wrong answers:

(A)   Personal conscience is innate, and all human beings develop it at the same rate.

(B)   By adulthood, all people judge moral issues in terms of self-chosen principles.

Hey, wait a minute. Where's the question? We've given you these two answer choices to demonstrate how common sense can play an important role in getting rid of wrong answer choices. Let's evaluate these two answer choices. (A) says that *personal conscience is innate, and all human beings develop it at the same rate*. Does that sound accurate? Even without knowing the question, it is hard to imagine that any psychologist would suggest that all human beings develop personal conscience at the same rate. You know this answer cannot be the answer to the question simply by using common sense. Cross it off.

How about (B): *By adulthood, all people judge moral issues in terms of self-chosen principles*. Again, is this statement true? Even if a lot of people judge moral issues in terms of self-chosen principles, it is rare that all people ever do anything the same way. The extreme language of this answer choice can help you determine that it is wrong. Without even knowing the question, you are able to eliminate two answer choices by using your common sense.

Do What You Want

Finally, in dealing with hard questions, remember that you don't need to do them all. You choose the difficult questions you want to do and in what order you want to do them. For example, after question 70, you may wish to concentrate on all the short-answer questions, because the long-answer questions are more time-consuming and difficult. Place a box around each question you skip so that you can go back to them, and make sure to be careful when bubbling in your answer sheet. If there are particular questions you want to go back to, mark them with a star.

CREATE YOUR PERSONAL STRATEGY

Finally, you will score your best on Section I of the AP Psychology Exam by developing your own optimal strategy. Use the tools we have given you; practice them to make them second nature (do the Test Breaks to help you fine-tune your skills). Once you are comfortable with your question strategy, do some timed work to help determine your personal pacing strategy. Determine what working *efficiently and effectively* means for you. And remember, you have an essay portion that will contribute to your final grade, as well. Emphasize your strengths to get the best grade you can. Oh yeah, and you better review some psychology too!

3

Cracking the Free-Response Section

Section II: Free-response. It has a nice ring to it, doesn't it? That word *free* gives it a melodic sound. Well, don't be fooled. On the AP Psychology Exam, "free-response" is simply a euphemism for *timed essays*. Here are the facts about Section II.

- You are required to answer two essays.

- There is no choice—two essays are presented and you must do both.

- Each essay is worth $16\frac{2}{3}\%$ of your score, or 25 out of the 150 points on the exam.

- Each essay has a specified number of pieces of information you need to provide, usually between 8 and 12.

SOUND FAMILIAR?

Often when a student realizes he needs to write an essay under timed conditions, panic sets in. As he begins to read the question, his heart races, and he has difficulty concentrating on what the question is asking. He knows he should outline something, but is afraid he will run out of time, so he just jumps in and starts writing. Midway through paragraph one, feeling a little light-headed, he realizes that he doesn't really understand the question. He glances back at the question but, worried that he's losing precious minutes, decides he needs to forge ahead.

Partway through paragraph two (yes, he did remember to use paragraphs), he realizes that he has skipped a big point he needs to make. Should he cross off what he has written, or do the verbal backpedal until he can work it in? "How much time is left, anyway?" he asks himself. And on it goes.

Relax: All of us at one time or another have felt our sympathetic nervous system kick into gear at the mention of a timed essay. How can you effectively write not one but two essays in a limited period of time? By being a smart tester, of course.

SMART-TESTER ESSAY WRITING

Compare the smart tester's approach to our panicked tester from above. The smart tester knows that she can't write an effective essay without understanding the question. She spends her first 1–2 minutes "working the question over," pulling it apart to make sure she knows exactly what she is being asked to do. Next, she sets up a chart and spends 3–5 minutes outlining the points she will make. She then counts up her points and sketches out the layout of the essay.

In that first 7–10 minutes, the smart-tester has done the bulk of the work for her essay without actually writing a word of it. She can then spend the next 15 minutes writing the essay whose framework she has already created; no skipped points, no major cross-outs. She may even be able to put in some impressive vocabulary.

How Do They Score Them?

Before the graders begin reading essays, they are given a "checklist" of points they should look for. The AP Psych bigwigs determine exactly how many points each essay is worth by doing a count. Keep in mind that the readers are locked into that scale—they will not give you an extra point for unrelated information or anything else.

BE THE SMART TESTER

Because you have read this far in the book, you must be a smart tester. We're now going to teach you all the secrets of writing a great essay (or two, for that matter) without activating your adrenal glands. To become the smart essay writer, you first need to know what the readers—the people who will grade your essays—are looking for.

WHAT'S IN AN ESSAY

There are lots of different ways to write a quality essay. However, you have a more specific goal in mind when it comes to the AP Psychology essays—you want a good grade. Therefore, you need to know what the graders want so that you can write an essay that will earn a good score. Let's start by taking a peek at what they say they want from a good essay.

According to the College Board's published materials on the AP Psychology free-response questions, you are expected to do the following:

- Describe an overarching framework.

- Be specific in both your references to and discussion of psychological principles or problems.

- Cite evidence and examples to illustrate your explanations.

- Clearly state the intent of your evidence (to support or contrast a claim).

- State your points clearly and directly.

"Huh?" you ask. Let's simplify. To get a good score on an AP Psych essay, you should do the following:

- Get right to the point—a sentence or two is enough of an introduction.

- Use psychology terms and proper names of theories, theorists, etc.

- Define all terms.

- Support everything with an example or study, preferably from your course work (*not* an example from your own personal life).

- Clearly state the purpose of the example or study (support or contrast).

- Be clear, concise, and direct.

- Underline all key terms.

WHAT NOT TO DO

In addition, there are a few no-nos that the College Board implies or states outright.

- Do *not* restate the question in your essay.

- Do *not* suggest anything that can be misconstrued as unethical.

- Do *not* write everything you know on the topic, stay focused on the question.

- Do *not* spend a lot of time writing your introduction and conclusion.

- Do *not* begin writing until you have a clue about what you are going to write.

Beginning to get the picture? Although this may seem like a tall order, let us ease your mind a bit: Each of your essays will receive approximately five minutes of the reader's time. What? All that work for a lousy five minutes? Yup. Check out how AP essays are scored.

THE READING

After the AP exams are given, the College Board and ETS get together a slew of high school teachers and college professors and stick them in a room for six days to do nothing but read essays. ETS and the Board fondly refer to this process as the Reading (always capitalized). During the Reading, the readers are typically required to read hundreds of essays.

The readers first create a rubric by which to grade the essays. Most essays require between 8 and 12 pieces of information. Each essay is then read and a point is given for each required component covered accurately and completely. The points are then added together. Here's an example: A particular essay question has 10 required pieces of information, of which you wrote accurately and completely about 7. In this case, 2.5 is the multiplier, because there were 10 points available ($2.5 \times 10 = 25$). Because you supplied 7 pieces of information correctly and accurately, 7 is multiplied by 2.5, giving you 17.5 out of a possible 25. Note that there are no deductions—just points given for discussing the information correctly and completely. Your essay may be read and scored by a number of readers. For the most recent essay questions you can read the individual rubrics and required information at www.collegeboard.com.

TALKIN' ABOUT GOOD NEWS

This is all good news for you because it means that you can put together a high-scoring essay without panicking about time constraints and exact wording. Let's work through the smart-tester strategies for writing a high-scoring essay, and then finish up with some pointers for adding the polish.

Smart-Tester Strategy #1: Work It

Imagine you are in the boxing ring of the AP Psychology Championship. You have already sustained 70 minutes of multiple-choice sparring and now you have to take on two more big questions in 50 minutes to come out the winner. When the proctor says "go," you come out of your corner ready to take on that essay question. You're not hanging back, passively reading the question, hoping to understand it. If you took that approach, you'd get pummeled, and so would your score. Instead, you get in there and work it over; you pull it apart, examine each piece, and determine what the important stuff is.

Work It

The first step is reading the entire question. Then start taking it apart piece by piece.

1.   Although popular in American culture, the efficiency of the "time-out" method in modifying children's behavior is under much debate.

Now you should "work over" the above statement. Circle the trigger words—words that indicate transitions, changes in the direction of the sentence, etc., and then underline the critical terms. Make notes as needed to ensure that you understand the point of the sentence.

Here's what we did:

1.   (Although) popular in American culture, the efficiency of the "time-out" method in modifying children's behavior is under much debate.

Popular here, but does it work?

Smart-Tester Strategy #2: Chart It

Most Section II essays begin with a statement like the one we just saw and then go on to ask you to do some detailed stuff. Often, the essays have two parts (A and B) that you have to write about. Look at one part at a time:

A.   Basing your answer on psychological knowledge, discuss both the pros and cons of the time-out in regard to each of the following:

Attachment

Cognitive Development

Adult Relationships

Let's work Part A together. The first phrase emphasizes the importance of using what you have learned, not just what you feel about the subject. This is the AP Psychology Exam, after all. Next, the statement says to discuss both the pros and cons of time-out in regard to the three topics. Before you go any further, draw a chart next to the list of three topics. At the top of one column, write "pros" and at the top of the other write "cons." You know you have to do at least two things for each of the topics: address the pros of each in regard to the time-out, and then the cons. The chart will help you keep track of what you are doing.

Next, look at each topic to make sure that you can: 1) define it and 2) illustrate it. Before you can list the pros and cons for any of the three topics, you will need to clarify what each is and give an appropriate example. You may wish to add a column to your chart in front of the other two that reminds you to define and illustrate each term.

This is what Part A should look like now:

A. ~~Basing your answer on psychological knowledge~~, discuss both the (pros) and (cons) of the time-out in regard to each of the following:

Attachment

Cognitive Development

Adult Relationships

def/illus	pro	con

So far, so good. Now let's look at Part B:

B. Explain how the following methods of teaching behavior could be used instead of the time-out:

Shaping

Positive Reinforcement

Once again, mark the critical stuff—what are you being asked to do? Define each method, and illustrate how each could be used in place of time-out. Draw a chart with two columns: "define" (you should always define the term even if the question doesn't ask you to) and "use instead" (illustrate how this method will be used in place of the time-out). Here's how the chart should look:

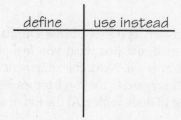

define	use instead

But Wait, There's More

You're well on your way to a great essay, but there are a few more things you need to do. And don't worry about this taking a long time; it won't after a little practice. Let's put everything together and look at what we have:

1. (Although) popular in American culture, the efficiency of the <u>"time-out" method</u> in modifying children's behavior is <u>under much debate</u>.

   Popular here, but does it work?

   A. Basing your answer on psychological knowledge, discuss both the (pros) and (cons) of the <u>time-out in regards to each of the following</u>:

   Attachment

   Cognitive Development

   Adult Relationships

def/illus	pro	con

   B. Explain how the following methods of teaching behavior could be used instead <u>of the time-out</u>:

   Shaping

   Positive Reinforcement

define	use instead

Before you write your essay, fill in your charts. Blank charts are not going to make your life easier. If you jot just a few notes under each column, you will be able to better organize your thoughts before you begin writing. Let's do the first part of A together:

For the "Attachment" part of A, write the following in your first column:

Bond with parents, ex. geese, separation anxiety

You will define attachment in your essay as critical bonding with primary care givers (parents). The first column shows that you plan to emphasize the critical nature of this attachment by explaining imprinting—the tendency of young animals, such as goslings, to attach to the first moving object they see (presumably their mother). Next, you will underscore the importance of human attachment with an explanation and illustration of separation anxiety.

What are the pros and cons of time-out in regard to attachment? Jot notes in your pros column such as:

Not many, authority figure, should attach after time-out

But What If?

What if you are unfamiliar with the topics the essay is addressing? You need to get working on those review chapters. The stuff you need to know to answer this question can be found in Chapter 12: Developmental Psychology.

These notes indicate that the time-out is not a benefit to attachment. However, it does establish the parent as the authority figure and can be done without significant damage to attachment if loving attachment is pursued at the conclusion of the time-out.

How about cons?

Mistrust of parent, separation anxiety

The time-out may in fact lead to problems associated with attachment, such as mistrust of the parent's care and affection or problems associated with separation anxiety. By taking the time to jot down your thoughts, you ensure that your essay is well on its way to being written—and well written, for that matter. Continue this process for the points of Part A and Part B.

SMART-TESTER STRATEGIES #1 AND #2

Let's review. Smart-Tester Strategy #1: Work It—work the question over so that you know exactly what you are being asked. While you are working over the question, you will also begin to do Smart-Tester Strategy #2: Chart It—draw your charts and, if you feel comfortable, fill them in at the same time (why add another step?). You may wish to give the question a quick read-through before you begin, but you don't need to artificially separate working the question from writing your outline. This entire process should take you between five and seven minutes.

SMART-TESTER STRATEGY #3: COUNT IT

Remember we said that your essay is scored on a scale ranging from 0 to usually between 8 and 12. You can actually estimate what that number is and use that information to make sure that you don't lose any points. Once you have finished the Work It and Chart It steps, take a minute to number all the possible points that you could earn. A point is given for each of the main things you are asked to do in a given essay. Flip back to the time-out essay question and number each part that you would consider "point-worthy." Then count up. We'll wait here.

Finished? What did you get? If you counted 13 points, that's right. Here's how we got it:

> If you write your essay well, you will get 3 points for each of the three categories in Part A (attachment, cognitive development, and adult relationships)—1 point will be awarded for defining each term, 1 point will be awarded for illustrating a con argument and 1 point for having a pro argument. Therefore, Part A is worth 9 points.

> Part B is worth 4 points, 1 point for each of the two topics that you address, 1 point awarded for the definition of each term and 1 point for each explanation of how they can be used instead of time-out. Part B is typically awarded fewer points than Part A.

Why should you care about how many points an essay is worth? Because you don't want to miss a major component and, consequently, lose points. You also will use this information to complete the last smart-tester strategy before you start to write the essay.

Smart-Tester Strategy #4: Sketch It

Sketch out your essay in the one minute or so before you begin to write. Insert your "points" so that you know exactly how the whole thing is organized. Then, use your sketch as your checklist while you write your essay.

First, draw a box to represent a paragraph. In the box, write the word *open* so that you don't forget your opening line and then insert the first points you will make:

```
Open

1    define and illustrate attachment

2    pros and cons re: time-out and attach.
```

Each time you think you need a new paragraph, draw a new box and insert your points.

```
3    define and illustrate cognitive dev.

4    pros and cons re: time-out and cogn. dev.
```

```
5    define and illustrate adult relationships

6    pros and cons re: time-out and adult relat.
```

```
7    define shaping—use instead of time-out

8    define pos. reinforcement—use instead of time-out

Closing
```

<aside>
But What If?

What if you don't know one of the terms in the question? Remember, you will get no points for supplying no information, so do your best to analyze (pull apart) the possible meaning of the word and then make up an answer.
</aside>

Smart-Tester Strategy #5: Write It

Now that you have a sketch, your essay will practically write itself. You just need to piece it together in a clear, concise manner. As you write, check off each point on your sketch as you complete it. That way you'll be sure not to skip anything. Keep in mind that the readers will not grade your charts or outlines. The essay must be written in paragraph form. Be sure to write in complete sentences. Don't use symbols or bulleted lists in defining or giving examples. If you are running out of time, continue writing pertinent information. Your essay should take about ten to fifteen minutes to write. Then it's on to the second essay!

The Opening

Did you think we'd desert you without first guiding you through the actual writing? Never. Let's review how to get a good score according to the College Board.

Essay-Writing Guidelines

- Write an introductory sentence that is *not* a repeat of the question.

- Use psychology terms and proper names of theories, theorists, etc.

- Define and underline all key terms.

- Support everything with an example or study, preferably from your course work (*not* an example from your own personal life).

- Clearly state the purpose of the example or study (support or contrast).

- Be clear, concise, and direct.

First, write an opening. Your opening sentence needs to introduce what you are going to say and to incorporate what the question says *without* simply rewriting the question. Restating the question is a big pet peeve of the College Board. Let's try an opening sentence for the "time-out" essay:

> Although the "time-out" has become an acceptable means in the United States of dealing with inappropriate behavior of children, it may have both positive and negative effects on the development of our youth.

Pretty good, huh? Says what it needs to, introduces your point, and tells the reader that you are going to look at both sides of the issue. From here, jump right into your discussion of attachment.

Choose Your Words Wisely

The more appropriate psychological terms you use, the better the point-value of your essay. In the "time-out" essay, a point-getter is to use the term *separation anxiety* relating to attachment issues. Even though the readers are scanning your essay pretty quickly, they have been trained to look for appropriate psychological terms. When they see one, they will slow down (possibly even smile a little) to read more carefully. But remember this, you cannot earn points if you do not define, illustrate, or give an example of the psychological term.

Examples, Examples, Examples

All the College Board literature clearly states that the graders like, and often expect, to see students' points supported by appropriate examples. When inserting examples, remember the following:

1. They should *not* come from your personal life.

2. They should be relevant to your point and should make a clear reference to the question being asked.

3. You should flag them with "for example."

A good example is something that you learned in your course, from your own reading, or from this book. A bad example is, "my little brother hates it when Mom puts him in time-out." Enough said.

Before you give the example, make it clear whether it is supporting your point or contesting your point. This procedure ties in perfectly with the third point about examples: Always flag your examples with an introductory phrase. Again, the readers are reading your essay quickly. They will pause if they see an example, and will be impressed by examples that are clearly delineated. If your example supports a point you just made, flag it with "for example." If it contrasts the point, insert a sentence that introduces it:

> Most will agree that the time-out is clearly an improvement over corporal punishment. However, attachment dysfunction can have far-reaching effects. For example…

Note that the word *however* introduces the change in direction of the paragraph. Putting your example after that sentence makes it clear that your example is in contrast to a previous point.

Closing

Once you have included all the points you need to make, write a final closing sentence that summarizes your overriding theme:

> Thus, while the time-out may have some benefits, the potential emotional scars it can leave behind should not be underestimated.

You tell 'em!

Plain, Good Writing

Finally, don't add in a lot of fluff. The AP Psych essay questions are pretty meaty. Your job is to write an essay that has no additives or fillers. At the same time it's important that your essay be complete. Don't skip over points. Your reader is counting up the 8, or 9, or 10 points you are to make. If you miss one, you lose a point. That also goes for running out of time. There is no reason to run out of time on an essay, and if you do it will hurt your score. To avoid this problem, use the plan on the following page.

Essay Smart-Tester Strategies	Total Time 7–10 minutes
#1 Work It	1–2 minutes
#2 Chart It	3–5 minutes
#3 Count It	1 minute
#4 Sketch It	1–2 minutes

Essay Smart-Tester Strategy #5	Total Time 10–15 minutes
# 5 Write It	Keep track of your own time. Finish the essay before time is called.

Follow this same time table for both essays. When you hit the 25-minute mark, you better hustle on to the second essay. If you are still working on essay number one, finish up as quickly as possible and move on.

Finishing Touches

Just a few more things to make sure you get all the points you can. First, when you've finished an essay, double check that you have addressed all the points you originally counted. Second, as you move from one thought to another, use trigger words and transitional phrases. For example:

Another important area to examine when considering the possible repercussions of the "time-out" is the cognitive development of children.

As compared with:

Cognitive development of children comes in stages.

Although there is nothing inherently wrong with the second sentence, the first sentence creates better flow and more overall cohesion to your essay.

Also, use the highest level of vocabulary that is comfortable for you. In other words, don't use too much slang, but don't write in a way that will sound awkward and forced. Do your best to use the most concise terminology possible.

Lookin' Good

Lastly, remember that first impressions count. In the case of your essays, the better they look, the more positive a reader is likely to regard them at the outset. Readers can't help but feel better about an essay that is legible and long enough to appear complete. Make sure you indent the paragraphs and neatly cross out mistakes (if you need to).

TIME!

Don't rely on your proctor to keep the time accurately or to remember to give you the 25-minute warning. If for some reason your proctor is a flake, you won't be able to use that excuse to explain why your essay is only half done. Wear a watch and keep your own time.

PUT IT ALL TOGETHER

Now that you have the knowledge to be a smart essay writer, put your skills to the test on the following question. When you are finished, check your work against ours (pages 207–208). You can find many more sample prompts from real tests to practice on at **www.collegeboard.com/student/testing/ap/psych/samp. html?psych**. Good luck and good writing!

2. More and more, stress is being cited as a major contributor to both physiological and psychological problems.

    A. Define how stress can have both physiological and psychological consequences in light of the each of the following scenarios:

        Daily hassles

        Significant life events

        Catastrophes

    B. What tactics can individuals employ to better cope with stress? Choose two methods that would effectively reduce the individual's stress level.

PART II

Psychology Review

4

History

LOGIC, PHILOSOPHY, AND HISTORY OF SCIENCE

Q: Why is psychology a science?

Psychology is the study of behavior and the mind. **Behavior**, a natural process subject to natural laws, refers to the observable actions of a person or an animal. The **mind** refers to the sensations, memories, motives, emotions, thoughts, and other subjective phenomena particular to an individual or animal that are not readily observed.

Psychology is a science because it uses systematic observation and collection of data to try to answer questions about the mind and behavior and their interactions. Psychology seeks to describe, predict, and explain behavior and the mental processes underlying behavior. As we discuss the history of psychology, we will encounter many theories that embody sets of assumptions and beliefs about the mind and behavior. In psychology, as in science in general, people tend to accept one theory and proceed under the assumptions of that theory. Psychologists accept the prevailing theory until sufficient data inconsistent with the theory are collected. At this point, what was the prevailing theory is replaced by another theory. Many theories are simply elaborations or revisions of previous ones. As you read over the history of psychology, pay attention to how theories relate to and influence one another.

Q: Define *dualism*.

The ancient Greeks were the first to speculate on the nature of the mind. Socrates considered the philosophical issues of beauty and justice and the rights of man. Socrates' student Plato argued that humans possess innate knowledge that is not obtainable simply by observing the physical world. Aristotle, a student of Plato, believed that we derive truth from the physical world. Aristotle's application of logic and systematic observation of the world laid the basis for the scientific method.

Q: What did Locke mean by *tabula rasa*?

The questions raised by the early Greeks pertain to the concept of **dualism**. Dualism divides the world and all things in it into two parts: body and spirit. Dualism is a theme that recurs often in psychology. The distinction between body and spirit mirrors the current debate around the difference between the brain (that is, the command center of the central nervous system) and the mind (that is, the sensations, memories, emotions, thoughts and other subjective experiences of a particular individual).

After the heyday of the Greek philosophers, there was a long period of time during which relatively little systematic investigation of psychological issues was conducted. This dearth of investigation was due, in part, to religious beliefs that said that the "spirit" portion of human nature could not be studied scientifically. These same prevailing theological views indicated that studying the natural world was only useful for what it demonstrated about God. These views changed with the advent of the scientific revolution (c. 1600–1700) when great discoveries were being made in biology, astronomy, and other sciences. These discoveries, along with corresponding movements in philosophy and art, made it clear that human nature was subject to scientific inquiry.

Q: Why is Wundt considered by some psychologists to be the founder of psychology?

René Descartes (1596–1650) conducted some of the most important speculation on the nature of man. He believed that the physical world is not under divine influence but rather follows a set of observable laws or rules. The world and all of the creatures in it are like machines, in that they behave in observable, predictable ways. Humans are the exception to this rule, because they possess minds. The mind, according to Descartes, is not observable and is not subject to natural laws. Descartes hypothesized that the mind and body interact, and that the mind controls the body while the body provides the mind with sensory input for it to decipher. Descartes believed that this interaction occurs in the **pineal gland**, which is located deep within the brain at the top of the brain stem. Finally, Descartes realized that some body movements, which he named reflexes, are not controlled by the mind. A reflex is an immediate, unconscious reaction to an environmental event, such as pulling your hand away from a flame.

John Locke (1632–1704) extended Descartes's application of natural laws to all things, believing that even the mind is under the control of such laws. Locke's school of thought is known as **empiricism**—the acquisition of truth through observations and experiences. In his book, *Essay Concerning Human Understanding,* Locke proposed that humans are born knowing nothing; Locke used the term *tabula rasa* (Latin for "blank slate") to describe the mind of a child. All knowledge that we have must be learned; nothing is innate. Locke felt that all knowledge must derive from experience. He emphasized nurture over nature as the greater influence on development.

Thomas Hobbes (1588–1679) believed that the idea of a soul or spirit, or even of a mind, is meaningless. Hobbes' philosophy is known as materialism, which is the belief that the only things that exist are matter and energy. What we experience as consciousness is simply a by-product of the machinery of the brain. Whereas Locke emphasized nurture over nature, Hobbes stressed the role played by nature. Hobbes philosophy of materialism greatly influenced **behaviorism**, which will be discussed later.

The nineteenth century was a time of great discovery in biology and medicine. These discoveries influenced the science of psychology to varying extents; however, one new theory revolutionized science—the theory of natural selection. **Charles Darwin** (1809–1882) published *On the Origin of Species* in 1859. In the book Darwin proposed a theory of **natural selection**, which said that all creatures have evolved into their present state over long periods of time. This evolution occurs because there exists naturally occurring variation among individuals in a species, and the individuals that are best adapted to the environment are more likely to survive to reproduce—and are likely to produce more successful offspring. Their offspring, in turn, will probably have some of the traits that made their predecessors more likely to survive. Over time, this process selects physical and behavioral characteristics that promote survival in a particular environment. Behavior evolves just like physiology: They both function to help individuals survive. **Evolutionary theory** set the stage for psychology by providing a way to explain differences between species and justifying the use of animals as a means to study the roots of human behavior.

Many credit **Wilhelm Wundt** (1832–1920) as the founder of the science of psychology. In 1879 in Leipzig, Germany, Wundt opened a laboratory to study consciousness. Wundt was trained in physiology and hoped to apply the methods that he used to study the body to the study of the mind. **Edward Titchener** (1867–1927) was a student in Wundt's laboratory and was one of the first to bring

A: Psychology is a science because it uses systematic collection and observation of data to try to answer questions about the mind and behavior and their interactions.

A: Dualism refers to the division of the world and all things in it into two parts: body and spirit.

A: *Tabula rasa* means "blank slate" and has been used (originally by Locke) to refer to the mind of a child. According to this view, all knowledge that we have must be learned; nothing is innate.

A: Wilhelm Wundt is sometimes viewed as the founder of psychology because he initiated the first psychology laboratory in Leipzig, Germany, in 1879.

the science of psychology to the United States. Titchener sought to identify the smallest possible elements of the mind, theorizing that understanding all of the parts would lead to the understanding of the greater structure of the mind. This theory is known as **structuralism**, and it means looking for patterns in thought, which are illuminated through interviews with a subject describing his or her conscious experience. This interview process is known as **introspection**. For example, Wundt would manipulate a stimulus in front of a subject, ask him or her to describe the conscious experience, and then he would work to identify commonalities among participants' conscious descriptions.

William James (1842–1910) was an American psychologist who opposed the structuralist approach. Instead, he argued that what is important is the function of the mind, such as how to solve a complex problem. James, who was heavily influenced by Darwin, believed that the important thing to understand is how the mind fulfills its purpose. This function-oriented approach is appropriately called **functionalism**.

APPROACHES

The theories discussed above laid the groundwork for modern psychology as a science. This next section will deal with eight of the most prominent approaches to modern psychology. The roots of these approaches are in the theoretical perspectives we discussed above.

APPROACH 1: BIOLOGICAL

Q: What is biological psychology?

Biological psychology is the field of psychology that seeks to understand the interactions between anatomy and physiology (particularly, the physiology of the nervous system) and behavior. This approach is practiced by directly applying biological experimentation to psychological problems, for example, in determining which portion of the brain is involved in a particular behavioral process. To accomplish this, researchers might use CAT scans, MRIs, EEGs, and PET scans.

APPROACH 2: BEHAVORIAL GENETICS

Behavioral Genetics is the field of psychology that emphasizes that particular behaviors are attributed to particular, genetically-based psychological characteristics. This perspective takes into account biological predispositions as well as the extent of influence that the environment had on the manifestation of that trait. For example, a person studying behavioral genetics might investigate to what extent risk-taking behavior in adolescents is attributable to genetics.

APPROACH 3: BEHAVIORAL

Behaviorism posits that psychology is the study of observable behavior. The mind or mental events are unimportant to the behaviorists, as they cannot be observed. **Classical conditioning**, first identified by Ivan Pavlov (1849–1936), was one of the behaviorists' most important early findings. Classical conditioning is defined as a basic form of learning in which a behavior comes to be elicited by a formally neutral stimulus. **John Watson** (1878–1958) and his assistant Rosalie Rayner applied classical conditioning to humans in the famed Little

Albert experiment. **B. F. Skinner** (1904–1990) was a behaviorist, who through the development of his Skinner Box, described operant conditioning in which a subject learns to associate a behavioral response will have an environmental outcome. Although behaviorism is no longer the prevailing approach, many behavioral principles are still used in **behavior modification**—a set of techniques in which psychological problems are considered to be the product of learned habits, which can be unlearned by the application of behavioral methods.

APPROACH 4: COGNITIVE

Cognitive psychology is an approach rooted in the idea that to understand people's behavior, we must first understand how they construe their environment—in other words, how they think. This approach combines both the structuralist approach of looking at the subcomponents of thought and the functionalist approach of understanding the purpose of thought. Cognitive psychologists use a variety of methods, including reaction-time tasks, computer models, and participants' self reports, to better understand thought. The cognitive approach largely replaced the behavioral approach as the predominant psychological method used in the United States. It remains popular today, and this approach has influenced and blended with others.

APPROACH 5: HUMANISTIC

The **humanistic approach** is rooted in the philosophical tradition of studying the roles of consciousness, free will, and awareness of the human condition. This is a holistic study of personality that developed in response to a general dissatisfaction with behaviorism's inattention to the mind and its function. Humanistic psychologists emphasize personal values and goals and how they influence behavior, rather than attempting to divide personality into smaller components. **Abraham Maslow** (1908–1970) proposed the idea of self-actualization, the need for individuals to reach their full potential in a creative way. Attaining **self-actualization** means accepting yourself and your nature, while knowing your limits and strengths. **Carl Rogers** (1902–1987) stressed the role of **unconditional positive regard** in interactions and the need for positive self-concept as critical factors in attaining self-actualization.

APPROACH 6: PSYCHOANALYTIC/PSYCHODYNAMIC

While laboratory psychology was passing through its various theories, a very different approach to psychology was forming. **Sigmund Freud** (1856–1939) developed a theory of human behavior known as **psychoanalytic theory**. Freud was concerned with individuals and their mental problems. Freud drew a distinction between the **conscious mind**—a mental state of awareness that we have ready access to—and the **unconscious mind**, those mental processes that we do not normally have access to but are yet influenced by in some way. The interaction of the forces of the conscious and unconscious mind shape behavior. Psychoanalytic theory stresses the importance of childhood experiences and a child's relationship with his or her parents to the development of personality. The focus of the psychoanalytic approach is on the resolution of unconscious conflicts through uncovering information that has been **repressed**, or buried in the unconscious.

A: Biological psychology is the field of psychology that seeks to understand the interactions between anatomy and physiology—particularly, the physiology of the nervous system—on the one hand, and behavior, on the other.

APPROACH 7: SOCIOCULTURAL

Those subscribing to the sociocultural approach believe that the environment a person lives in has a great deal to do with how the person behaves and how others perceive that behavior. According to this approach, cultural values vary from society to society and must be taken into account when trying to understand, predict, or control behavior.

APPROACH 8: EVOLUTIONARY

Similar to the behavioral genetics approach, the **evolutionary approach** focuses on the theories of Darwin. Behavior can best be explained in terms of how adaptive that behavior is to our survival. For example, fear is an adaptive evolutionary response; without fear our survival would be jeopardized.

The distinctions among the different approaches in psychology are absolutely one of the most essential ideas for you to understand for the AP Psychology exam. Let's use the common example of risk-taking in adolescence and explore that using each of the eight different approaches.

Approach	Question	Cause of Behavior	Methods
Biological	How are high risk takers physiology different than non-risk takers?	Physiology	Brain scans
Behavioral Genetics	Which genes contribute to the development of risk taking?	Genes	Genetic analysis
Behavioral	How does rewarding or punishing a risk-taker affect his or her behavior?	Learning and reflexes	Behavior modification
Cognitive	How do risk-takers think and solve problems?	Thoughts	Computer models of memory networks
Humanistic	How does the adolescent's self-esteem encourage or discourage risk-taking behavior?	Self-concept	Talk therapy
Psychodynamic	How might a child's early experiences affect risk taking in adolescence?	Unconscious mind	Dream analysis, talk therapy
Sociocultural	How might an adolescent's culture lead to risk-taking?	Cultural environment	Cross-cultural studies
Evolutionary	Is risk taking an evolutionary adaptable trait?	Natural selection	Species comparison

KEY TERMS

History

    behavior
    brain
    mind
    dualism
    René Descartes
    John Locke
    empiricism
    Thomas Hobbes
    behaviorism
    Charles Darwin
    natural selection
    evolutionary theory
    Wilhelm Wundt
    Edward Titchener
    structuralism
    introspection
    William James
    functionalism

Approaches

    biological psychology
    behavioral psychology
    classical conditioning
    B.F. Skinner
    behavior modification
    cognitive psychology
    humanistic approach
    Abraham Maslow
    self-actualization
    Carl Rogers
    Sigmund Freud
    psychoanalytic theory
    conscious mind
    unconscious mind
    sociocultural psychology
    evolutionary psychology

REVIEW QUESTIONS

See Chapter 18 for answers and explanations.

1. A cognitive psychologist would likely be most interested in

    (A) concentration of neural transmitters in the spinal cord
    (B) unconditional positive regard in the therapeutic setting
    (C) token economies in prisons
    (D) perceptual speed on word association tests
    (E) development of fine motor skills in toddlers

2. The concept of *tabula rasa*, or "blank slate" (the idea that human beings come into the world knowing nothing, and thereafter acquire all of their knowledge through experience), is most closely associated with

    (A) David Hume
    (B) Charles Darwin
    (C) John Locke
    (D) Sigmund Freud
    (E) Erich Fromm

3. The concept of dualism refers to the division of all things in the world into

    (A) thought and action
    (B) body and spirit
    (C) structural and functional
    (D) theoretical and practical
    (E) dependent and independent

4. The humanistic approach to psychology emphasizes the importance of

    (A) childhood experiences
    (B) biological predispositions
    (C) maladaptive thoughts
    (D) free will and conscious awareness
    (E) cultural experiences

5. Psychologists who emphasize the importance of repressed memories and childhood experiences subscribe to which of the following perspectives?

    (A) Cognitive
    (B) Behavioral
    (C) Psychodynamic
    (D) Social cultural
    (E) Medical/biological

5

Methods and Approaches

EXPERIMENTAL, CORRELATIONAL, AND CLINICAL RESEARCH

Q: Define *independent variable*.

Psychologists conduct three main types of research: experimental, correlational, and clinical. An **experiment** is an investigation seeking to understand relations of cause and effect. The experimenter changes a variable (cause) and measures how it, in turn, changes another variable (effect). At the same time, the investigator tries to hold all other variables constant so she can attribute any changes to the manipulation. The manipulated variable is called the **independent variable**. The **dependent variable** is what is measured. For example, an experiment is designed to determine whether watching violence on television causes aggression in its viewers. Two groups of children are randomly placed either in front of violent or nonviolent television programs for one hour. This would be considered the independent variable since it is able to be manipulated by the experimenter. Afterwards, a large doll may be placed in front of each child for one hour while the experimenter records the number of times that child hits, kicks, or punches the doll. This would be considered the dependent variable since it is the variable that remains constant and is being measured.

Q: Define *dependent variable*.

Other terms to remember include the following: The group receiving or reacting to the independent variable is the **experimental group;** the **control group** does not receive the independent variable but should be kept identical in all other respects. Using two groups allows for comparison to be made and causation to be determined.

In order to draw conclusions about the result of the controlled experiment, it is important that certain other conditions are met. The researcher identifies a specific **population,** or group of interest, to be studied. Because the population may be too large to study effectively, a **representative sample** of the population may be drawn. **Representativeness** is the degree to which a sample reflects the diverse characteristics of the population that is being studied. **Random sampling** is a way of ensuring maximum representativeness. Once sampling has been addressed, subjects are **randomly assigned** into both the experimental and control groups. Random assignment is done to assure that each group has minimal differences.

Q: What are three measures of central tendency?

Sometimes researchers or subjects inadvertently influence the results. To avoid this, researchers use a **single- or double-blind design**. Single-blind design means that the subjects do not know whether they are in the control or experimental group. In a double-blind design, neither the subjects nor the researcher know who is in the two groups. Double-blind studies are designed so that the experimenter does not inadvertently change the responses of the subject, such as by using a different tone of voice with members of the control group than with the experimental group. Obviously, a third party has the appropriate records so that the data can be analyzed later. In some double-blind experiments, the control group is given a **placebo**, a seemingly therapeutic object or procedure that causes the control group to believe they are in the experimental group but actually contains none of the tested material.

Correlational research involves assessing the degree of association between two or more variables or characteristics of interest that occur naturally. It is important to note that in this type of design, researchers do not directly manipulate variables but rather observe naturally occurring differences. If the characteristics under consideration are related, they are correlated. It is important to note that **correlation does not prove causation**; it simply shows the strength of the relationship among variables. For example, poor school performance may be correlated with lack of sleep. However, we do not know if lack of sleep caused the poor performance, or if the poor school performance caused the lack of sleep, or if some other unidentified factor influenced them both. If an unknown factor is playing a role, it is known as a **confounding (3rd variable)** problem. One way to gather information for correlational studies is through surveys. Using either questionnaires or interviews, one can accumulate a tremendous amount of data and study relationships among variables. Such techniques are often used to assess voter characteristics, teen alcohol and drug use, and criminal behavior. For example, survey studies might examine the relationship between socioeconomic status and educational levels. Correlational studies can be preferred to experiments because they are less expensive, not as time consuming, and easier to conduct.

A: The independent variable is manipulated by the experimenter.

    Clinical research often takes the form of case studies. **Case studies** are intensive psychological studies of a single individual. These studies are conducted under the assumption that an in-depth understanding of single cases will allow for general conclusions about other similar cases. Case studies have also been used to investigate the circumstances of the life of notable figures in history. Frequently, multiple case studies on similar cases are combined to draw inferences about these issues. Researchers must be careful though, because case studies, like correlational ones, cannot lead to conclusions regarding causality. Sigmund Freud and Carl Rogers used numerous case studies to draw their conclusions about psychology. The danger of assessing the outcome of case studies is that the individual studied may be atypical of the larger population. This is why researchers try to ensure that their studies are **generalizable**; that is, applicable to similar circumstances because of the predictable outcomes of repeated tests.

A: The dependent variable is what is measured.

    Two important research methods associated with developmental psychology are cross-sectional and longitudinal studies (see Chapter 12).

EXPERIMENTAL DESIGN

    Two important features of studies are the **conceptual definition** and the **operational definition**. Whereas the conceptual definition is the theory or issue being studied, the operational definition is how that theory or issue will be directly observed or measured in the study. For example, in a study on the effects of adolescent substance abuse, "the way in which taking drugs affects adolescent behavior" is the conceptual definition, while the number of recorded days the student is absent from school due to excessive use of substances is the operational definition.

A: Mean, median, and mode

    Operational definitions have to be internally and externally valid. **Internal validity** is the certainty with which the results of an experiment can be attributed to the manipulation of the independent variable rather than to some other, confounding variable. **External validity** is the extent to which the findings of a study can be generalized to other contexts in the "real world". Another key factor is if a study has reliability, which is whether or not the same results appear if the experiment is repeated under similar conditions.

STATISTICS

Psychologists and other scientists collect data. These data are then subjected to statistical analysis. Statistical methods can be divided into descriptive and inferential statistics. **Descriptive statistics** summarize data, whereas **inferential statistics** allow researchers to test hypotheses about data and to determine how confident they can be in their inferences about the data.

DESCRIPTIVE

Descriptive statistics do just what their name implies—they describe data. They do not allow for conclusions to be made about anything other than about the particular set of numbers they describe. Commonly used descriptive statistics are the mean, the mode, and the median. These descriptive statistics are measures of **central tendency,** that is, they characterize the typical value in a set of data.

The **mean** is the arithmetic average of a set of numbers. The **mode** is the most frequently occurring value in the data set. The **median** is the number that falls exactly in the middle of a distribution of numbers. These statistics can be represented by a **normal curve.** In a perfectly normal distribution, the mean, median, and mode are identical.

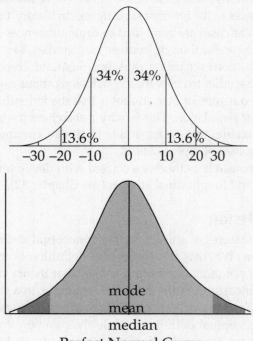

Perfect Normal Curve

The graph of the normal distribution depends on two factors—the mean and the standard deviation. The mean of the distribution determines the location of the center of the graph, and the standard deviation determines the height and width of the graph. When the standard deviation is large, the curve is short and wide; when the standard deviation is small, the curve is tall and narrow. All normal distributions look like a symmetric, bell-shaped curve, as shown on the following page.

In a typical distribution of numbers, about 68 percent of all scores are within 1 standard deviation above or below the mean, and about 95 percent of all scores are within 2 standard deviations above or below the mean. So, for example, IQ is typically said to have a mean of 100, and a standard deviation of 15, so a person with a score of 115 is one standard deviation above the mean.

Be aware that math questions about normal distributions can appear on the test. Since skewed distributions do not all share the same mathematical properties, questions about percentages and these distributions are often trick questions.

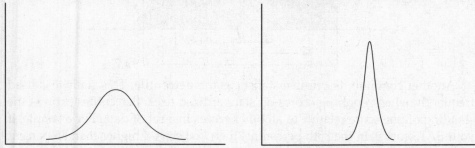

The curve on the left is shorter and wider than the curve on the right, because the curve on the left has a bigger standard deviation.

In skewed distributions, the median is a better indicator of central tendency than the mean. A right or **negative skew** means that there are more exceptionally small values than exceptionally large values. A left or **positive skew** means the opposite; there are more exceptionally large values.

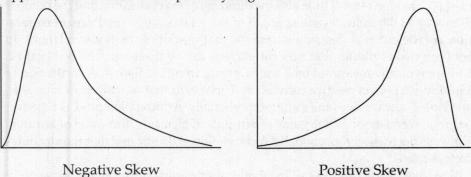

Negative Skew   Positive Skew

Although the mean, the mode, and the median give approximations of the central tendency of a group of numbers, they do not tell us much about the variability in that set of numbers. **Variability** refers to how much the numbers in the set differ from each other. The **standard deviation** measures a function of the average dispersion of numbers around the mean and is a commonly used measure of variability. Therefore, we can have a set of numbers that has a mean of 100. If most of those numbers are close to 100, say, ranging from 95 to 105, then the standard deviation will be small. However, if the mean of 100 comes from a set of numbers ranging from 50 to 150, then the standard deviation will be large.

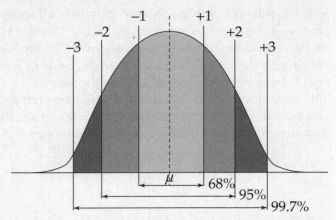

Another common descriptive statistic is the **percentile**. This statistic is used frequently when reporting scores on standardized tests. Percentiles express the standing of one score relative to all other scores in a set of data. For example, if your SAT score is in the 85th percentile, then you scored higher than 85 percent of the other test takers.

When looking at correlational data, as described above, we need statistical techniques to describe how the attributes we are studying relate to one another. The **correlation coefficient** is a statistic that will give us such information. Correlation coefficient is a numerical value that indicates the degree and direction of the relationship between two variables. Correlation coefficients range from +1.00 to –1.00. The sign (+ or –) indicates the direction of the correlation and the number (0 to + or –1.00) indicates the strength of the relationship. The **Pearson correlation coefficient** is a descriptive statistic that describes the linear relationship between two attributes. Pearson correlations can be positive, zero, or negative, and are typically measured on a scale ranging from 1 to 0 to –1. A correlation of 1 indicates a perfect positive correlation. This means that as attribute X increases, attribute Y always does the same proportionally. A correlation of –1 is a perfect negative correlation: As the value of attribute X increases, the value of attribute Y always decreases proportionally. A correlation of 0 indicated that the attributes are not related.

Positive Correlation (As years of education increases, income increases)

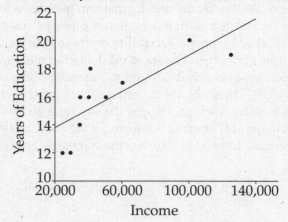

Negative Correlation (As absences for math lessons increase, math score decreases)

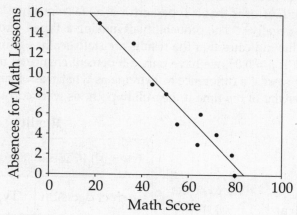

INFERENTIAL

Inferential statistics are used to determine our level of confidence in claiming that a given set of results would be extremely unlikely to occur if the result was only up to chance. When experiments are conducted, they are typically conducted using a small group of people. However, psychologists typically want to be able to **generalize** the results of the experiment to a larger group of people, perhaps even to all people. The small group of people in the experiment constitutes the **sample**, and the large group to whom the psychologist is trying to generalize is called the **population**. It is important that the sample reflects the characteristics of the population as a whole. If it does, then the sample is referred to as being **representative**.

Inferential statistics are tools for hypothesis testing. The **null hypothesis** states that a treatment had no effect in an experiment. The **alternative hypothesis** is that the treatment did have an effect. Inferential statistics allow us the possibility of rejecting the null hypothesis with a known level of confidence, that is, of saying that our data would be extremely unlikely to have occurred were the null hypothesis true. Tests such as these are statistically significant because they enable us to examine whether effects are likely to be a result of treatment, or are likely to be simply the normal variations that occur among samples from the same population. If a result is found to be statistically significant, then that result may be generalized with some level of confidence to the population.

Alpha is the accepted probability that the result of an experiment can be attributed to chance rather than the manipulation of the independent variable. Given that there is always the possibility that an experiment's outcome can happen by chance, no matter how improbable, psychologists have set alpha at 0.05, which means that an experiment's results will be considered statistically significant if the probability of the results happening by chance is less than 5%.

Two primary types of errors can occur when testing a hypothesis. **Type I error** refers to the conclusion that a difference exists when in fact this difference does not exist. **Type II error** refers to the conclusion that there is no difference when in fact there is a difference. Psychologists pay particularly close attention to the

Type I error because they want to be conservative in their inferences: They do not want to conclude that a difference exists if in fact it does not. A good analogy for Type I and Type II error is that a Type I error is a "false positive" and a Type II error is a "false negative." The probability of making a Type I error is called the *p*-value. A *p*-value indicates that the results are statistically significant (not due only to chance). If $p = 0.05$, we have only a 5 percent chance of making a Type I error. In other words, a difference as extreme as what was obtained would be found only 5 percent of the time if the null hypothesis were correct.

Q: What is informed consent?

Reality

Your Statistical Decision		The null is True	The null is False
	Fail to reject the null	Correct decision	**Type II error**
	Reject the null	**Type I error**	Correct decision

Statistical Decision Making: The Four Possible Outcomes

ETHICS IN RESEARCH

Q: What are Type I and Type II errors?

Occasionally psychological experiments involve deception, which may be used if informing participants of the nature of the experiment might bias results. This deception is typically small, but in rare instances it can be extreme. For example, in the 1970s **Stanley Milgram** conducted obedience experiments in which he convinced participants that they were administering painful electric shocks to other participants, when, in fact, no shocks were given. The shocked "participants" were actually collaborating with Milgram. Those giving the shocks were the real participants. Many people felt that this study was unethical, because the participants were not aware of the nature of the study and could have believed that they had done serious harm to other people. Since this time, ethical standards have been set forth by the American Psychological Association to ensure the proper treatment of animal and human subjects. Institutional Review Boards (IRBs) assess the research plans before the research is approved to ensure that it meets all ethical standards. Additionally, participants must give **informed consent**; in other words, they only agree to participate in the study after they have been told what their participation entails. Participants are also allowed to leave the experimental situation if they become uncomfortable about their participation. After the experiment is concluded, participants must receive a **debriefing** in which they are told the exact purpose of their participation in the research and of any deception that may have been used in the process of experimentation.

Pain, both physiological and psychological, is also an issue in experiments. In the past, shock was an acceptable technique with human participants. However, physical pain is infrequently used in experiments today. Psychological stress is also minimized.

Confidentiality is another area of concern for psychology. Many experiments involve collecting sensitive information about participants that the participants might not want to be revealed. For this reason, most psychological data are collected anonymously, with the participant's name not attached to the collected data. If such anonymity is not possible, it is the researcher's ethical obligation to ensure that names and sensitive information about participants are not revealed.

Animal rights within psychological experiments are a topic of controversy. According to animal-rights activists, animals often endure both physiological and psychological stress in experiments. Often the animals are euthanized at the end of the research. Psychologists counter that many life-saving drugs could not be tested were it not for tests with animals. Moreover, animal models afford a level of experimental control that is not attainable with human participants. Of course, no ethical researcher wants to cause unnecessary pain or discomfort to any subject—animal or human.

A: Informed consent is an agreement to be in a study only after hearing about what types of experiences will be confronted in the study. Informed consent allows participants to leave the experimental situation at any time without penalty.

SUBFIELDS IN PSYCHOLOGY

Psychology can be divided into two broad areas—applied and basic. **Applied psychology** is psychology put directly into practice: for example, when a therapist meets with a client. School psychology is another example. **Basic psychology** is grounded in research and is often conducted at universities and private laboratories. Other subfields of psychology include experimental, developmental, and social psychology. These subfields can be both applied and basic, such as clinical and industrial/organizational psychology, which may deal with both clients and research. Industrial psychology is the study of human organization and the application of these principles in solving the complex problems present in a variety of workplaces.

Note the difference between psychology and psychiatry. Psychiatry is the study of mental disorders, and its practitioners are medical doctors and can prescribe medication, whereas "psychology" is a much broader category.

A: Type I error refers to the conclusion that a difference exists when in fact this difference does not exist. Type II error refers to the conclusion that there is no difference when in fact there is a difference.

KEY TERMS

Experimental, Correlational, and Clinical Research

independent variable
dependent variable
experimental group
control group
population
representativeness
representative sample
random sampling
double-blind
single-blind
placebo
correlational research
confounding variable
clinical research
case studies
generalizable
conceptual definition
internal validity
external validity
alpha
reliability
operational definition
group matching
naturalistic observation

Statistics

descriptive statistics
inferential statistics
mean
median
mode
normal curve
negative skew
positive skew
variability
standard deviation
percentile
correlation coefficient
Pearson correlation coefficient
inferential statistics
null hypothesis
alternative hypothesis
Type I error
Type II error
p-value
Stanley Milgram
informed consent
debriefing
confidentiality
applied psychology
basic psychology

REVIEW QUESTIONS

See Chapter 18 for answers and explanations.

1. In a double-blind experimental design, which of the following would be true?

   (A) The experimental subjects know whether they are in an experimental group or in a control group, but the researchers do not.
   (B) The researchers know whether particular subjects have been assigned to an experimental group or a control group, but the experimental subjects do not.
   (C) Both the researchers and the experimental subjects know whether the latter have been assigned to an experimental group or a control group.
   (D) Neither the researchers nor the experimental subjects know whether the latter have been assigned to an experimental group or a control group.
   (E) The observers are unable to see the responses or behaviors of the experimental group during the course of the experimental manipulation.

2. In a normal distribution of scores, approximately what percentage of all scores will occur within one standard deviation from the mean?

   (A) 34
   (B) 68
   (C) 95
   (D) 97.5
   (E) 100

3. When testing a hypothesis, a Type II error would involve

   (A) concluding a difference between groups exists after the experimental manipulation when in fact a difference does not exist
   (B) concluding a difference between groups does not exist after the experimental manipulation when in fact a difference does exist
   (C) concluding a score is two standard deviations above the mean when in fact it is two standard deviations below the mean
   (D) concluding a score is two standard deviations below the mean when in fact it is two standard deviations above the mean
   (E) rejecting the null hypothesis when in fact it should have been accepted

4. Which of the following would NOT be considered essential for a proposed research design to meet the requirements for ethicality?

(A) Research subjects must consent to participate in the project, and a full description of what their participation consists of must be spelled out before they are asked to give consent.

(B) Participants must be allowed to withdraw from the project at any time.

(C) Both the subjects and the researchers must know which of the subjects will be part of the experimental group.

(D) If deception is involved, a full debriefing of the subjects must occur soon after the completion of the project.

(E) In keeping with protecting the privacy and confidentiality of the subjects, data should be obtained as anonymously as possible.

5. The correlation between two observed variables is –0.84. From this, it can be concluded that

(A) as one variable increases, the other is likely to increase, showing a direct relationship

(B) as one variable increases, the other is likely to decrease, showing an inverse relationship

(C) the two variables are unrelated

(D) one variable causes the other variable to occur

(E) one variable causes the other variable not to occur

6

Biological Bases
of Behavior

Physiological psychology is the study of behavior as influenced by biology. It draws its techniques and research methods from biology and medicine to examine psychological phenomena.

PHYSIOLOGICAL TECHNIQUES

Many different techniques are used to examine the interrelationship between the brain and behavior. The **EEG** (electroencephalogram) measures subtle changes in brain electrical activity through electrodes placed on the head. These data can be filtered mathematically to yield evoked potentials, which allow for localization of functions in the brain. This technique has allowed psychologists to get an electrical picture of brain activity during various cognitive states or tasks.

Computerized axial tomography scans, better known as **CAT scans**, generate cross-sectional images of the brain using a series of X-ray pictures taken from different angles. **MRI** (magnetic resonance imaging) uses extremely powerful electromagnets and radio waves to get 3-D structural information from the brain. These techniques only capture "snapshots" of the brain. They do not allow observation of the brain in action over time. Functional MRI **(fMRI)** and **PET scans** (positron emission tomography) are techniques that allow scientists to view the brain as it is working. Functional MRI provides such viewing by rapid sequencing of MRI images. PET scans provide images via diffusion of radioactive glucose in the brain. Glucose is the primary "fuel" of brain cells; the more glucose being used in a given brain area, the more that area is in active use. This procedure allows psychologists to observe what brain areas are at work during various tasks and psychological events.

FUNCTIONAL ORGANIZATION OF THE NERVOUS SYSTEM

The **nervous system** can be divided into two distinct subsystems, the **central nervous system** (CNS)—comprising the brain and the spinal cord—and the **peripheral nervous system** (PNS)—comprising all other nerves in the body.

The brain is located in the skull and is the central processing center for thoughts, motivations, and emotions. The brain, as well as the rest of the nervous system, is made up of neurons, or nerve cells. The neurons form a network that extends to the spinal cord, which is encased in the protective bones of the spine, or the vertebrae. Both the brain and the spinal cord are bathed in a protective liquid called cerebrospinal fluid. In the spinal cord the neurons are bundled into strands of interconnected neurons known as nerves. The nerves of the spine are responsible for conveying information to and from the brain and the PNS. Nerves sending information to the brain are sensory (or **afferent**) neurons; those conveying information from the brain are motor (or **efferent**) neurons. A memory tip for afferent and efferent is that **a**fferent connections are **a**rriving to the brain and **e**fferent are **e**xiting the brain. Although most movements are controlled by the brain, a certain small subset of movements are controlled by direct transmission from afferent to efferent cells at the level of the spinal cord. These responses, known as **reflexes**, are quick and involuntary responses to environmental stimuli. The path of a reflex arc goes from sensory neurons to motor neurons.

The PNS comprises all of the nerve cells in the body with the exception of those in the CNS (the brain and spinal cord). The PNS can be subdivided into the **somatic nervous system** and the **autonomic nervous system**. The somatic nervous system is responsible for voluntary movement of large skeletal muscles. The autonomic nervous system controls the nonskeletal or smooth muscles, such as those of the heart and digestive tract. These muscles are typically not under voluntary control. The autonomic nervous system can be further divided into the sympathetic and parasympathetic nervous systems.

The **sympathetic nervous system** is associated with processes that burn energy. This is the system responsible for the heightened state of physiological arousal known as the **fight-or-flight reaction**—an increase in heart rate and respiration, accompanied by a decrease in digestion and salivation. The **parasympathetic nervous system** is the complementary opposite system responsible for conserving energy. When the sympathetic system is aroused in a fight, for example, digestion ceases, blood transfers to skeletal muscle, and heart rate increases. When the fight ends, however, the parasympathetic system becomes active, sending blood to the stomach for digestion and slowing the heart rate and conserving energy. This returns the body to homeostasis.

A: The sympathetic nervous system is associated with processes that burn energy. This is the system responsible for the heightened state of physiological arousal known as the *fight-or-flight reaction*.

A: The parasympathetic system is the system responsible for conserving energy.

NEUROANATOMY

The brain is divided into three distinct regions that have evolved over time. These are the **hindbrain**, **midbrain**, and the **forebrain (limbic system and cerebral cortex)**.

THE HINDBRAIN

- The oldest part of the brain to develop in evolutionary terms

- Composed of the cerebellum, medulla oblongata, reticular activating system (RAS), pons, and thalamus

- **Cerebellum**—controls muscle tone and balance

- **Medulla oblongata**—controls involuntary actions, such as breathing, digestion, heart rate, and swallowing (basic life functions)

- **Reticular activating system (RAS)**—controls arousal (wakefulness and alertness). This is also known as reticular formation.

- **Pons**—Latin for "bridge, the pons is a way station, passing neural information from one brain region to another. The pons is also implicated in REM sleep.

- **Thalamus**—relays sensory information; receives and directs sensory information from visual and auditory systems

A. The somatic nervous system is responsible for voluntary movement of large skeletal muscles.

A: The autonomic system controls the nonskeletal or smooth muscles, such as those of the heart and digestive tract.

THE MIDBRAIN

- Major components of the midbrain are **tectum** and **tegmentum**

- These two act as the brain's roof (tectum) and floor (tegmentum).

- Tectum and tegmentum govern visual and auditory reflexes, such as orienting to a sight or sound.

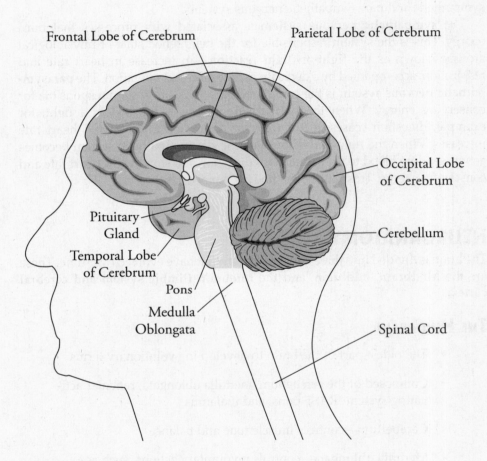

Frontal Lobe of Cerebrum

Parietal Lobe of Cerebrum

Occipital Lobe of Cerebrum

Cerebellum

Pituitary Gland

Temporal Lobe of Cerebrum

Pons

Medulla Oblongata

Spinal Cord

THE FOREBRAIN

- Contains the **limbic system**, or emotional center of the brain

- Composed of the hippocampus, amygdala, and hypothalamus

- **Hippocampus**—involved in processing and integrating memories. Damage to the hippocampus does not eliminate existing memories because memories are stored in the neocortex, but rather it prevents the formation of new memories. This condition is known as anterograde amnesia.

- **Amygdala**—implicated in the expression of anger and frustration

- **Hypothalamus**—controls the temperature and water balance of the body; controls hunger and sex drives; orchestrates the activation of the sympathetic nervous system and the endocrine system; it can be divided into the **lateral hypothalamus** and **ventromedial hypothalamus**, the combination of which regulates eating behaviors and body weight. The lateral hypothalamus is the "on switch" for eating while the ventromedial hypothalamus is the "off switch." A lesion to the latter would cause obesity and death from overeating, while a lesion to the former will lead to decreased hunger drive.

- Also contains the **cerebral cortex**, or the wrinkled outer layer of the brain.

- The cortex is involved in higher cognitive functions such as thinking, planning, language use, and fine motor control.

- This area receives sensory input (**sensory cortex**) and sends out motor information (**motor cortex**).

- The cortex covers two symmetrical-looking sides of the brain known as the **left and right cerebral hemispheres**. These hemispheres are joined together by a band of connective nerve fibers called the **corpus callosum**.

- The left hemisphere is typically specialized for language processing, as first noticed by **Paul Broca**, who observed that brain damage to the left hemisphere in stroke patients resulted in **expressive aphasia**, or loss of the ability to speak (also referred to as simply "aphasia"). This area of the brain is known as **Broca's area**. Another researcher, **Carl Wernicke**, discovered an area in the left temporal lobe that, when damaged in stroke patients, resulted in **receptive aphasia**, or the inability to comprehend speech. This is called **Wernicke's Area**.

- Others have noted that the right hemisphere processes certain kinds of visual and spatial information. **Roger Sperry** demonstrated that the two hemispheres of the brain can operate independently of each other. He did this by performing experiments on **split-brain patients**, who had their corpus callosums severed to control their epileptic seizures. Split brain patients can describe objects without deficit if presented in the right visual field (processed on the left, more verbal side of the brain), but have great difficulty drawing the image; whereas if the image is presented in the left visual field (and processed in the more visual right side of the brain), the person can draw or choose the object but cannot explain it verbally. This is called **contralateral processing**.

- The cortex can be divided into four distinct lobes: the frontal, the parietal, the temporal, and the occipital.

  - The **frontal lobe** is responsible for higher-level thought and reasoning. That includes working memory, paying attention, solving problems, making plans, forming judgments, and performing movements.

  - The **parietal lobe** handles somatosensory information and is the home of the primary somatosensory cortex. This area receives information about temperature, pressure, texture, and pain.

  - The **temporal lobe** handles auditory input and is critical for processing speech and appreciating music.

  - Finally, the **occipital lobe** processes visual input. This information crosses the **optic chiasma**.

- Much of the cerebral cortex is composed of **association areas**, which are responsible for associating information in the sensory and motor cortices (this is the plural of cortex!). Damage to these association areas can lead to a variety of dysfunctions, including **apraxia**, the inability to organize movement; **agnosia**, a difficulty processing sensory input; and **alexia**, the inability to read.

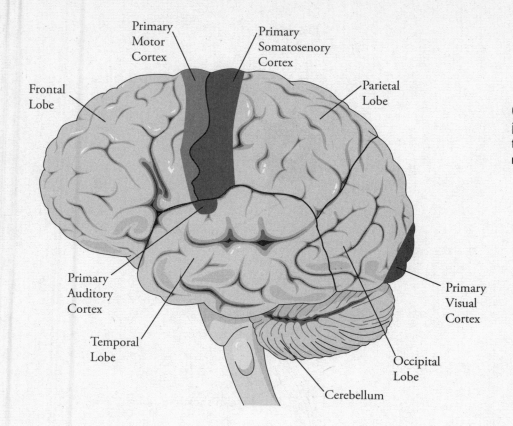

Primary
Motor
Cortex

Primary
Somatosenory
Cortex

Frontal
Lobe

Parietal
Lobe

Primary
Auditory
Cortex

Primary
Visual
Cortex

Temporal
Lobe

Occipital
Lobe

Cerebellum

Q: The two hemispheres are joined together in the center of the brain by a dense band of nerves called the _____.

NEURAL TRANSMISSION

Much of our discussion has involved the idea of information or stimulation being passed along nerves. **Nerves** are bundles of **neurons**, the basic unit of the nervous system. Neurons are cells with a clearly defined, nucleated cell body, or **soma**. Branching out from the soma are **dendrites**, which receive input from other neurons through receptors on their surface. The **axon** is a long, tubelike structure that responds to input from the dendrites and soma. The axon transmits a neural message down its length and then passes its information on to other cells. Some neurons have a fatty coating known as a **myelin sheath** surrounding the axon. Myelin serves as insulation for the electrical impulses carried down the axon and also speeds up the rate at which electrical information travels down the axon. The better insulated the myelin sheath, the fatter and more efficient the sending of action potentials. The myelin looks like beads on a string. The small gaps between the "beads" are known as the **nodes of Ranvier**. These nodes help speed up neural transmission. The axons end in **terminal buttons**, knobs on the branched end of the axon. The terminal buttons come very close to the cell body and dendrites of other neurons, but they do not touch. The gap between them is known as a **synapse**. The terminal buttons release **neurotransmitters**, chemical messengers, across the synapse, where they bind with receptors on subsequent dendrites.

Q: What purpose does myelin serve?

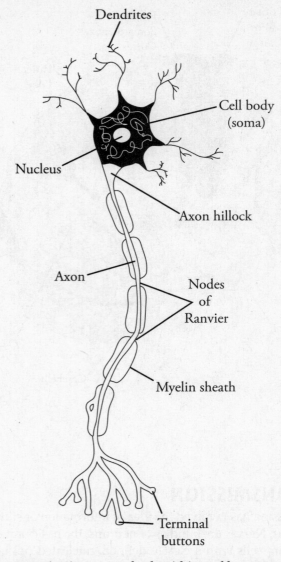

Dendrites

Cell body
(soma)

Nucleus

Axon hillock

Axon

Nodes
of
Ranvier

Myelin sheath

Terminal
buttons

A: Corpus callosum

A: Myelin serves as insulation for the electrical impulses carried down the axon, and also speeds up the rate at which electrical information travels down the axon.

Neuronal communication occurs both within and between cells. Communication within cells is electrochemical. For such communication to occur, a cell must reach a certain level of stimulation known as the threshold of excitation. Once this threshold is surpassed, an action potential forms. The **action potential** is also referred to as a **nerve impulse**. When an action potential occurs, the neuron "fires," causing the permeability of the cell membrane to change, which permits electrically charged ions of potassium and sodium to enter the cell. This event repeats down the axon, which allows the action potential to travel to terminal buttons, where it causes the release of a neurotransmitter. Action potentials are "all or none," meaning that they are either generated or not, with nothing in between. They are always of a fixed strength, never weaker nor stronger. After a neuron fires, it passes through an absolute refractory phase, during which no amount of stimulation can cause the neuron to fire again. The absolute refractory phase is followed by the relative refractory phase, in which the neuron needs much more stimulation than usual to fire again.

Communication between cells happens via neurotransmitters, which bind to receptors on the dendrites of the adjacent neurons. **Excitatory** messages from neurotransmitters serve to excite the cell or cause the neuron to fire. **Inhibitory** messages inhibit (or stop) cell firing. After a neurotransmitter is released and has conducted the impulse to the next cell or cells, it is either broken down by **enzymes** or is absorbed back into the cell that released it in a process called **reuptake**. A helpful metaphor for the process of cell communication is thinking of neurotransmitters as keys that open the locks on the postsynaptic cell.

The following are a few key neurotransmitters:

- **Acetylcholine**, which affects memory function, as well as muscle contraction, particularly in the heart

- **Serotonin**, which is related to arousal, sleep, pain sensitivity, and mood and hunger regulation

- **Dopamine**, which is associated with movement, attention, and reward; dopamine imbalances may play a role in Parkinson's disease and in schizophrenia

- **GABA**, or *gamma*-Aminobutyric acid, which is an inhibitory neurotransmitter

- **Norepinephrine**, which affects levels of alertness; a lack of norepinephrine is implicated in depression

- **Endorphins**, which are the body's natural painkillers

- **Glutamate**, which is an excitatory neurotransmitter and the all-purpose counterpart to GABA

ENDOCRINE SYSTEM

The **endocrine system** provides another way by which various parts of our bodies relay information to one another. This system works through groups of cells known as glands, which release substances called hormones. Hormones affect cell growth and proliferation. The primary gland is the **pituitary gland**, which is also known as the master gland. The pituitary releases **hormones**, which in turn control hormonal release by many other glands. Hormones are different from neurotransmitters in many ways. Neurotransmitters are released locally, while hormones are not. Hormones coordinate a wide range of responses, while neurotransmitters trigger highly localized and specific reactions. Hormones are present in the bloodstream, while neurotransmitters work in the synapse. Hormones also affect the body for long periods of time compared to neurotransmitters. The pituitary is located just under the part of the brain that controls it—the hypothalamus. Stressful situations cause the pituitary to release **adrenocorticotropic hormone (ACTH)**, which stimulates the **adrenal glands**, resulting in fight-or-flight reactions. The adrenal glands secrete **epinephrine** (adrenaline) and **norepinephrine** (noradrenaline). The **thyroid gland**, located at the front of the neck, produces **thyroxine**, which is important for regulating cellular metabolism.

GENETICS

Behavioral genetics is the application of the principles of evolutionary theory to the study of behavior. **Traits** are distinctive characteristics or behavior patterns that are determined by genetics. Genes are the basic biological elements responsible for carrying information about traits between successive generations. A **dominant trait** is more likely to be expressed in offspring than is a **recessive trait**. A **genotype** comprises all of the possible combinations of genes. Whenever a dominant gene is paired with a recessive gene, the dominant one typically will be shown in the **phenotype**, the observable result. The phenotype typically shows the recessive trait only when two recessive genes are paired together. Genes reside on rod-shaped chromosomes. Humans have 46 chromosomes, with one set of 23 inherited from each parent, so that half of our genetic makeup comes from each parent.

As mentioned earlier, the behavioral-genetics approach examines the ways in which we are different from one another. The term **heritability** is used here to discuss the degree of variance among individuals that can be attributed to genetic variations. Many physical and psychological characteristics are inherited. However, genes do not determine everything about us. **Environmentality** is the degree to which a trait's expression is caused by the environment in which an organism lives. Psychology has long been concerned with the relative influences of genetics and environment. This controversy is known as the **nature vs. nurture debate**. Today, the debate is no longer nature vs. nurture, but rather nature and nurture working together; our psychological makeup is largely the result of the interaction of the two forces.

Some disorders are the result of genetic abnormalities. **Down's syndrome** occurs when there are three copies of the twenty-first chromosome, which generally causes some degree of mental retardation. **Huntington's chorea** is a genetic disorder that results in muscle impairment that does not typically occur until after age 40. It is caused by the degeneration of the structure of the brain known as the basal ganglia and it is fatal. Because of the late onset of the disease, it is frequently passed down to the next generation before its symptoms are manifested. New genetic mapping techniques are revealing other relationships between specific genes and disorders, and scientists are trying to address ways to correct genetic flaws and provide genetic counseling.

KEY TERMS

Physiology and the Nervous System

electroencephalogram (EEG)

magnetic resonance imaging (MRI) scan

positron emission tomography (PET)
   scan

computerized axial tomography (CAT)
   scan

functional MRI (fMRI)

central nervous system (CNS)

peripheral nervous system (PNS)

afferent neurons

efferent neurons

reflexes

somatic nervous system

autonomic nervous system

sympathetic nervous system

fight-or-flight reaction

parasympathetic nervous system

Neuroanatomy

hindbrain

midbrain

forebrain

cerebral cortex

cerebellum

medulla oblongata

reticular activating system (RAS)

pons

thalamus

limbic system

hippocampus

tectum

tegmentum

amygdala

hypothalamus

lateral hypothalamus

ventromedial hypothalamus

sensory cortex

motor cortex

left and right cerebral hemispheres

Paul Broca

expressive aphasia

Carl Wernicke

receptive aphasia

Roger Sperry

split-brain patients

contralateral processing

corpus callosum

Broca's area

Wernicke's area

frontal lobe

parietal lobe

temporal lobe

occipital lobe

optic chiasma

association areas

agnosia

apraxia

alexia

Neural Transmission

nerves

neurons

axons

dendrites

soma

myelin sheath

nodes of Ranvier

terminal buttons

synapse

neurotransmitters

nerve impulse

action potential

acetylcholine

serotonin

dopamine

GABA

norepinephrine

endorphins

Endocrine System

pituitary gland

adrenal glands

hormones

adrenocorticotropic
   hormone (ACTH)

epinephrine

norepinephrine

thyroid gland

thyroxine

Genetics

dominant trait

recessive trait

genotype

phenotype

heritability

environmentality

Down's syndrome

Huntington's chorea

REVIEW QUESTIONS

See Chapter 18 for answers and explanations.

1. Damage to the Broca's area in the left cerebral hemisphere on the brain would likely result in which of the following?

   (A) A repetition of the speech of others
   (B) A loss of the ability to speak
   (C) A loss of the ability to visually integrate information
   (D) A loss of in the ability to comprehend speech
   (E) An inability to solve verbal problems

2. In the neuron, the main function of the dendrites is to

   (A) release neurotransmitters to signal subsequent neurons
   (B) preserve the speed and integrity of the neural signal as it propagates down the axon
   (C) perform the metabolic reactions necessary to nourish and maintain the nerve cell
   (D) receive input from other neurons
   (E) connect the cell body to the axon

3. Veronica is having trouble balancing as she walks, and her muscles seem to have lost strength and tone. A neuroanatomist looking into her condition would most likely suspect a problem with Veronica's

   (A) medulla oblongata
   (B) right cerebral hemisphere
   (C) cerebellum
   (D) occipital lobes
   (E) thalamus

4. Which of the following neurotransmitters is generally associated with the inhibition of continued neural signaling?

   (A) Dopamine
   (B) Adrenaline
   (C) GABA
   (D) Serotonin
   (E) Acetylcholine

5. A phenotype is best defined as

   (A) an observable trait or behavior that results from a particular genetic combination
   (B) the underlying genetic composition of a species
   (C) a biological unit within which genetic information is encoded
   (D) a recessive genetic combination that remains physically unexpressed
   (E) the genetic combination given by a parent to its offspring

6. John is constantly overeating and can't seem to control his appetite, no matter how hard he tries. It is possible that John may have damage in which of the following brain structures?

   (A) Thalamus
   (B) Pons
   (C) Hypothalamus
   (D) Amygdala
   (E) Association areas

7

Sensation and Perception

To study **sensation** is to study the relationship between physical stimulation and its psychological effects. Sensation is the process of taking in information from the environment. **Perception** is how we recognize, interpret, and organize our sensations.

THRESHOLDS

We can divide thresholds into **detection thresholds** and **discrimination thresholds**. Detection is the act of sensing a stimulus. In **psychophysics**, the branch of psychology that deals with the effects of physical stimuli on sensory response, researchers determine the smallest amount of sound, pressure, taste, or other stimuli that an individual can detect. Psychologists conducting this type of experiment are attempting to determine the **absolute threshold**—the minimal amount of stimulation needed to detect a stimulus and cause the neuron to fire 50 percent of the time. At the absolute threshold we cannot detect lower levels of stimuli but we can detect higher levels.

In a typical absolute-threshold experiment an experimenter plays a series of tones of varying volume to determine at exactly what volume the participant first reports that she can hear the tone. Another approach to measuring detection thresholds involves **signal detection theory (SDT)**. This theory takes into consideration that there are four possible outcomes on each trial in a detection experiment: the signal (stimulus) is either present or it is not, and the participants respond that they can detect a signal or they cannot. Therefore, we have the following four possibilities:

- **Hit**—the signal was present, and the participant reported sensing it.

- **Miss**—the signal was present, but the participant did not sense it.

- **False alarm**—the signal was absent, but the participant reported sensing it.

- **Correct rejection**—the signal was absent, and the participant did not report sensing it.

SDT takes into account response bias, moods, feelings, and decision-making strategies that affect our likelihood of making a given response.

Another type of threshold is the discrimination threshold, which is the ability to distinguish the difference between two stimuli. The minimum amount of distance between two stimuli that can be detected as distinct is called the **just noticeable difference (JND)** or **difference threshold**. In this case, the experiment might involve playing pairs of tones of varying volumes. The participants would

try to determine if the tones that they heard were the same or different.

Ernst Weber (1795–1878) noticed that at low weights, say one ounce, it was easy to notice one-half-ounce increases or decreases in weight; however, at high weights, say 32 ounces, participants were not well able to judge one-half-ounce differences. The observation that the JND is a proportion of stimulus intensity is called **Weber's law**. Simply put, this law states that the greater the magnitude of the stimulus, the larger the differences must be to be noticed.

Subliminal perception is a form of preconscious processing that occurs when we are presented with stimuli so rapidly that we are not consciously aware of them. When later presented with the subliminally presented stimuli for a longer period of time, we recognize them more quickly than stimuli we were not subliminally exposed to. Clearly there was some processing (preconscious) occurring, even if we were not aware of it. Another example of preconscious information processing can be seen in the **tip-of-the-tongue phenomenon**, in which we try to recall something that we already know that is available but not easily accessible to consciousness. This phenomenon demonstrates that certain preconscious information may be available to the conscious mind but quite difficult to access.

A: Sensation is the relationship between physical stimulation and its psychological effects.

RECEPTOR PROCESSES

Sensory organs have specialized cells, known as **receptor cells**, which are designed to detect specific types of energy. For example, the visual system has specialized receptor cells for detecting light waves. The area from which our receptor cells receive input is the **receptive field**. Incoming forms of energy to which our receptors are sensitive include mechanical (such as in touch), electromagnetic (such as in vision), and chemical (such as in taste). No matter what the form of the input at the level of the receptor, it must first be converted, or transduced, into the electro-chemical form of communication used by the nervous system. Through a process called **transduction**, the receptors convert the input, or stimulus, into neural impulses, which are sent to the brain. For example, when we hear something, tiny receptor cells in the inner ear first convert mechanical vibrations into electrochemical signals. These signals are then carried by neurons to the brain. Transduction takes place at the level of the receptor cells, and then the neural message is passed to the nervous system. The incoming information from all of our senses except for smell travels to the sensory neurons of the thalamus. The thalamus, as you will recall from the neuroanatomy section, redirects this information to various sensory cortices in the cerebral cortex where it is processed. It is at the level of the thalamus that the **contralateral shift** occurs, in which much of the sensory input from one side of the body travels to the opposite side of the brain. Olfaction, or the sense of smell, travels in a more direct path to the cerebral cortex, without stopping at or being relayed by the thalamus.

A: Perception is the study of how we recognize, interpret, and organize our sensations.

A: The receptive field is the area from which our receptor cells receive input.

A: Contralateral shift refers to the switch of sensory input from one side of the body to the opposite side of the brain.

SENSORY MECHANISMS

Sensory receptors deal with a wide range of stimuli, and we experience a wide variety of input within each given sensory dimension. Imagine, for example, the gamut of colors and intensities that the eye can sense and relate to the brain. **Sensory coding** is the process by which receptors convey such a range of information to the brain. Every stimulus has two dimensions: what it is (i.e., its qualitative dimension) and how much of it there is (i.e., its quantitative dimension). The qualitative dimension is coded and expressed by which neurons are firing. For example, neurons firing in the occipital lobe would indicate that the sensory information is light, and neurons firing in the temporal lobe might

A: Subliminal perception is a form of preconscious processing that occurs when we are presented with stimuli so quickly that we are not consciously aware of them.

indicate that the sensory stimulus is sound. In contrast, the quantitative information is coded by the number of cells firing. Bright lights and loud noises involve the excitation of more neurons than those brought on by dim lights and quiet noises. The wavelengths of light and frequency of sound are perceived as hue and pitch, respectively. The physical characteristic of amplitude is perceived as brightness for light and loudness for sound. Similarly, the physical trait of complexity is known as saturation when dealing with light and timbre when referring to sound. Sensory neurons respond to differing environmental stimuli by altering their firing rate and the regularity of their firing pattern. **Single cell recording** is a technique by which the firing rate and pattern of a single receptor cell can be measured in response to varying sensory input.

Sensation occurs in differing ways for the various sensory systems. **Visual sensation** occurs when the eye receives light input from the outside world. Note that the object as it exists in the environment is known as the **distal stimulus**, whereas the image of that object on the retina is called the **proximal stimulus**. Because of the shape of the retina and the positions of the cornea and the lens, the proximal stimulus is inverted. The brain, through sensation perception processes, is then capable of interpreting this image correctly.

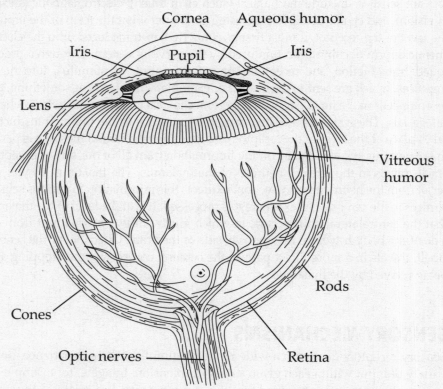

Q: What are the two types of receptors in the eye, and what are their functions?

Visual sensation is a complex process. First light passes through the **cornea**, which is a protective layer on the outside of the eye. Just under the cornea is the **lens**. The curvature of the lens changes to accommodate for distance. These changes are called, logically, **accommodations**. The **retina** is at the back of the eye and serves as the screen onto which the proximal stimulus is projected. The retina is covered with receptors known as **rods** and **cones**. Rods, located on the periphery of the retina, are sensitive in low light. Cones, concentrated in the center of the retina, or **fovea**, are sensitive to bright light and color vision. After light stimulates the receptors, this information passes through horizontal cells to **bipolar** and **amacrine cells**. Some low-level information processing may occur here. The stimulation then travels to the ganglion cells of the **optic nerves**. The optic nerves cross at the **optic chiasma**, sending half of the information from each visual field to the opposite side of the brain. Each visual field includes information from both the left and right eye. From here information travels to the primary visual cortex areas for processing. The brain processes the information received from vision—color, movement, depth, and form—in parallel, not serial, fashion. In other words, the brain is simultaneously identifying the patterns of what is seen. **Serial processing** occurs when the brain computes information step-by-step in a methodical and linear matter, while **parallel processing** happens when the brain computes multiple pieces of information simultaneously. Over time and through practice, serial processes can turn into parallel processes, just as riding a bike initially requires a person to consider each decision, but later is done seemingly automatically. **Feature detector** neurons "see" different parts of the pattern such as a line set at a specific angle to background. Like pieces of a jigsaw puzzle, these parts are amalgamated to produce the pattern in the environment. This process starts at the back of the occipital lobe and moves forward. As the information moves forward, it becomes more complex and integrated. This process, by which information becomes more complex as it travels through the sensory system, is known as convergence and occurs across all sensory systems. Once lines and colors have been sensed, the information travels through two pathways: the dorsal stream and the ventral stream. The ventral stream is the "what" pathway that connects to the prefrontal cortex, allowing a person to recognize an object. The dorsal stream is the "where" pathway that integrates visual information with the other senses through a connection to the somatosensory cortex at the top of the brain.

Two different processes contribute to our ability to see in color. The first is based on the **Young-Helmholtz** or **trichromatic theory**. According to this theory, the cones in the retina of the eyes are activated by light waves associated with blue, red, and green. We see all colors by mixing these three much as a television does. However, this does not tell the whole story. Another theory, known as **opponent process theory**, contends that cells within the thalamus respond to opponent pairs of receptor sets—namely, black/white, red/green, and blue/yellow. If one color of the set is activated, the other is essentially turned off. For example, when you stare at a red dot on a page and then you turn away to a blank piece of white paper, you will see a green dot on the blank piece of paper because the red receptors have become fatigued and, in comparison, the green receptors are now more active. This is known as an **afterimage**. **Color blindness** responds to this theory as well. Most color-blindness occurs in males, which provides strong evidence that this is a sex-linked genetic condition. Dichromats are people who cannot distinguish along the red/green or blue/yellow continuums. Monochromats see only in shades of black and white (this is much more rare). Most color blindness is genetic.

A: Rods and cones. Rods are sensitive in low light, whereas cones are responsible for vision in bright light and for color vision.

AUDITORY MECHANISMS

Auditory input in the form of sound waves enters the ear by passing the outer ear, the part of the ear that is on the outside of your head, and into the ear canal.

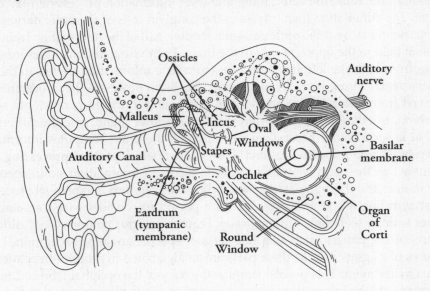

The outer ear collects and magnifies sound waves. The vibrations then enter the middle ear, first vibrating the **tympanic membrane**. This membrane abuts the **ossicles**, the three tiny bones that comprise the middle ear. Vibration of the tympanic membrane vibrates the ossicles. The last of the three ossicles is the **stapes**, which vibrates against the oval window. The oval window is the beginning of the inner ear. The vibrations further jiggle the cochlea. Within the cochlea are receptor cells, known as hair cells, so named for their hair-like cilia which move in response to the vibrations. The hair cells line a structure in the cochlea called the basilar membrane. From the cochlea, sound energy is transferred to the auditory nerve and then to the temporal lobe of the auditory cortex. The inner ear is also responsible for balance and contains **vestibular sacs**, which have receptors sensitive to tilting.

Various theories have been suggested for how hearing occurs. Current thinking relies on the work of Georg von Békésy, which asserts that a traveling wave energizes the basilar membrane. As frequencies get higher so do the peaks of the traveling wave, increasing the stimulation of the receptors for hearing. This accounts for recognition of sound above 150 Hz. However, humans can hear from 20 to 20,000 Hz. The volley principle—which states that receptor cells fire alternatively, increasing their firing capacity—appears to account for the reception of sound in the lower ranges.

Place theory asserts that sound waves generate activity at different places along the basilar membrane. **Frequency theory** in hearing states that we sense pitch because the rate of neural impulses is equal to the frequency of a particular sound.

Deafness can occur from damage to the ear structure or the neural pathway. **Conductive deafness** refers to injury to the outer or middle ear structures, such as the eardrum. Impairment of some structure or structures from the cochlea to the auditory cortex results in **sensorineural**, or nerve deafness.

Olfaction (smell) is a chemical sense. Scent molecules reach the olfactory epithelium, deep in the nasal cavity. The scent molecules contact receptor cells at this location. Axons from these receptors project directly to the olfactory bulbs of the brain. From there information travels to the olfactory cortex and the limbic system.

Gustation (taste) is also a chemical sense. The tongue is coated with small protrusions known as papillae. Located on the papillae are the taste buds, the receptors for gustatory information. There are five basic tastes: sweet, salty, bitter, sour, and umami (savory). These five tastes may have evolved for specific reasons. For example, sweetness, which we tend to like, is often accompanied by calories. Most poisonous plants, in contrast, taste bitter, a taste we generally do not like. Information from the taste buds travels to the medulla oblongata and then to the pons and the thalamus. This information is then relayed to the gustatory areas of the cerebral cortex, as well as the hypothalamus and limbic system.

The skin has **cutaneous** and **tactile receptors** that provide information about pressure, pain, and temperature. The receptor cells sensitive to pressure and movement are fast-conducting myelinated neurons, which send information to the spinal cord. From here the information goes to the medulla oblongata, the thalamus, and finally, to the somatosensory cortex. Pain information is sent via two types of neurons, C fibers are unmyelinated and responsible for the throbbing sense of chronic pain, while myelinated A-delta fibers send information about acute pain. The pain signal first reaches the spinal cord and triggers the release of "substance P" (which is a neuropeptide, or chemical signal similar to a neurotansmitter, that alerts the spinal cord to the presence of a painful stimulus). The signal then travels to the thalamus and to the cingulated cortex, which is responsible for attention. Once pain is perceived, the brain begins to reduce the intensity of the signal through a process known as "pain-gating." A signal is sent from the brain to opiate receptors in the spinal cord, which reduces the sensation of pain. This information projects to the limbic system, and then to the somatosensory cortex. The receptor cells for temperature can be divided into **cold fibers**, which fire in response to cold stimuli, and **warm fibers**, which are sensitive to warm stimuli.

Other senses include the **vestibular sense**, which involves sensation of balance. This sense is located in the semicircular canals of the inner ear. **Kinesthesis**, found in the joints and ligaments, transmits information about the location and position of the limbs and body parts.

Use this table to compare and contrast different sensory systems.

Sensory system	Receptor cells location	Type of energy	Transduction	Processing center location
Visual	Eye	Light	Rods and cones in the retina	Occipital lobe
Auditory	Ear	Sound	Cochlea	Temporal lobe
Tactile	Tactile and cutaneous cells on the skin	Pressure	Tactile cells	Somatosensory cortex
Olfaction (smell)	Nose	Chemical	Olfactory receptor cells	Olfactory bulb
Gustation (taste)	Tongue	Chemical	Taste buds	Cerebral cortex

Q: What is habituation?

Q: What is dishabituation?

Q: Describe the cocktail party phenomenon.

SENSORY ADAPTATION

Our sensory systems need to do more than simply detect the presence and absence of stimulation. They also need to do more than detect the intensity or quality of stimuli. A key feature of our sensory systems is that they are dynamic, that is, they detect changes in stimuli intensity and quality. Two processes are used in responding to changing stimuli: adaptation and habituation.

Adaptation is an unconscious, temporary change in response to environmental stimuli. An example of this process is our adaptation to being in darkness. At first it is difficult to see, but our visual system soon adapts to the lack of light. Sensory adaptation to differing stimuli leaves our sensory systems at various adaptation levels. The adaptation level is the new reference standard of stimulation against which new stimuli are judged. A familiar example is that of the swimming pool. If you enter a 75-degree swimming pool directly from an air-conditioned room, it will feel warm, as your adaptation level is set for the cold room. If, however, you are on a hot beach and then enter the same pool, it will feel cold, as your adaptation level is set for the heat of the beach.

Habituation is the process by which we become accustomed to a stimulus, and notice it less and less over time. **Dishabituation** occurs when a change in the stimulus, even a small change, causes us to notice it again. A good example of this pair of processes is in the noise from an air conditioner. We may notice a noisy air conditioner when we first enter a room, but after a few minutes, we barely even notice it; we have habituated to the noise. However, when the air conditioner's compressor turns on, slightly altering the sound being generated, we once again notice the noise. This noticing is dishabituation. Although habituation is not typically a conscious process, we can control it under certain circumstances. If, in the examples above, we are unaware of the air-conditioner noise, but then someone asks us if the noise of the air conditioner sounds like something else, we can force ourselves to dishabituate, and again notice the noise. This control over our information processing is the key to distinguishing habituation from sensory adaptation: You cannot control sensory adaptation; for example you cannot force your eyes to dark adapt by mere force of will. You can, however, force yourself to pay attention to things to which you have habituated.

A: Habituation is the process by which we become accustomed to a stimulus and notice it less and less over time.

A: Dishabituation occurs when a change in a stimulus, even a small change, causes us to notice the stimulus again.

ATTENTION

The term **attention** refers to the processing through cognition of a select portion of the massive amount of information incoming from the senses and contained in memory. In common terms, attention is what allows us to focus on one small aspect of our perceptual world, such as a conversation, while constantly being assailed by massive input to all of our sensory systems. Attention serves as a bottleneck or funnel that channels out some information in order to focus on other information. This process is essential because the brain is not equipped to process and pay attention to all of the information it is presented with at a particular moment. The fact that the brain must take shortcuts and focus on particular information is a key issue in perception, which explains why the brain can be tricked through illusions. A good example of attention in action is **selective attention**, by which we try to attend to one thing while ignoring another. For

A: The cocktail party phenomenon refers to our ability to carry on and follow a single conversation in a room full of conversations.

example, we try to attend to a movie, while trying to ignore the people having a conversation behind us. An example of selective attention is called the "**cocktail party phenomenon**," which refers to our ability to carry on and follow a single conversation in a room full of conversations. At the same time, our attention can quickly be drawn to another conversation by key stimuli, such as someone saying our name. This recognition of our name is a demonstration that, although we are not paying very much attention to those other conversations, we are definitely attending to information we are not consciously aware of at that moment. This phenomenon has been studied in the laboratory with headphones, by playing a different message in each of a participant's ears. The participant is instructed to repeat only one of the conversations. This repetition is referred to as **shadowing**. The message played into the nonshadowed ear is largely ignored, however. Changes in that message or key words, like names, can draw attention to that message. There are two main types of theories explaining selective attention; filter theories and attentional resource theories. **Filter theories** propose that stimuli must pass through some form of screen or filter to enter into attention. Donald Broadbent proposed a filter at the receptor level. However, the notion of a filter at this level has generally been discarded, based on findings showing that meaningful stimuli, such as our own names, can catch our attention. Therefore the filter must be at a higher processing level than that of the receptors. It is easiest, though, for people to tell the difference between the messages when they are physically different, such as when one message is spoken by a woman and the other by a man.

Attentional resource theories, in contrast, posit that we have only a fixed amount of attention, and that this resource can be divided up as is required in a given situation. So, if you are deeply engrossed in this book, you are giving it nearly all of your attentional resources. Only strong stimulation could capture your attention. This theory is also inadequate, however, because all attention is not equal. For example, a conversation occurring near you is more likely to interfere with your reading than is some other nonverbal noise.

Divided attention, trying to focus on more than one task at a time, is most difficult when attending to two or more stimuli that activate the same sense, as in watching TV and reading. The ability to successfully divide attention declines with age.

PERCEPTUAL PROCESSES

When we were describing sensory mechanisms, we talked about how environmental stimuli affect the receptor systems. This section deals with **perceptual processes**—how our mind interprets these stimuli. There are two main theories of perception—bottom-up and top-down.

Bottom-up processing achieves recognition of an object by breaking it down into its component parts. It relies heavily on the sensory receptors. Bottom-up processing is the brain's analysis and acknowledgement of the raw data. **Top-down processing**, by contrast, is when the brain labels a particular stimulus or experience. For example, let's think about the first time a person tastes the

Remember This!

Sensation = bottom-up process

Perception = top-down process

sourness of a lemon. In this example, the neurons firing to alert the brain of the presence of some taste in the mouth is a bottom-up process, whereas labeling it "sour" is the top-down process. However, the next time the person sees a lemon, they might salivate or wince before ever tasting the lemon. This is top-down processing because the expectation based on experience influences the perception of the lemon.

Visual perception is quite complex. We need to perceive depth, size, shape, and motion. Depth perception is facilitated by various perceptual cues. Because of the limited ability of the brain to process information, it must take certain shortcuts and educated guesses based on how the world is normally structured. As such, the brain uses these cues but can also fall victim to illusions.

These cues can be divided into monocular and binocular cues. **Monocular depth cues** are those that we need only one eye to see. As such, they can be depicted in two-dimensional representations. **Relative size** refers to the fact that images that are farther from us project a smaller image on the retina than do those that are closer to us. Therefore, we expect an object that appears much larger than another to be closer to us. Related to this idea is the idea of **texture gradient**. Textures, or the patterns of distribution of objects, appear to grow more dense as distance increases. If we are looking at pebbles in the distance, they appear smooth and uniform, but close up may appear jagged and rough. Another monocular depth cue is **interposition**, also known as occlusion, which occurs when a near object partially blocks the view of an object behind it. **Linear perspective** is a monocular cue based on the perception that parallel lines seem to draw closer together as the lines recede into the distance. Picture yourself standing on a train track, looking at the two rails. As the rails move away from you, they appear to draw closer together. The place where the rails seem to join is called the **vanishing point**. This is the point at which the two lines become indistinguishable from a single line, and then disappear. Objects present near the vanishing point are assumed to be farther away than those along the tracks at a point where they diverge greatly. **Aerial perspective**, another perceptual cue, is based on the observation that atmospheric moisture and dust tend to obscure objects in the distance more than they do nearby objects. An example of this notion occurs when one is driving in the fog; a far-off building looks more distant than it really is through the fog, but its image quickly becomes clearer and clearer as you approach. **Relative clarity** is a perceptual clue that explains why less distinct, fuzzy images appear to be more distant. **Motion parallax** is the difference in the apparent movement of objects at different distances, when the observer is in motion. For example, when riding on a train, a person sees distant objects out of a window as seeming to move fairly slowly; they may appear to move in the same direction as the train. Near objects seem to move more quickly, and in the opposite direction to the movement of the train. Note that motion parallax differs from other monocular depth cues in that it requires motion and cannot be represented in a two-dimensional image.

Binocular depth cues rely on both eyes viewing an image. They result from the fact that each eye sees a given image from a slightly different angle. **Stereopsis** refers to the three-dimensional image of the world resulting from binocular vision. **Retinal convergence** is a depth cue that results from the fact that your eyes must turn inward slightly to focus on near objects. The closer the object, the more the eyes must turn inward. The complement to stereopsis is **binocular disparity**, which results from the fact that the closer an object is, the less similar the information arriving at each eye will be. This process can be demonstrated by covering one eye, and then the other, while looking at something directly in front of you. This procedure reveals two very different views of the object. Repeat this procedure with an object across the room, however, and the two views appear more similar.

Together, the binocular cues for vision enable us to have depth perception. To test whether depth perception was innate (nature) or learned (nurture), researchers **Eleanor Gibson and Richard Walk** developed the **visual cliff** to test depth perception. The visual cliff was a glass tabletop that appeared to be clear on one side and had a checkerboard design visible on the other side. The infants were placed on the "cliff" to see if they would cross over to the deep side. Most infants did not cross over, only after they learned to crawl, which implied that depth perception was at least partially innate. Because the infant had to be a few months old, it was unclear how much learning had influenced depth perception. With other animals that they tested, chicks, pigs, kittens, turtles, it was concluded that the animal's visual skills depended on the importance of vision to the organism's survival.

As previously stated, the visual system also needs to perceive and recognize form, that is, size and shape. The **Gestalt approach** to form perception is based on a **top-down theory**. This view holds that most perceptual stimuli can be broken down into figure-ground relationships. Figures are those things that stand out, whereas the ground is the field against which the figures stand out. The famous vase-face example shows us that figure and ground are often reversible.

Some basic Gestalt principles of figure detection include the following:

- **Proximity**—the tendency to see objects near to each other as forming groups

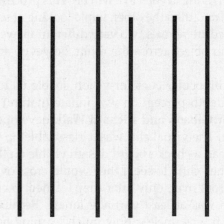

The Gestalt Principle of Proximity: We tend to see these as three pairs of lines, rather than six individual lines.

- **Similarity**—the tendency to prefer to group like objects together

Q: What are some Gestalt principles of perception?

The Gestalt Principle of Similarity: We tend to see these as rows of circles and squares, rather than columns of circles then squares.

- **Symmetry**—the tendency to perceive preferentially forms that make up mirror images

The Gestalt Principle of Symmetry: We tend to see the top figures as a single circle, and the lower figures as forming a single triangle.

- **Continuity**—the tendency to perceive preferentially fluid or continuous forms, rather than jagged or irregular ones

A: Proximity, Similarity, Symmetry, Continuity, Closure.

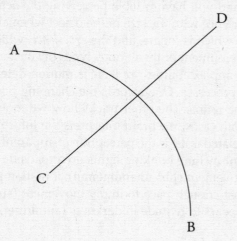

The Gestalt Principle of Continuity: We tend to see this as two lines, one from point A to point B, the other from C to D, rather than seeing it as A to D and C to B.

- **Closure**—the tendency preferentially to "close up" objects that are not complete

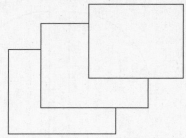

The Gestalt Principle of Closure: We tend to see this
as three squares, even though there is actually only
one square that is completely visible.

These Gestalt principles represent the **law of Pragnanz**, or minimum tendency, meaning that we tend to see objects in their simplest forms.

A different theory of form recognition is based on a **feature detector approach**. This approach differs from the law of Pragnanz, which reduces an image to its simplest form by positing that organisms respond to specific aspects of a particular stimulus. For example, when driving a car we use feature detection to anticipate the movement of other cars and pedestrians that demand our immediate attention, helping us to be more aware of the environment.

Constancy is another important perceptual process. Constancy means that we know that a stimulus remains the same size, shape, brightness, weight, and/or volume even though it does not appear to. People who have never seen airplanes on the ground will have trouble perceiving the actual size of a plane because of their experience with the size of the object when airborne. The *ability* to achieve constancy, which is innate, and the *experience*, which is learned, both contribute to our development of the various types of constancy.

One of the most complex abilities we have is **motion detection**. We perceive motion through two processes. One records the changing position of the object as it moves across the retina. The other tracks how we move our head to follow the stimuli. In both cases, the brain interprets the information with special motion detectors. A related issue is the perception of **apparent motion**. Examples of apparent movement include blinking lights on a roadside arrow, which give the appearance of movement (**phi phenomenon**); a motion picture, where still pictures move at a fast enough pace to imply movement (**stroboscopic effect**); and still light that appears to twinkle in darkness (**autokinetic effect**).

KEY TERMS

Thresholds
sensation perception
detection thresholds
discrimination thresholds
absolute threshold
psychophysics
signal detection theory (SDT)
just noticeable difference (JND)
Ernst Weber
Weber's law
subliminal perception
tip-of-the-tongue phenomenon

Receptor Processes
receptor cells
receptive field
transduction
contralateral shift

Sensory Mechanism
sensory coding
single cell recording
visual sensation
distal stimulus
proximal stimulus
cornea
lens
accomodations
bipolar
amacrine cells
iris
pupil
aqueous humor
vitreous humor
cones
rods
fovea
retina
optic nerves
optic chiasma
serial processing
parallel processing
feature detector
Young-Helmholtz theory
trichromatic theory
afterimage

color blindness
opponent process theory
auditory input
tympanic membrane
cochlea
ossicles
malleus
incus
stapes
vestibular sacs
place theory
frequency theory
deafness
conductive deafness
sensorineural
auditory canal
auditory nerve
olfaction
gustation
cutaneous receptors
tactile receptors
cold fibers
warm fibers
vestibular sense
kinesthesis

Sensory Adaptation
adaptation
habituation
dishabituation

Attention
selective attention
cocktail-party phenomenon
shadowing
attentional resource theories
filter theories
divided attention

Perceptual Processes
- bottom-up processing
- top-down processing
- visual perception
- texture gradient
- monocular depth cues
- relative size
- linear perspective
- vanishing point
- aerial perspective
- relative clarity
- Eleanor Gibson and Richard Walk
- motion parallax
- binocular depth cues
- retinal convergence
- stereopsis
- binocular disparity
- visual cliff
- Gestalt approach
- law of Pragnanz
- constancy
- apparent motion
- proximity
- similarity
- symmetry
- continuity
- closure
- feature detector approach
- motion detection
- phi phenomenon
- stroboscopic effect
- autokinetic effect

REVIEW QUESTIONS

See Chapter 18 for answers and explanations.

1. Which of the following is NOT an example of a monocular visual depth perception cue?

    (A) Texture gradient
    (B) Motion parallax
    (C) Interposition
    (D) Opponent process
    (E) Relative size

2. The five basic gustatory sensations that most animals possess are

    (A) bitter, salty, sweet, tangy, sour
    (B) salty, sweet, bitter, sour, umami
    (C) smooth, grainy, cold, hot, prickly
    (D) grain, fruit, meat, vegetable, dairy
    (E) salty, sharp, umami, sour, bitter

3. Cats tend to notice slight movements under low lighting conditions with greater ease than do humans; they do not, however, find it easy to distinguish colors. This is primarily due to their retinas containing, in comparison to humans

    (A) relatively fewer numbers of amarcine cells and relatively more bipolar cells
    (B) relatively fewer numbers of ganglion cells and relatively more osmoreceptors
    (C) relatively fewer numbers of cilia and relatively more optic nerve cells
    (D) relatively fewer numbers of cones and relatively more rods
    (E) relatively fewer numbers of mechanoreceptors and relatively more ossicles

4. The Gestalt concept of perceptual continuity refers to

    (A) our tendency to see objects near to each other as belonging to the same group
    (B) our tendency to see objects that are closer to us as larger than objects that are farther away
    (C) our tendency to see fluid or complete forms rather than irregular or incomplete ones
    (D) our tendency to see similar-looking objects as part of the same group
    (E) our tendency to see two slightly different images from each of our eyes

5. Which of the following would be the best illustration of Weber's law?

    (A) As sound increases to 80 decibels from 40 decibels, most people can recognize that one sound is louder than the other. However, if the two sounds are given at 80 and 82 decibels respectively, most people would not recognize the difference between the two sounds.
    (B) A person can recognize an imperceptible amount of perfume in a ten foot-by-ten-foot room.
    (C) People cannot attend to more than one stimulus at a time.
    (D) A person has the ability to tell the difference between a 20 watt bulb and a 100 watt bulb 50 percent of the time.
    (E) All auditory stimuli above a certain frequency "sound" as if their frequencies are the same.

TEST BREAK #1

Throughout the rest of this book, you will find "Test Breaks"—drills designed to help you hone your test-taking skills while giving you a break from your psychology review. Use these Test Breaks to practice the various smart-tester strategies you have learned.

SMART-TESTER STRATEGY #1: ASK IT LIKE IT IS

Before you can answer a question, you need to know what it is asking. To avoid careless errors, put the question into your own words before you try to answer it. On some questions, you may find it useful to circle the key word(s) in the question. Use the following drill questions to practice Smart-Tester Strategy #1: Ask It Like It Is. The answers are on page 212.

7. Which of the following best summarizes the differences between the psychoanalytic and the behaviorist perspectives?

22. Louis is suffering from severe headaches and occasional moments of disorientation or even mental paralysis. His doctors are interested in examining the brain for lesions. Which of the following technologies would prove most useful in examining various regions of Louis's brain?

39. The somatosensory cortex is the primary area of the

58. In the processing of visual information, a fully integrated image does not appear until the information has reached which of the following regions of the brain?

78. If a participant does not report a stimulus when no stimulus is present in a signal-detection experimental trial, it is known as a

89. The lower the p-value of a study, the

8

States of
Consciousness

CONSCIOUSNESS

Q: Define *consciousness*.

A **state of consciousness** enables us to evaluate the environment and to filter information from the environment through the mind, while being aware of the occurrence of this complex process. Philosophers and psychologists have debated the nature of consciousness for generations. **William James** referred to consciousness as the **stream of thought**. The cognitive psychologist Robert Sternberg refers to consciousness as a **mental reality** that we create in order to adapt to the world. It serves to establish our personal identity.

Consciousness serves two important functions. First, consciousness is responsible for monitoring, or keeping track of, ourselves, our environment, and our relationship with the environment. Additionally, consciousness serves a controlling role, planning our responses to the information gathered by monitoring. We typically think of ourselves as fully conscious, but there are lower levels of consciousness, specifically the preconscious and unconscious levels.

The **preconscious level** contains information that is available to consciousness, but that is not always in consciousness. It can be retrieved when needed. This is where directions to frequently visited places might be stored. The preconscious is also where many automatic behaviors are stored. You use these behaviors in tasks that you can do nearly without thought, such as riding a bicycle.

Consciousness exists on a continuum—starting from **controlled processing**, where we are very aware of what we are doing, and moving on to **automatic processing**, where we perform tasks mechanically, such as brushing our teeth. The continuum proceeds through daydreaming, a state in which we can regain consciousness in a moment, and meditation. Then come sleep and dreaming and then, at the far end of the spectrum, coma and unconsciousness.

SLEEP AND DREAMING

Sleep is an altered state of consciousness. Interestingly, scientists still do not precisely understand the function of sleep. One theory holds that sleep is necessary for restorative processes. If this theory is correct, then some chemical in the body should be associated with sleep. Researchers have discovered some neurochemicals, notably **melatonin**, that play a role in sleep, yet a definitive cause-and-effect relationship between a brain chemical and the control of sleep has not been demonstrated.

Another theory of sleep is based on evolution. According to this point of view, our ancestors who survived to pass on their genes were diurnal (awake during the day and asleep at night). Our nocturnal ancestors were more likely to meet with disaster and die off before passing on their genes, as their visual system was not built to survive at night and avoid nocturnal predators.

In addition to conducting chemical investigations of sleep, psychologists investigate the functions of sleep by depriving animals or humans of it. It is difficult to deprive organisms of sleep, as the need for sleep is very strong. One 24-hour cycle without sleep is tolerable, but the second such cycle is considerably more difficult. By the third 24-hour cycle, **hallucinations** can begin, as well as **illusions**. Four 24-hour cycles of sleep deprivation can lead to paranoia and other psychological disturbances. All of the symptoms of sleep deprivation disappear when the deprived person is allowed to sleep again.

Another approach to the study of sleep is to investigate the pattern of sleeping. Sleeping generally occurs in humans during the time their area of the world is in darkness; that is, at night. People who live in extreme northern or southern exposures, where it may be light for close to 24 hours, generally try to create conditions of darkness in order to sleep. Our body temperature and other physiological markers follow a day-to-night type of pattern, known as a **circadian rhythm.** Because of the nature of the relationship of the earth and the sun, this natural day-night rhythm is a 24-hour one. Our circadian rhythms generally match this pattern. However, if all time cues (sunlight, clocks, television, etc.) are removed, then we tend to follow roughly a 25-hour rhythm, called free-running rhythm.

External stimuli are important to setting our circadian rhythms. Rapidly changing these stimuli, such as in the case of traveling across time zones, can disturb circadian rhythms. In this example, the result can be the unpleasant feelings associated with jet lag.

Sleep itself is not a uniform process. Rather, sleep can be divided into stages based on brain-wave patterns. Brain waves usually are measured with **electroencephalograms (EEGs)**, which provide a picture of the electrical activity of the brain. When we are awake and focused, **beta wave** activity is happening. While still awake but more relaxed, we drift into **alpha waves**. Then, when we drift off to sleep, **theta wave** activity takes over. In stage 2 sleep, a pattern of waves known as **sleep spindles** appears. These spindles are occasionally broken up by **K complexes**, which are large, slow waves. The skeletal muscles relax during this portion of sleep. In stages 3 and 4, **delta waves** are most common, with a larger proportion of delta waves occurring during stage 4 sleep. The last stage of sleep is called **REM (rapid eye movement)** sleep. In all other stages of sleep, which often are referred to collectively as NREM or non-REM sleep, the eyes are relatively still. Researchers **Aserinsky** and **Kleitman** discovered that the eyes move

A: Consciousness is the process of evaluating the environment and filtering this information through the mind, while being aware of this process's occurrence.

vigorously during the REM stage. This stage of sleep is typically associated with dreaming, although it is not the only stage of sleep in which dreaming occurs. In REM sleep, our brain waves are mostly theta and beta. The fact that this is a very deep stage of sleep, characterized by suppressed skeletal muscle tone, yet our brain waves resemble those observed when we are nearly awake, has led investigators to refer to REM sleep as **paradoxical sleep**.

Q: What forms can insomnia take?

Each sleep cycle is approximately 90 minutes long; therefore, if we sleep 7 and one half hours we will experience 5 cycles. We drift through the stages of sleep as follows:

- Stage 1: for up to 5 minutes

- Stage 2: for about 20 minutes

- Stage 3: for another 10 minutes

- Stage 4: for about 30 minutes

- Then back up through stage 3 for 10 minutes

- Stage 2: for 10 minutes

- Stage 1: for 1 or 2 minutes

- Then into REM sleep for 10 minutes

As the period of sleep progresses, stages 3 and 4 diminish and eventually disappear. Meanwhile the REM or dream sleep gets longer, until near morning the dreams are approximately one hour long. Because of their proximity to an awakened state and their length, dreams occurring toward the end of sleep are more easily remembered. Psychologists note that the big difference in sleep is between REM and non-REM.

Sleep researcher **William Dement** studied the effects of the deprivation of REM sleep. By depriving participants of REM sleep (waking them every time they entered a REM period) and then allowing them to sleep normally after the experimental period, participant's REM periods increased from the normal 90 minutes of REM per night to 120 minutes of REM sleep in the period immediately following the deprivation. This is known as **REM rebound** and it helps reinforce the idea that we need to sleep.

Given that sleep is such an important factor in our lives, it is not surprising that psychologists are interested in disorders of sleep. **Insomnia** is a lack of sleep, which can take the form of an inability to fall asleep or the inability to maintain sleep. Stress can cause temporary insomnia, as can the use of alcohol or stimulants such as caffeine.

Q: What is narcolepsy?

Narcolepsy is the inability to stay awake. A narcoleptic has irresistible urges to sleep throughout the day and at inappropriate times, such as when driving. Interestingly, when narcoleptics fall asleep, it is typically only for a few minutes, and the sleep is almost all REM sleep. Although narcolepsy can be treated, the cause of the disorder is unknown.

Sleep apnea is a disorder in which a person repeatedly stops breathing while sleeping. This disorder can occur hundreds of times in a night, leaving the sufferer exhausted during the day. Sleep apnea is associated with obesity and also may be linked to alcohol consumption. **Sudden infant death syndrome (SIDS)** may also be linked to sleep apnea.

Sleepwalking, or **somnambulism**, occurs when an individual walks around, and sometimes even talks, while sleeping. Scientists have shown that sleepwalking is not simply acting out dreams, as it occurs during stage 3 and 4 sleep, not during REM.

Dreams, like sleep itself, are mysterious. We all dream every night, yet we do not always remember our dreams, and the function of dreams remains unknown. Freud hypothesized that dreams are the expression of unconscious wishes or desires. In psychoanalytic theory, the **manifest content**, or storyline and imagery of the dream, offers insight into and important symbols relating to unconscious processes. The **latent content** is the emotional significance and underlying meaning of the dream. The **activation-synthesis hypothesis of dreaming** postulates that dreams are the product of our awareness of neural activity due to sensory input while we are sleeping. The problem-solving theory of dreaming holds that dreams provide a chance for the mind to work out issues that occupy its attention during waking hours. Neural repair, consolidation of memories, and protein synthesis seem to occur during dreams.

A **nightmare** is an elaborate dream sequence that produces a high level of anxiety or fear for the dreamer. The dreamer may experience a sense of physical danger to himself, or his loved ones, or a strong sense of embarrassment about doing something unacceptable. These dreams are vivid and can often be elaborately described by the dreamer upon awakening; they generally occur during REM sleep. In contrast, **night terrors** occur in much deeper sleep states; these involve behaviors such as screaming, crying, and jerking/lunging movements while asleep. This state is thought to overlap with somnambulism, as a person suffering a night terror may also be quite mobile, going through all the motions of being attacked by some horror, and yet be fully asleep.

A: Insomnia can take the form of an inability to fall asleep, or the inability to maintain sleep. Stress can cause temporary insomnia, as can the use of alcohol or stimulants such as caffeine.

HYPNOSIS

Hypnosis is an altered state of consciousness in which the hypnotized person is very relaxed and open to suggestion. Hypnotized persons can be convinced that they see things that are not there, or that they are having experiences that they are not having. Hypnotized people can sometimes recall things that they could not recall when they were in a normal state of consciousness. Typically, a person who is hypnotized has no recollection of the hypnosis upon returning to normal consciousness. Some theories hold that hypnosis is a state of deep relaxation, whereas other theories hold that hypnosis is not a real effect at all, but is rather a form of the participant's living up to the expectations of the hypnotist or experimenter. Another theory of hypnosis is the **neodissociative theory**. According to **Hilgard's** theory of the **hidden observer**, hypnosis somehow divides or dissociates the mind into two parts. One part obeys the hypnotist, while the other part, referred to as the hidden observer, silently observes everything. While this theory may explain the phenomenology of hypnotism, the physiology of hypnotism remains unexplained. Explaining hypnosis is made more difficult by the finding that hypnotic suggestibility varies on a normally distributed curve—in other words, some people are more susceptible to hypnosis than others.

A: Narcolepsy is the inability to stay awake. A narcoleptic has irresistible urges to sleep at inappropriate times.

Hypnosis has some clinical applications. In some types of psychoanalysis, hypnotism is used to extract memories so terrible that they were repressed from the conscious into the unconscious mind. It is controversial whether such repressed memories really exist. Such reports of repressed memories are controversial in a legal setting and have been used to falsely accuse people of crimes they did not commit. People who are hypnotized may also be susceptible to **posthypnotic suggestion**. Posthypnotic suggestions are instructions given to people when they are hypnotized that are to be implemented after they wake. Such suggestions have had limited success in treating chronic pain, reducing blood pressure, and even in helping people quit smoking.

PSYCHOACTIVE DRUG EFFECTS

Q: Why are narcotics effective?

Drug	Effect on CNS	Effect on the Brain	Effect on Behavior
Alcohol	Depressant	Decreases dopamine levels	Dizziness, slurred speech, impaired judgment At high doses can result in respiratory depression and death
Barbiturates Examples: Seconal, Nebutal	Depressant	Inhibits neural arousal centers	Decreases anxiety; increases relaxation At high doses can result in respiratory depression and death Can be very addictive and dangerous when mixed with other depressants or alcohol
Tranquilizers Examples: Xanax, Valium, Librium	Depressant	Inhibits neural arousal centers	Reduces anxiety without inducing sleep

Drug	Effect on CNS	Effect on the Brain	Effect on Behavior
Caffeine	Stimulant	Accelerates heart rate, constricts blood vessels Reduces levels of adnenosine, a neurochemical regulator of norepinephrine release	Can lead to irritability, anxiety, insomnia
Amphetamines Examples: Diet pills, Ritalin	Stimulant	Increases body temperature and heart rate Increases production of dopamine and norepinephrine	Can be addictive Produces feelings of euphoria At high doses can lead to motor dysfunction
Cocaine	Stimulant	Stimulates heart rate and blood pressure Increases dopamine, serotonin, and norepinephrine release	Users feel as though they have increased mental abilities and social ability Can be highly addictive
Nicotine	Stimulant	Stimulates acetylcholine transmission Increases heart rate	Has depressant behavioral effects such as decreasing appetite while increasing heart rate and respiration Can sometimes cause euphoria and dizziness

A: They are effective because they bear a striking resemblance to the endogenous endorphins, neurochemicals responsible for pain relief and are implicated in pleasant feelings and euphoria.

Drug	Effect on CNS	Effect on the Brain	Effect on Behavior
Narcotics Example: Heroin	Stimulant	Stimulate receptors for endogenous endorphins	Induces relaxation and euphoria, can relieve pain May cause impaired cognitive ability, sweating, nausea, and respiratory depression Highly addictive and are available only by prescription or through illicit means
Hallucinogens Examples: LSD and marijuana	Distort sensory perceptions	May increase serotonin levels	May induce sensory synesthesia, in which stimuli from one sense, such as hearing, produce sensory effects in other modalities, such as vision Occasionally the perceptual alterations are extremely unpleasant and terrifying. This state may also be accompanied by paranoia.

In discussing psychoactive drugs, it is important to distinguish among dependence, tolerance, and withdrawal. **Dependence** occurs when an individual continues using a drug despite overarching negative consequences in order to avoid unpleasant physical and/or psychological feelings associated with not taking it. (This term has generally replaced the term *addiction* in psychological and health circles.) A person has developed **tolerance** to a drug when increasingly larger doses are needed in order for the same effect to occur. It is possible to develop tolerance without being dependent. **Withdrawal** refers to the process of weaning off a drug one has become dependent upon; this often involves physical and psychological symptoms of a highly unpleasant nature. It can be said those dependent on drugs are, among other things, avoiding symptoms of withdrawal.

KEY TERMS

Consciousness

William James
stream of thought
mental reality
preconscious
unconscious
controlled processing
automatic processing

Sleep and Dreaming

melatonin
hallucinations
circadian rhythm
electroencephalograms (EEGs)
beta waves
alpha waves
theta waves
delta waves
sleep spindles
K complexes
rapid eye movement (REM)
REM rebound
Aserinsky and Kleitman
paradoxical sleep
William Dement
insomnia
narcolepsy
sleep apnea
sudden infant death
    syndrome (SIDS)
somnambulism
manifest content
latent content
activation-synthesis
    hypothesis of
    dreaming
nightmare
night terrors

Hypnosis

neodissociative theory
Hilgard's theory of the hidden
    observer
posthypnotic
    suggestion

Psychoactive Drug Effects

depressants
stimulants
barbiturates
tranquilizers
amphetamines
narcotics
hallucinogens
dependence
tolerance
withdrawal

REVIEW QUESTIONS

See Chapter 18 for answers and explanations.

1. The brain wave patterns known as "sleep spindles" are most characteristic of which stage of sleep?

   (A) Stage 1 sleep
   (B) Stage 2 sleep
   (C) Stage 3 sleep
   (D) Stage 4 sleep
   (E) REM sleep

2. Subliminal perception is a form of preconscious processing that occurs when stimuli are presented too rapidly for us to be consciously aware of them. The fact that these stimuli were perceived and processed on some level can be demonstrated by

   (A) immediate recognition of these stimuli
   (B) subtle influence to do or say something that has been presented subliminally
   (C) inability of the stimuli to be subject to the tip-of-the-tongue phenomenon
   (D) greater tendency of these stimuli to be subject to proactive interference
   (E) slower recall of these stimuli in a matched pairs trial

3. If all external time cues are removed or blocked, the human circadian "free-running" rhythm tends to cycle every

   (A) 20 hours
   (B) 24 hours
   (C) 25 hours
   (D) 27 hours
   (E) 36 hours

4. All of the following are differences between nightmares and night terrors EXCEPT

   (A) nightmares typically occur during REM sleep, while night terrors typically occur during other sleep stages
   (B) nightmares are often recalled vividly and in detail upon waking, whereas night terrors are not
   (C) people are usually relatively still during nightmares, while they may move around quite a lot, even sleepwalk, during night terrors
   (D) while people may vocalize during nightmares, night terrors are more likely to involve screaming, crying, or shouting
   (E) nightmares are generally expressions of the dreamer's conscious issues, while night terrors reflect unconscious concerns

5. Which of the following is not a member of the class of psychoactive drugs collectively known as narcotics?

   (A) codeine
   (B) morphine
   (C) heroin
   (D) opium
   (E) cocaine

Learning

Q: Define *classical conditioning*.

Learning is a relatively permanent or stable change in behavior as a result of experience. Such changes may be associated with certain changes in the connections within the nervous system. Learning occurs by various methods, including classical conditioning, operant conditioning, and social learning. Cognitive factors are also implicated in learning, particularly in humans.

CLASSICAL CONDITIONING

Classical conditioning was first described by **Ivan Pavlov**, and is sometimes called **Pavlovian conditioning**. Classical conditioning occurs when a neutral stimulus, paired with a previously meaningful stimulus, eventually takes on some meaning itself. For example, if you shine a light in your fish tank, the fish will ignore it. If you put food in the tank, they will all typically swim to the top to get the food. If, however, each time you feed the fish, you shine the light in the tank before putting in the food, the fish will begin to learn about the light. Eventually, the light alone will cause the fish to swim to the top, as if food had been placed in the tank. The previously neutral light has now taken on some meaning. If you are having a difficult time understanding the different parts of classical conditioning, note that *conditioning* is another word for *learning*. For instance, *unconditioned response* is just another way of saying *unlearned response*.

Psychologists use specific terms for the various stimuli in classical conditioning. The **conditioned stimulus (CS)** is the initially neutral stimuli, in our example, the light. The **unconditioned stimulus (US)** is the initially meaningful stimulus. In our example, the US is food. The response to the US does not have to be learned; this naturally occurring response is the **unconditioned response (UR)**. In our example the UR is swimming to the top of the tank. The **conditioned response (CR)** is the response to the CS after conditioning. Again, in our example the CR is swimming to the top.

Q: What is CTA?

What has just been presented is the simplest case of classical conditioning. The CS and the US can be paired into classical conditioning in a number of ways. **Forward conditioning**, in which the CS is presented before the US, can be further divided into **delay conditioning**, in which the CS is present until the US begins, and **trace conditioning**, in which the CS is removed some time before the US is presented. For the most part, the CS or neutral stimulus should come before the US. In the fish example above, this point is true because if the US was present first, the fish could be distracted from noticing the presence of the CS and will therefore not learn the association. Forward conditioning has been found to be the most effective at modifying behavior.

John Watson and his assistant Rosalie Rayner demonstrated classical conditioning with a child known now as Little Albert. Albert was first tested and found to have no fear of small animals, though he did show fear whenever a steel bar was banged loudly with a hammer. Watson then presented Albert repeatedly with a small, harmless white rat, and at the same time, banged the steel bar, making the child cry. Afterwards, Albert cringed and cried any time he was presented with the rat—even if the noise wasn't made. Furthermore, Albert showed that he was afraid of other white fluffy objects; the closer they resembled the white rat, the more he cried and cringed. This is known as **generalization**. If Albert could distinguish among similar but distinct stimuli, he would be exhibiting **discrimination**. We can use this example to demonstrate other terms related to classical conditioning. **Acquisition** takes place when the pairing of the natural and neutral stimuli (the loud noise and the rat) have occurred with enough frequency that the neutral stimulus alone will elicit the conditional response (cringing and crying). **Extinction**, or the elimination of the conditioned response, can be achieved by presenting the CS without the US repeatedly (in other words, the white rat without the loud noise). Eventually, the white rat will not produce the unpleasant response. However, **spontaneous recovery**, where the original response disappears on its own, but then is elicited again by the previous CS at a later time, is also possible under certain circumstances. Spontaneous recovery occurs when the CR reappears quickly but less strongly after the subject has been re-exposed to the pairing of the original neutral stimulus and US. For example, if Little Albert was again presented with a loud noise and a white rat, his fearful response to white, fluffy objects would reappear without him having to be retrained. Spontaneous recovery demonstrates that even though the learning is not evident during the extinction period, the association between the CS and CR is still stored in the brain.

A: Classical conditioning occurs when a neutral stimulus, paired with a meaningful stimulus, eventually takes on a certain related meaning itself.

In **second-order conditioning**, a previous CS now is used as the US. In our example, the fish would now be trained with a new CS, such as a tone, which would be paired with the light, which would now serve as the US. If the conditioning were successful, the fish would learn to swim to the top in response to the tone. Second-order conditioning is a special case of higher order conditioning, which in theory can go up to any order as new CSs are linked to old ones. In practice, higher-order conditioning is rarely effective beyond the second order.

There are two distinct theories as to why classical conditioning works. Pavlov and Watson believed that the pairing of the neutral (eventual CS) and the natural (US) stimuli occurred because they are paired in time. This is the **contiguity approach**. Robert Rescorla believes that the CS and US get paired because the CS comes to predict the US. The fish from the initial example come to expect food upon seeing the light. This is known as the **contingency approach**. Rescorla demonstrated this effect through blocking, where a natural stimulus was paired with two neutral stimuli. Only one neutral stimulus elicited the CR; the other did not, as it did not predict the US.

A: CTA, or conditioned taste aversion, can occur when animals eat a food that results in nausea induced by a drug or radiation; the animals often will not eat that food if they ever encounter it again.

OPERANT CONDITIONING

Operant conditioning (also called **instrumental conditioning**) involves an organism's learning to make a response in order to obtain a reward. The response is an action not typically associated with obtaining a particular reward. **B.F. Skinner** pioneered the study of operant conditioning, although the phenomenon first was discovered by **Edward L. Thorndike**, who proposed the law of effect, which states that a behavior is more likely to recur if reinforced. Skinner ran many operant-conditioning experiments. He often used a specially designed testing apparatus known as an operant chamber, or a Skinner Box.

Q: Define *operant conditioning*.

This box typically was empty except for a lever and a hole through which food pellets could be delivered. Skinner trained the rats to press the lever (not a typical behavior for rats) in order to get food. To get the rats to learn to press a lever, the experimenter would use a procedure called **shaping**, in which a rat first receives a food reward for being near the lever, then for touching the lever, and finally for pressing the lever. In the end, the rat is only rewarded for pressing the lever. This process is also referred to as **differential reinforcement of successive approximations**.

Q: Define *extinction*.

In a typical operant conditioning experiment, pressing the bar is the type of response (also called an operant), and food is the reinforcer. Food is a form of **natural reinforcement** that doesn't need to be learned to be reinforced. These types of natural reinforcers, such as food, water, and sex, provide **primary reinforcement**. **Secondary reinforcement** is provided by learned reinforcers. Money is a good example of a secondary reinforcer. Money is simple paper and has no intrinsic value. We have learned, however, that money can be exchanged for other forms of reinforcement.

Q: What are secondary reinforcers?

Reinforcement can be divided into positive and negative reinforcement. **Positive reinforcement** is a reward or event that increases the likelihood that a particular type of response will be repeated. For example, picture an experiment in which a rat is given a food pellet every time it presses a lever. The food provides positive reinforcement, increasing the likelihood that the rat will press the lever again. **Negative reinforcement** is the removal of an aversive event in order to encourage the behavior. An example of negative reinforcement occurs in an experiment in which a rat is sitting on a mildly electrified cage floor. Pressing a bar in the cage turns off the electrical current. The removal of the negative experience (shock) is rewarding. Note that negative reinforcement is not the same as punishment. Negative reinforcement increases the probability that a given type of response will be repeated, whereas punishment tends to decrease the probability that a given type of response will be repeated. In punishment, an aversive stimulus is administered in order to decrease the frequency of the behavior. **Omission training** also seeks to decrease the frequency of behavior, by withholding the reward until the desired behavior is demonstrated.

Q: What is a token economy?

Behaviorists use various schedules of reinforcement in their experiments. A **schedule of reinforcement** refers to how often an organism receives reinforcement for a given type of response. In a **continuous reinforcement schedule**, every correct response that is emitted results in a reward. This produces rapid learning, but also results in rapid extinction, where extinction is a decrease and eventual disappearance of a response once the behavior is no longer reinforced.

Q: Define *negative reinforcement*.

Schedules of reinforcement in which not all responses are reinforced are called **partial (or intermittent) reinforcement schedules**. A **fixed-ratio schedule** is one in which the reward always occurs after a fixed number of responses. For example, a rat might have to press a lever 10 times in order to receive a food pellet. This schedule is called a 10:1 ratio schedule. Fixed-ratio schedules produce strong learning, but the learning extinguishes relatively quickly, as the rat quickly detects that the reinforcement schedule no longer is operative. A **variable-ratio schedule** is one in which the ratio of responses to reinforcement is variable and unpredictable. A good example of this is slot machines. The response, putting in money and pulling the lever, is reinforced with a payoff in a seemingly random manner. Reinforcement can come at any time. This type of schedule takes longer to condition a response; however the learning that occurs is resistant to extinction. A **fixed-interval schedule** is one in which reinforcement is presented as a function of fixed periods of time, as long as there is at least one response. This schedule is similar to being a salaried employee. Every two weeks the paycheck arrives, regardless of your work performance (as long as you show up at all). Finally, in the **variable-interval schedule**, reinforcement is presented at differing time intervals, as long as there is at least one response. This schedule of reinforcement is illustrated by a teacher who gives pop quizzes. The time at which the quiz will be given is always changing. Variable-interval, like variable-ratio, is more difficult to extinguish than fixed schedules.

Operant conditioning techniques are used quite frequently in places that have controlled populations, such as in a prison or mental institution. These institutions set up a **token economy**—an artificial economy based on tokens. These tokens act as secondary reinforcers, in that the tokens can be used for purchasing primary reinforcers, such as food. The participants in a token economy are reinforced for desired behaviors (responses) with tokens; this reinforcement is designed to increase the number of positive behaviors that occur.

Learned helplessness occurs when consistent effort fails to bring rewards. If this situation persists, the subject will stop trying. Psychologist Martin Seligman sees this condition as possibly precipitating depression in humans. If people try repeatedly to succeed at work, school, and/or relationships, and find their efforts are in vain no matter how hard they try, depression may result.

BIOLOGICAL FACTORS

The biological basis of learning is of great interest to psychologists. Neuroscientists have tried to identify the neural correlates of learning. In other words, what physiological changes are brought about when we learn?

In the 1960s, psychologists noticed that neurons themselves could be affected by environmental stimulation. Experiments were conducted in which some rats were raised in an enriched environment, while others were raised in a deprived environment. The enriched environment included things to explore and lots of room in which to move, whereas the deprived environment was just a small, empty cage. At the end of the experiment, the rats were sacrificed and the brains of the rats were examined. The experimenters found that the rats from the enriched environment had thicker cortexes, higher brain weight, and greater neural connectivity in their brains. This pattern of results suggests that neurons can change in response to environmental stimuli.

Donald Hebb proposed that human learning takes place by neurons forming new connections with one another or by the strengthening of connections that already exist. To study how learning affects specific neurons, scientists study the sea slug aplysia. This is a good animal to study because it has about 20,000 neurons, whereas humans have millions. Aplysia can be classically conditioned to withdraw their gill, a protective response. **Eric Kandel**, a neuroscientist,

A: Operant conditioning (also called instrumental conditioning) involves training an animal to make a response in order to obtain a reward.

A: Extinction is the decrease and eventual cessation of a response once the reinforcement is no longer presented.

A: Secondary reinforcement is provided by learned reinforcers. Money is a good example of a secondary reinforcer.

A: A token economy is an artificial economy based on tokens, which act as secondary reinforcers, in that the tokens can be used for purchasing primary reinforcers, such as food. The participants in a token economy are reinforced for desired behaviors with tokens.

A: Negative reinforcement is the removal of a negative event. Negative reinforcement increases the frequency of a learned response.

Q: What is vicarious learning?

examined classical conditioning in aplysia. Kandel paired a light touch (CS) with a shock (US). This pairing causes the aplysia to withdraw its gill (UCR). After training, the light touch alone can elicit the gill withdrawal (now a CR). Kandel found that when a strong stimulus, such as a shock, happens repeatedly, special neurons called modulatory neurons release neuromodulators. **Neuromodulators** strengthen the synapses between the sensory neurons (the ones that sense the touch) and the motor neurons (the ones that withdraw the gill) involved. Additionally, new synapses were created. In other words, the neurons sensing shock and those that withdrew the gill became more connected than they were before. This experiment illustrated a neural basis for learning, namely, a physiological change that correlates with a relatively stable change in behavior as a result of experience. This is known as **long-term potentiation** (LTP). The same basic process has been shown to be the neural basis of learning in mammals. An easy way to remember this information is that "neurons that fire together, wire together."

SOCIAL LEARNING

Q: What is latent learning?

Classical and operant conditioning obviously do not account for all forms of learning. A third kind of learning is **social learning** (also called observational learning), which is learning based on observing the behavior of others as well as the consequences of that behavior. Because this learning takes place by observing others, it is also referred to as **vicarious learning**.

Albert Bandura conducted some of the most important research on social learning. One example of this research involved having children watch films of adults beating up an inflatable clown doll called Bobo. In some films the adults were rewarded for this behavior; in others they were punished. The children were then allowed to interact with a similar doll. Bandura additionally demonstrated that observing a response-reward relationship was not necessary for observational learning to occur. In another experiment, Bandura had children watch either a film in which an adult attacked an inflatable doll or another film in which the adult ignored the doll. No consequences of their actions were shown. When the children were allowed to interact with similar dolls, those who observed the adults acting aggressively tended to attack the doll, while those who saw the adults ignore the doll did not tend to act aggressively. This illustrated the power of **modeling** in effecting changes in behavior. This finding calls into question the behaviorist's assertion that learning must occur through direct experience.

Bandura concluded that four conditions must be met for observational learning to occur. First, the learner must pay attention to the behavior in question. Second, there must be retention of the observed behavior, meaning that it must be remembered. Third, there must be a motivation for the learner to produce the behavior at a later time. Finally, the potential for reproduction must exist, that is, the learner must be able to reproduce the learned behavior.

Observational learning is a phenomenon frequently discussed in the debate over violence in the media. This issue is a particularly relevant one for television programs designed for children, as studies have shown that young children are particularly likely to engage in observational learning.

COGNITIVE PROCESSES IN LEARNING

The behaviorist view, championed by Skinner, is that behavior is a series of behavior-reward pairings and cognition is not as important to the learning process. In more recent years, many psychologists have abandoned this view. One more recent view of learning posits that organisms start the learning process by observing a stimulus; then they continue the process by evaluating that stimulus; then they move on to a consideration of possible responses; finally they make a response. Various lines of evidence indicate that cognitive factors play a role in both animal and human learning. For example, if humans are conditioned to salivate to the word *style*, they also are likely to salivate to the word *fashion*. These words do not sound alike, so this pattern of behavior is clearly the result of a **cognitive** evaluation of the words, which have related meanings.

Perhaps a more profound demonstration of a similar phenomenon comes from work with pigeons. Pigeons were shown pictures containing either trees or no trees. They were trained to peck a key for food, but only when a picture of a tree was shown. As you might expect, they would peck the key only when tree pictures were shown, even after reinforcement stopped. They even pecked at pictures of trees that they had never seen before. Therefore, the birds must have formed a concept of trees, where a concept is defined as a cognitive rule for categorizing stimuli into groups. Any new stimuli were categorized according to the concept.

An example of classical conditioning worthy of special mention is **conditioned taste aversion (CTA)**, also known as the **Garcia effect**, after the psychologist who discovered it. John Garcia demonstrated that animals that eat a food that results in nausea induced by a drug or radiation, will not eat that food if they ever encounter it again. This effect is profound and can be demonstrated with forward or backward conditioning. It is also highly resistant to extinction. A notable feature of this phenomenon is that it works best with food. It is hard to condition an aversion to a light paired with illness, for example. Psychologists have used this finding as evidence that animals are biologically predisposed to associate illness with food, as opposed to, say, light. This predisposition is a useful feature for a creature that samples many types of food, such as a rat. Humans also experience CTA. If you have ever eaten a food and vomited afterwards, you may never want to eat that food again, even if you know that the food itself did not cause you to be ill.

CTA demonstrates another learning phenomenon: **stimulus generalization**. Let's say that you eat a peach and get sick. You may never want to eat a peach again, but you may also develop an aversion to other similar fruits, such as nectarines. The two fruits are similar, so you generalize from one stimulus (the peach) to the other (the nectarine).

Garcia's research is profound for two reasons: (1) it shows that certain species are built to learn certain associations more easily than others; (2) it shows that classical conditioning might be occurring through the access of some concept. The fact that someone might get sick by eating a peach, and then will refuse to eat all fruit, suggests that this person has attached that negative feeling to the concept of fruit. If it was simple classical conditioning, this effect would not occur because the person did not have direct experience getting sick while eating other types of fruit. There must be some concept at work, which discredits the

A: Vicarious learning is learning based on observing the behavior of others and the consequences of that behavior.

A: Latent learning is learning that is not outwardly expressed through observable performance until the situation calls for it.

"black box" theory of the brain held by behaviorists. It also calls into question the assertion that direct experience is necessary to learn and associate. Looking at this learning as cognitive provides the explanation for why someone would develop food aversion even though that person doesn't become sick until hours after he/she has eaten the food. That person must access the concept of what they ate earlier and attach the association with getting sick. Finally, this is a cognitive issue because sometimes people develop food aversion to a food item they think made them ill, such as sushi, even though it could have been something else that brought upon the illness, such as bacteria in the water at the sushi restaurant.

Other evidence for a cognitive component to learning derives from the work of **Edward Tolman**. Rats permitted to explore a maze without being reinforced would find the exit after following an indirect path; the time it took them to exit the maze without reinforcement decreased quite slowly. However, when reinforcers were applied after several trials without reinforcement, the rats' time to exit the maze decreased dramatically, indicating that the rats knew how to navigate to a specific location within the maze and so had formed a **cognitive map**, or mental representation of the maze. This demonstrates **latent learning**, or learning that is not outwardly expressed until the situation calls for it.

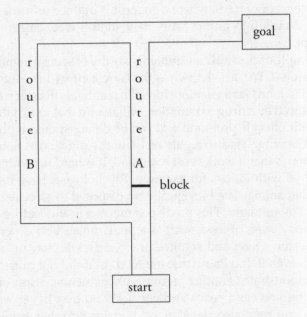

KEY TERMS

learning

Classical Conditioning

Ivan Pavlov
Pavlovian conditioning
conditioned stimulus
unconditioned stimulus
unconditioned response
conditioned response
forward conditioning
delay conditioning
trace conditioning
generalization
discrimination
acquisition
extinction
spontaneous recovery
second-order conditioning
contiguity approach
contingency approach

Operant Conditioning

operant conditioning
B.F. Skinner
Edward L. Thorndike
shaping
differential reinforcement
   of successive approximations
natural reinforcement
primary reinforcement
secondary reinforcement
positive reinforcement
negative reinforcement
omission training
reinforcement schedules
continuous reinforcement
   schedule
partial reinforcement schedule
fixed-ratio schedule
variable-ratio schedule
fixed-interval schedule
variable-interval schedule
token economy
learned helplessness

Biological Factors

Donald Hebb
Eric Kandel
neuromodulators
long-term potentiation

Social Learning

social learning
   (observational learning)
Albert Bandura
modeling

Cognitive Processes In Learning

cognitive
conditioned taste aversion
Garcia effect
stimulus generalization
Edward Tolman
cognitive map
latent learning

REVIEW QUESTIONS

See Chapter 18 for answers and explanations.

1. After having been struck by a car, a dog now exhibits fear responses every time a car approaches. The dog also exhibits a fear response to the approach of a bus, a truck, a bicycle, and even a child's wagon. The dog has undergone a process of

   (A) stimulus discrimination
   (B) stimulus generalization
   (C) spontaneous recovery
   (D) backward conditioning
   (E) differential reinforcement

2. Which of the following would be an example of second-order conditioning?

   (A) A cat tastes a sour plant that makes it feel nauseated and will not approach that plant again.
   (B) A horse that is fed sugar cubes by a particular person salivates every time that person walks by.
   (C) A pigeon that has received food every time a red light is presented exhibits food-seeking behavior when a yellow light is presented.
   (D) A rabbit that has repeatedly seen a picture of a feared predator paired with a musical tone exhibits a fear response to the musical tone as well as to a flashed light alone that had been repeatedly paired with the tone.
   (E) Wild rats instinctively avoid canine predators, but domesticated rats show little fear of the domesticated dogs they encounter, and may even join them in exploration or play.

3. The reinforcement schedule that generally provides the most resistance to response extinction is

   (A) fixed ratio
   (B) fixed interval
   (C) variable ratio
   (D) variable interval
   (E) continuous

4. The importance of enrichment and stimulation of the brain during critical periods in development can be seen in all of the following EXCEPT

   (A) an increase in the number of neurons
   (B) an increase in the number of connections between neurons
   (C) strengthening of already existing connections between neurons
   (D) an increase in the size of neurons
   (E) higher levels of neurotransmitters

5. According to Albert Bandura, observational learning can occur even in the absence of

   (A) observed consequences of behavior
   (B) direct attention to the behavior
   (C) retention of the observed behavior over time
   (D) ability to reproduce the behavior
   (E) motivation to reproduce the behavior at a later time

TEST BREAK #2

SMART-TESTER STRATEGY #2: ANSWER BEFORE YOU ANSWER

Before you even think about looking at the answer choices, you need to have an idea of what the answer to the question might be; otherwise, you will be adrift in a sea of confusion, tricks, and traps. Use the following questions to practice both Ask It Like It Is and Answer Before You Answer. Speaking of answers, see page 215 to check your work on these questions.

5. Thomas knows how to roast meat, cook vegetables, and prepare salad. In order for him to learn to prepare a meal for twenty people, Thomas will most likely employ which of the following learning techniques?

What does the question ask?

What's your answer?

22. The endocrine system is a collection of glands that

What does the question ask?

What's your answer?

35. A major contribution of the behaviorist perspective to psychology is

What does the question ask?

What's your answer?

45. Which of the following best explains why regeneration is essential for taste receptors?

What does the question ask?

What's your answer?

72. Which of the following technologies is most useful in the study of brain waves?

What does the question ask?

What's your answer?

10
Cognition

MEMORY

Q: What is the sensory memory?

According to the **modal model**, memory is divided into three separate storage areas: **sensory**, **short term**, and **long term**. Each type of memory has four components: storage capacity, duration of code, nature of code, and how information is lost. Consider each in turn.

SENSORY MEMORY

The **sensory memory** is the gateway between perception and memory. This store is quite limited. Information in the sensory memory is referred to as **iconic** if it is visual, and **echoic** if it is auditory. The iconic store only lasts for a few tenths of a second while the echoic store lasts for three or four seconds. The items in the sensory memory are constantly being replaced by new input, with only certain items entering into the short-term memory.

Q: What is the short-term memory?

The nature of the sensory memory is clarified by certain types of events. If you have ever watched someone jump rope quickly, you may have noticed the perception of the rope being at many points in its rotation at once. A quickly moving fan also may generate such a perception. This phenomenon is called visual persistence. Sensory information in the sensory memory remains in attention briefly; the speed of the rope or fan causes the sensory information to run together.

In 1960, researcher **George Sperling** experimented on memory and **partial report**. He first presented participants with a matrix of three rows of four letters each for just tenths of a second.

G Z E P
R K O D
B T X F

He paired each line with either a high-, medium-, or low-pitched sound and asked participants to recall what they had seen. Their memories of the letters increased significantly from the first test. Sperling called this ability to recall these lines of letters **short-term visual memory**, or **iconic memory**. The fact that participants in Sperling's study could access one line of the matrix, even after it was no longer present, meant that they had a roughly exact picture of the matrix in their memory for a limited duration.

THE SHORT-TERM MEMORY (STM)

Q: How do items leave STM?

The short-term memory holds information for a few seconds up to about a minute. The information stored in this portion of memory is primarily acoustically coded, despite the nature of the original source. Short-term memory can hold about seven items, plus or minus two (convenient for telephone numbers). Items in the short-term store are maintained there by rehearsal. Rehearsal can be divided into two types: **maintenance rehearsal** and **elaborative rehearsal**. Maintenance rehearsal is simple repetition to keep an item in the short-term memory until it can be used (as when you say a phone number to yourself over and over again until you can dial it). Elaborative rehearsal involves organization and understanding of the information that has been encoded in order to transfer the information to the long-term memory (as when you try to remember the name of someone you have just met at a party). Elaborative rehearsal is more effective than maintenance rehearsal for ensuring short-term memory information is sent to long-term memory, and, therefore, is a preferred way to study.

Items in the short-term memory may be forgotten or they may be **encoded** (stored and able to be recalled later) into the long-term memory. Items that are forgotten exit the short-term memory either by **decay**, that is, the passage of time, or by **interference**, that is, they are displaced by new information. One type of interference is **retroactive interference**; by which new information pushes old information out of the short-term memory.

An additional feature of the short-term memory is that it seems to store items from a list sequentially. This sequential storage leads to our tending to remember the first few and last few items in a list better than the ones in the middle. These effects are called **primacy** (remembering the first items) and **recency** (remembering the last items). The recency effect tends to fade in about a day; the primacy effect tends to persist longer. The overall effect is called the **serial position effect**.

A: The sensory memory is the gateway between perception and memory.

A: The short-term memory holds information for a few seconds up to about a minute.

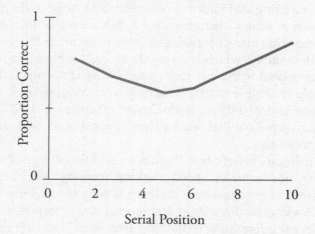

The Serial Position Effect

An interesting feature of the short-term memory is that its limit of about seven items is not as limiting as it would seem. The reason is that what constitutes an item need not be something as simple as a single digit. In fact, it can be a fairly large block of information. Grouping items of information into units is called **chunking**. For example, when learning a friend's phone number (typically seven digits), you probably chunk the information into a 3-digit and a 4-digit number in order to better retain the information.

THE LONG-TERM MEMORY (LTM)

The long-term memory is the repository for all of our lasting memories and knowledge and it is organized like a gigantic network of interrelated information. It is capable of permanent retention for the duration of our lives. Evidence suggests that information in this store is primarily **semantically encoded**, that is, encoded in the form of word meanings. Certain types of information in this store can, however, be **visually or acoustically encoded**. Remembering song lyrics is an example of acoustic encoding.

A: Items leave the short-term memory either by decay, that is, the passage of time, or by interference, when they are displaced by other information.

Q: Define *flashbulb memory.*

Q: What is the long-term memory?

Q: What are phonemes?

Information in the long-term store can be stored in different ways, depending on the type of information it is. One kind of storage is through **episodic memory**, or memory for events that we ourselves have experienced. Another kind is through **semantic memory**, also known as declarative, which comprises facts, figures, and general world knowledge. A third type of memory is **procedural**— that is, consisting of skills and habits. Because these memories are stored in the striatum, they are frequently not subject to damage and injury. A final way to classify memory is into categories based on whether or not it can be accessed consciously or not. **Declarative (or explicit) memory** is a memory a person can consciously consider and retrieve, such as episodic and semantic memory. In contrast, **nondeclarative (or implicit) memory** is beyond conscious consideration and would include procedural memory, priming, and classical conditioning.

Recalling items in long-term memory is subject to the **state-dependent memory**. This principle states that information is more likely to be recalled if the attempt to retrieve it occurs in a situation similar to the situation in which it was encoded. For example, if you memorize information about psychology while in a classroom, you should remember it better in that same classroom than if the information was memorized at home. State-dependent learning also applies to states of mind, meaning that information memorized when under the influence of a drug is easier to access when in a similar state than when not on that drug.

A phenomenon that many psychologists believe occurs in the long-term store is the **flashbulb memory**, which is a very deep, vivid memory in the form of a visual image associated with a particular emotionally arousing event. For example, many people remember exactly what they were doing when they heard that planes had crashed into the World Trade Center on September 11, 2001. However, some psychologists believe that recall of such events is no more accurate than recall of other memories.

Some psychologists believe that there is an additional type of memory, not included in the modal model, called **working memory**. Working memory is sometimes viewed as encompassing that part of long-term memory that is currently in use. Working memory is used to process new information and its relationship to relevant information in the long-term store. Working memory is located in the prefrontal cortex.

Sometimes what we remember only happened in part or even not at all. Memory **reconstruction** occurs when we fit together pieces of an event that seem likely. **Source amnesia** is one likely cause of memory reconstruction. In this case we attribute the event to a different source than it actually came from. For example, if children read and reread a story, they may come to think the events of the story happened to them rather than to the character. Similarly, childhood memories of both trivial and serious events can be reconstructed (falsified) by repeated suggestion. Elizabeth Loftus and other psychologists are studying the existence of false memories. They have demonstrated that repeated suggestions and misleading questions can create false memories. This is called **framing**. Similarly, eyewitness accounts, thought to be very strong evidence in courts of law, are only accurate about half the time. This is particularly true when dealing with children as eyewitnesses. The degree of confidence in the testimony of the witness does not necessarily correlate to accuracy of the account.

Before we move on, let's mention types of interference that we discussed briefly in the short-term memory section. Retroactive interference is when newly memorized information interferes with the ability to remember previously memorized information. **Proactive interference** is when previously memorized information interferes with the ability to learn and memorize new information. To give an example of retroactive interference, when you learn a new language (e.g., Spanish), it can interfere with your memory of a language that you learned previously (e.g., Italian).

A: A flashbulb memory is a very deep, vivid memory in the form of an image associated with a particular traumatic or otherwise emotionally arousing event.

LANGUAGE

Language is the arrangement of sounds to communicate ideas. Language has several key features.

- First, language is arbitrary, that is, words rarely sound like the ideas that they convey.

- Second, language has a structure that is additive in a certain sense. For example, words are added together to form sentences, sentences to form paragraphs, and so on.

- Third, language has multiplicity of structure, meaning that it can be analyzed and understood in a number of different ways.

- Fourth, language is productive, meaning that there are nearly endless meaningful combinations of words.

- Finally, language is dynamic, meaning that it is constantly changing and evolving.

A: The long-term memory is the repository for all of our lasting memories and knowledge. It is capable of permanent retention for the duration of a person's life.

Language can be broken down into subcomponents. **Phonemes** are the smallest units of speech sounds in a given language that are still distinct in sound from each other. Phonemes combine to form **morphemes**, the smallest semantically meaningful parts of language. **Grammar**, the set of rules by which language is constructed, is governed by syntax and semantics. **Syntax** is the set of rules used in the arrangement of morphemes into meaningful sentences; this can also be thought of as word order. **Semantics** refers to word meaning or word choice. **Prosody** is the rhythm, stress, and intonation of speech.

Children acquire language in stages. Infants make cooing noises, which consist of the utterance of phonemes that do not correspond to actual words, until roughly 4 months of age. The next stage after cooing is babbling, which is the production of phonemes only within the infants' own to-be-learned language. Sounds not relevant to this language drop out at this stage, which usually lasts until the first year of life. Soon the infant uses single words to convey demands and desires. These single words filled with meaning are called **holophrases**. Holophrases are single terms that are applied by the infant to broad categories of things. For example, it is not uncommon to hear an infant call any passing woman "mama." This type of error is known as an **overextension**, and results

A: Phonemes are the smallest units of speech sounds in a particular language that are still distinct from each other. Phonemes combine to form morphemes, the smallest meaningful parts of language.

from the infant not knowing enough words to express something fully. **Under-extension** is when a child thinks that his or her "mama" is the only "mama." Infants develop vocabulary as time goes on and tend to have up to one hundred words in their vocabulary by eighteen months.

At about two years of age, infants start combining words. Two- or three-word groups are termed **telegraphic speech**. This speech lacks many parts of speech. For example, a two-year-old would say, "mommy food," which means "mommy give me food." This is called "telegraphic speech" because people used to remove what they deemed unnecessary words when sending telegrams, in order to save money.

Vocabulary is increasing rapidly at this point. By age three, children know more than 1,000 words, but frequently make **overgeneralization** errors. These are errors in which the rules of language are overextended, such as in saying, "I goed to the store." *Go* is an irregular verb, but the child applies the standard rules of grammar to it. By age five, most grammatical mistakes in the child's speech have disappeared, and the child's vocabulary has expanded dramatically. At ten years old, a child's language is essentially the same as an adult's.

Noam Chomsky postulated a system for the organization of language based on the concept of what he referred to as **transformational grammar**. Transformational grammar differentiates between the **surface structure of language**—the superficial way in which the words are arranged in a text or in speech—and **the deep structure of language**—the underlying meaning of the words. Chomsky was struck by the similarities between the grammars of different languages, as well as by the similarities of language acquisition in children, regardless of the language they were learning. Based on this similarity, he proposed an innate **language acquisition device**, which facilitates the acquisition of language in children, and a critical period for the learning of language. **B.F. Skinner**, noted behaviorist, counters Chomsky's argument for language acquisition. Skinner explored the idea of the "language acquisition support system," which is the language–rich or language–poor environment the child is exposed to while growing up. Chomsky's language acquisition device (LAD) provides the foundational structure of language, while the language acquisition support system (LASS) provides the scaffolding to help young children learn language.

Language and thought are interactive processes. Language can influence thought and cognition can influence language. **Benjamin Lee Whorf**, in collaboration with **Edward Sapir**, proposed a **theory of linguistic relativity**, according to which speakers of different languages develop different cognitive systems as a result of their differences in language. A popularly cited example of this idea is illustrated by the Garo people of Burma, who have many words for rice. English speakers have only a few words to describe rice. The hypothesis is that rice is critical to the Garo way of life and so involves more categorization and complexity of thought than it does for someone in an English-speaking culture.

Q: Who posed the idea of a language acquisition device?

CONCEPTS

We are constantly being inundated by information about our surroundings. In order to organize all of this information, we devise concepts. A **concept** is a way of grouping or classifying the world around us. For example, chairs come in a large variety of sizes and shapes, yet we can identify them as chairs. The concept of chairs allows us to identify them without learning every possible trait of all chairs. **Typicality** is the degree to which an object fits the average. What are the average characteristics of a chair? When we picture "chair," an image emerges in our brain. This typical picture that we envision is referred to as a **prototype**. But we can imagine other images of a chair that are distant from the prototype to varying degrees.

Concepts can be small or large, more or less inclusive. A **superordinate concept** is very broad and encompasses a large group of items, such as the concept of "food." A **basic concept** is smaller and more specific—for example, "bread." A **subordinate concept** is even smaller and more specific, such as "rye bread." Concepts are essential for thinking and reasoning. Without such categorization we would be so overwhelmed by our surroundings that we would be incapable of any deeper thought.

COGNITION

Cognition encompasses the mental processes involved in acquiring, organizing, remembering, using, and constructing knowledge.

A: Noam Chomsky

Reasoning, the drawing of conclusions from evidence, can be further divided into deductive and inductive reasoning. **Deductive reasoning** is the process of drawing logical conclusions from general statements. **Syllogisms** are deductive conclusions drawn from two premises. For example, consider the following argument:

> All politicians are trustworthy.
>
> Janet is a politician.
>
> Therefore, Janet is trustworthy.

The logical conclusion is that Janet is trustworthy. This is drawn from the general statements that all politicians are trustworthy, and that Janet is a politician. In general, statements can be sound (the conclusion follows from the premises), unsound, valid (the conclusion is true—Janet is trustworthy), or invalid.

Inductive reasoning is the process of drawing general inferences from specific observations. For example, you might notice that everybody on the football team seems to be a good student. You could infer that all people who play football are good students. However, this is not necessarily true. You are drawing an inference based on a common occurrence. Inductive reasoning, while useful, is not as airtight as deductive reasoning.

PROBLEM SOLVING AND CREATIVITY

Problem solving involves the removal of one or more impediments to the finding of a solution in a situation. The problems to be solved can be either well structured, with paths to solution (for example, "What is the square footage of my room?"), or ill structured, with no single, clear path to solution (for example, "How can I succeed in school?"). In order to solve problems, we must decide whether the problem has one or more solutions. If many correct answers are possible, we use a process known as **divergent thinking**. Brainstorming is an example of divergent thinking. If the problem can be solved only by one answer, **convergent thinking** must be used. Convergent thinking, then, requires narrowing of the many choices available.

Q: What are the two main types of problems?

When solving well-structured problems, we often rely on **heuristics**, or intuitive rules of thumb that may or may not be useful in a given situation. There are a number of types of heuristics and all may lead to incorrect conclusions. The **availability heuristic** means that the rule of thumb is judged by what events come readily to mind. For example, many people mistakenly believe that air travel is more dangerous than car travel because airplane crashes are so vividly and repeatedly reported. The **representativeness heuristic** also can lead to incorrect conclusions. In this case, we judge objects and events in terms of how closely they match the prototype of that object or event. For example, many people view high school athletes as less intelligent. However, most high schools athletes must meet certain academic standards in order to participate in sports. A person's particular view of the athlete will determine whether the **representativeness heuristic** is leading to a correct or incorrect conclusion. Unfortunately, such erroneous conclusions are how racism, sexism, and ageism persist. Heuristics contrast with **algorithms**, which are systematic, mechanical approaches that guarantee an eventual answer to a problem.

Ill-structured problems often require insight to be solved. **Insight** is the sudden understanding of a problem or a potential strategy for solving a problem that usually involves conceptualizing the problem in a new way. A famous example of insight is the example of Kohler's chimps. **Wolfgang Kohler** had a chimp in a cage with two sticks. Outside of the cage were some bananas. The chimp wanted the bananas, but could not reach them with either stick. After struggling for a while, the chimp took the two sticks, and put the thinner end of one into the hollow end of the other, making one long stick of sufficient length to reach the bananas. The novel approach of combining the sticks was presumably the result of an insight. Recent studies have demonstrated that insight is more likely to occur when the problem solvers are able to create some mental and/or physical space between themselves and the problem.

Problems requiring insight are often difficult to solve because we have a **mental set**, or fixed frame of mind, that we use when approaching the problems. An example of a mental set is **functional fixedness**, which is the tendency to assume that a given item is only useful for the task for which it was designed. For example, many people might see this AP Psychology book as a source of information for the AP exam, but it can also serve as a bed support, a writing surface, a source of kindling, or much more!

Other obstacles to problem solving include confirmation bias, hindsight bias, belief perseverance, and framing. **Confirmation bias**, the search for information that supports a particular view, also hinders problem solving, by distorting objectivity. The **hindsight bias**, or the tendency after the fact to think you knew what the outcome would be, also distorts our ability to view situations objectively. Similarly, **belief perseverance** affects problem solving. In this mental error, a person only sees the evidence that supports a particular position, despite evidence presented to the contrary. **Framing**, or the way a question is phrased, can alter the objective outcome of problem solving or decision making.

Creativity can be defined as the process of producing something novel yet worthwhile. The elusive nature of creativity makes it a difficult topic to study. For example, what is truly novel, and who is the judge of what is or is not worthwhile? Briefly, creative people tend to be motivated to create, primarily for the sheer joy of creation, rather than for financial or material gain. Creative people also seem to exhibit care and consideration when choosing a specific area of interest to pursue. Once they have chosen that area, they tend to immerse themselves in it and to develop extensive knowledge of all aspects of the topic. Creativity seems to correlate with nonconformity to the rules governing the area of creativity. For example, Copernicus had to disregard the common belief that the earth was the center of the solar system to make his discoveries about planetary motion.

A: Problems are either well structured, with clear paths to solution, or are ill structured, with no clear paths to solution.

KEY TERMS

Memory

modal model
sensory memory
short-term memory
long-term memory
iconic
echoic
George Sperling
partial report
maintenance rehearsal
elaborative rehearsal
encoded
interference
decay
primacy
recency
serial position effect
retroactive interference
chunking
semantic memory
visually or acoustically
    encoded
episodic memory
procedural
declarative memory
nondeclarative memory
state-dependent memory
flashbulb memory
working memory
reconstruction
source amnesia
framing
proactive interference

Language

phoneme
morpheme
grammar
syntax
semantics
prosody
holophrases
overextension
underextension
telegraphic speech
overgeneralization
Noam Chomsky
transformational grammar
surface structure
deep structure
language acquisition device
B.F. Skinner
Benjamin Lee Whorf
Edward Sapir
linguistic relativity

Concepts and Cognition

typicality
prototype
basic concept
superordinate concept
subordinate concept
cognition
deductive reasoning
inductive reasoning
syllogisms

Problem Solving and Creativity

divergent thinking
convergent thinking
heuristics
availability heuristic
representativeness
    heuristic
algorithms
insight
Wolfgang Kohler
mental set
functional fixedness
confirmation bias
hindsight bias
belief perseverance
framing
creativity

REVIEW QUESTIONS

See Chapter 18 for answers and explanations.

1. The main difference between auditory and visual sensory memory is that
   (A) visual memory dominates auditory memory
   (B) visual sensory memory lasts for a shorter period of time than auditory sensory memory
   (C) visual sensory memory has a higher storage capacity than auditory sensory memory
   (D) a phone number read to an individual will be lost before a phone number that was glanced at for 15 seconds
   (E) if both visual and auditory stimuli are presented at the same time, the visual stimulus is more likely to be transferred to the long-term memory than is the auditory stimulus

2. The greater likelihood of recalling information from memory while in the same or similar environment in which the memory was originally encoded is an example of
   (A) retroactive interference
   (B) chunking
   (C) elaborative rehearsal
   (D) encoding specificity
   (E) procedural memory

3. The term given to that part of language composed of tones and inflections that add or change meaning without alterations in word usage is
   (A) syntax
   (B) grammar
   (C) phonemics
   (D) schematics
   (E) prosody

4. Which of the following would NOT be an example of a two-year-old's usage of telegraphic speech?
   (A) "Where ball?"
   (B) "Boy hurt."
   (C) "Milk."
   (D) "Mommy give hug."
   (E) "Go play group."

5. Students are given a reasoning task in which they are asked, in sixty seconds, to come up with as many ways as possible to use a spoon that do not involve eating or preparing food. The number and diversity of responses could most accurately reflect the students'
   (A) divergent thinking abilities
   (B) convergent thinking abilities
   (C) intelligence quotients
   (D) working memories
   (E) subordinate concepts

11

Motivation and Emotion

BIOLOGICAL BASES

Q: What are the primary drives?

Motivation is defined as a need or desire that serves to energize or direct behavior.

Learning is motivated by biological and psychological factors. Without motivation, action and learning do not occur. Animals are motivated to act by basic needs critical to the survival of the organism. For a given organism to survive, it needs food, water, and sleep. For the genes of the organism to replicate, reproductive behavior is needed to produce offspring and to foster their survival. Hunger, thirst, the need to sleep, and the drive to reproduce are **primary drives**. The desire to obtain learned reinforcers, such as money or social acceptance, are **secondary drives**.

The interaction between the brain and motivation was noticed when **Olds and Milner** discovered that rats would press a bar in order to send a small electrical pulse into certain areas of their brains. This phenomenon is known as intercranial self-stimulation. Further research demonstrated that if the electrode was implanted into certain parts of the limbic system, the rat would self-stimulate nearly constantly. The rats were motivated to stimulate themselves. This finding also suggests that the limbic system, particularly the nucleus accumbens, must play a pivotal role in motivated behavior, and that dopamine, which is the prominent neurotransmitter in this region, must be associated with reward-seeking behavior. Three primary theories attempt to explain the link between neurophysiology and motivated behavior: instinct theory, arousal theory, opponent process theory, and drive-reduction theory.

Q: What are the secondary drives?

Instinct theory, supported by evolutionary psychology, posits that the learning of species-specific behavior motivates organisms to do what is necessary to ensure their survival. For example, cats and other predatory animals have an instinctive motivation to react to movement in their environment to protect themselves and their offspring.

Arousal theory states that there is an optimum level of arousal, that is, of alertness and activation, at which performance on a given task is optimal. Arousal is a direct correlate of nervous system activity. A moderate arousal level seems optimal for most tasks, but keep in mind that what is optimal varies by person as well as task. The **Yerkes-Dodson law** states that tasks of moderate difficulty, neither too easy nor too hard, elicit the highest level of performance. The Yerkes-Dodson law also posits that high levels of arousal for difficult tasks and low levels of arousal for easy tasks are detrimental, while high levels of arousal for easy tasks and low levels of arousal for difficult tasks are preferred.

Q: What is homeostasis?

The **opponent process theory** is a theory of motivation that is clearly relevant to the concept of addiction. It posits that we start off at a motivational baseline, at which we are not motivated to act. Then we encounter a stimulus that feels good, such as a drug or even a positive social interaction. The pleasurable feelings we experience are the result of neuronal activity in the pleasure centers of the brain (i.e., the nucleus accumbens). We now have acquired a motivation to seek out the stimulus that made us feel good. Our brains, however, tend to revert back to a state of emotional neutrality over time. This reversion is a result of an opponent process, which works in opposition to the initial motivation toward seeking the stimulus. In other words, we are motivated to seek stimuli that make us feel emotion, after which an opposing motivational force brings us back in the

Q: What are the two hypotheses for the regulation of feeding?

direction of a baseline. After repeated exposure to a stimulus, its emotional effects begin to wear off, that is, we begin to habituate to the stimulus. The opponent process, however, does not habituate as quickly, so that what used to cause a very positive response now barely produces one at all. Additionally, the opponent process overcompensates, producing withdrawal. As with drugs, we now need larger amounts of the formerly positive stimuli just to maintain a baseline state. In other words, we are addicted.

The **drive-reduction theory** of motivation posits that psychological needs put stress on the body and that we are motivated to reduce this negative experience. Another way to view motivation is using the homeostatic regulation theory, or homeostasis. **Homeostasis** is a state of regulatory equilibrium. When the balance of that equilibrium shifts, we are motivated to try to right the balance. A good example is hunger. The body needs fuel, namely, food. If you do not eat for a while, you may notice that you feel hungry. Try to avoid eating for too long, however, and soon you will be famished, and very motivated to eat. A key concept in the operation of homeostasis is the negative feedback loop. When we are running out of something, like fuel, a metabolic signal is generated that tells us to eat food. When our nutrient supply is replenished, a signal is issued to stop eating. The common analogy for this process is a home thermostat in a heating-cooling system. It has a target temperature, called the **set-point**. The job of the thermostat is to maintain the set-point. If body weight rises above the set point, the action of the **ventromedial hypothalamus** will send messages to the brain to eat less and to exercise more. Conversely, when body weight falls below the set point, the brain sends messages to eat more and exercise less through the **lateral hypothalamus**.

HUNGER, THIRST, AND SEX

The homeostatic regulation model provides a biological explanation for the efficacy of primary reinforcers such as hunger and sex. The brain provides a large amount of the control over feeding behavior. Specifically, the **hypothalamus** has been identified as an area controlling feeding. This control can be demonstrated by lesion studies in animals. If the ventromedial hypothalamus (VMH) is lesioned, the animal eats constantly. The negative feedback loop that should turn off eating has been disrupted. If we damage a neighboring portion of the hypothalamus, the lateral hypothalamus (LH), then the animal stops eating, often starving to death. In more normal circumstances, **leptin** plays a role in the feedback loop between signals from the hypothalamus and those from the stomach. Leptin is released in response to a buildup of fat cells when enough energy has been consumed. This signal is then interpreted by the satiety center in the hypothalamus, working as a safety valve to decrease the feeling of hunger.

The feedback loop controlling eating can be broken by damaging the hypothalamus, but the operation of this mechanism raises the question of what is actually monitored and regulated in normal feeding behavior. Two prime candidates exist. The first candidate hypothesis is **blood glucose**. This idea forms the basis for the **glucostatic hypothesis**. Glucose is the primary fuel of the brain and most other organs. When **insulin** (a hormone produced by the pancreas to regulate glucose) rises, glucose decreases. To restore glucostatic balance, a person needs to eat something. If cellular fuel gets low, then it needs to be replenished. The glucostatic theory of energy regulation gains support from the finding that the hypothalamus has cells that detect glucose.

The glucostatic theory is not without flaws, however. Blood glucose levels are very transient, rising and falling quite dramatically for a variety of reasons. How could it be, then, that such a variable measure could control body weight, which remains relatively stable from early adulthood onward? Another phenomenon inconsistent with a glucostatic hypothesis is diabetes, a disorder of insulin production. Diabetics have greatly elevated blood glucose, but are no less hungry than everyone else.

A second candidate hypothesis is called the **lipostatic hypothesis**. As you might have guessed, this theory states that fat is the measured and controlled substance in the body that regulates hunger. Fat provides the long-term energy store for our bodies. The fat stores in our bodies are fairly fixed, and any significant decrease in fat is a result of starvation. The lipostatic hypothesis gained support from the discovery of leptin, which is a hormone secreted by fat cells. Leptin may be the substance used by the brain to monitor the amount of fat in the body.

In reality, both glucose and body fat are probably monitored, with glucostatic homeostasis responsible for the starting and stopping of individual meals, and lipostatic homeostasis responsible for larger long-term patterns of eating behavior.

There are several disorders related to eating habits, body weight, and body image that have their roots in psychological causes. **Anorexia nervosa**, which is more prevalent in females, is an eating disorder characterized by an individual being 15% below ideal body weight. **Body dysmorphia**, or a distorted body image, is key to understanding this disorder. Another related eating disorder is **Bulimia nervosa,** which is characterized by alternating periods of binging and purging.

Another great motivator of action in humans and animals is thirst. A human can live for weeks without food, but only for a few days without water. Water leaves the body constantly through sweat, urine, and exhalation. This water needs to be replaced, and the body regulates our patterns of intake so that water is consumed before we are severely water depleted. The lateral hypothalamus is implicated in drinking: Lesions of this area greatly reduce drinking behavior. Another part of the hypothalamus, the preoptic area, is also involved. Lesions of the preoptic area result in excessive drinking.

As mentioned earlier, biological drives are those that ensure the survival not only of the individual, but also the survival of the individual's genes. Like that of feeding and drinking, the motivation to reproduce relies on the hypothalamus, which stimulates the **pituitary gland** and which results in the production of androgens and estrogens. **Androgens** and **estrogens** are the primary sexual hormones in males and females, respectively. Without these hormones, sexual desire is eliminated in animals and is greatly reduced in humans.

Q: What are the receptor cells for thirst called?

THEORIES OF MOTIVATION

BIOLOGICAL THEORY

As discussed in the "biological bases" of motivation, early theories on motivation relied on a purely biological explanation of motivated behavior. Animals, especially lower animals, are motivated by **instinct**, genetically programmed patterns of behavior. These early theories, along with arousal theory and drive-reduction theory, have given us an understanding of nature's role in motivating behavior.

HUMANISTIC THEORY

Abraham Maslow proposed a hierarchical system for organizing needs. This hierarchy can be divided into five levels. Each lower level need must be met in order for an attempt to be made to fill the next category of needs in the hierarchy, which is illustrated in the diagram below.

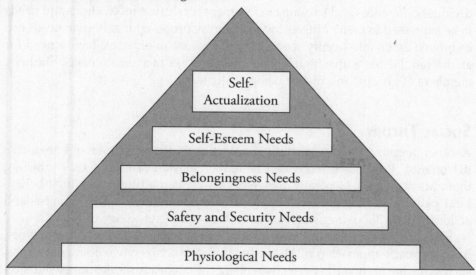

Self-actualization occurs when people creatively and meaningfully fulfill their own potential. This is the ultimate goal of human beings according to Maslow's theory.

COGNITIVE THEORIES

Cognitive psychologists divide the factors that motivate behavior into **intrinsic** and **extrinsic** factors; that is, factors originating from within ourselves, and factors coming from the outside world, respectively. A single type of behavior can be motivated by either intrinsic or extrinsic factors. For example, we may read because we enjoy it. In this case, reading is a behavior motivated by an intrinsic need. However, we may read because we need to know some information that will be on a test. Here, reading is driven by extrinsic motivation. Extrinsic motivators are often associated with the pressures of society, such as getting an education, having a job, and being sociable. Intrinsic motivators, in contrast, are associated with creativity and enjoyment. Over time, our intrinsic motivation

A: Osmoreceptors and volumetric receptors.

may decrease if we receive extrinsic rewards for the same behavior. This phenomenon is called the **overjustification effect**. For example, a person may love to play the violin for fun but when he is a paid concert performer, he will play less for fun and view using the violin as part of his job.

Q: What is the drive reduction theory of motivation?

An important intrinsic motivator is the need for **self-determination**, or the need to feel competent and in control. This need frequently conflicts with the pressures brought to bear by extrinsic motivators. The goal is to seek a balance between the fulfillment of the two categories of need. Related to the concept of self-determination is **self-efficacy**, or the belief that we can or cannot attain a particular goal. In general, the higher the level of self-efficacy, the more we believe that we can attain a particular goal and the more likely we are to achieve it as well.

Q: What is self-actualization?

Although physiological needs form the basis for motivation, humans are not automatons, simply responding to biological pressures. Various theories have attempted to describe the interactions among motivation, personality, and cognition. **Henry Murray** believed that, although motivation is rooted in biology, individual differences and varying environments can cause motivations and needs to be expressed in many different ways. Murray proposed that human needs can be broken down into twenty specific types. For example, people have a **need for affiliation**. People with a high level of this need like to avoid conflicts, like to be members of groups, and dislike being evaluated.

SOCIAL THEORY

Q: Describe the James-Lange theory of emotion.

Another cognitive theory of motivation concerns the need to avoid **cognitive dissonance**. People are motivated to reduce tension produced by conflicting thoughts or choices. Generally, they will change their attitude to fit their behavioral pattern, as long as they believe they are in control of their choices and actions. This will be discussed further in the Social Psychology chapter.

Sometimes, motives are in conflict. **Kurt Lewin** classified conflicts into four types. In an **approach-approach** conflict, one has to decide between two desirable options, such as having to choose between two colleges of similar characteristics. **Avoidance-avoidance** is a similar dilemma. Here one has to choose between two unpleasant alternatives. For example, a person might have to choose between the lesser of two evils. In **approach-avoidance** conflicts, only one choice is presented, but it carries both pluses and minuses. For example, imagine that only one college has the major the student wants but that college is also prohibitively expensive. The last set of conflicts is **multiple approach-avoidance**. In this scenario, many options are available, but each has positives and negatives. Choosing one college out of many that are suitable, but not ideal, represents a multiple approach-avoidance conflict.

Q: Describe the Cannon-Bard theory of emotion?

Q: Describe the typical reactions of Type-A and Type-B personalities to stress.

THEORIES OF EMOTION

Emotions are experiential and subjective responses to certain internal and external stimuli. These experiential responses have both physical and behavioral components. Various theories have arisen to explain emotion.

One class of theories relies on physiological explanations of emotion. The **James-Lange theory** posits that environmental stimuli cause physiological changes and responses. The experience of emotion, according to this theory, is a result of a physiological change. In other words, if an argument makes you angry, it is the physiological response (increased heart rate, increased respiratory rate) that prompts the experience of emotion.

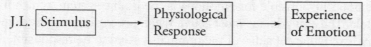

There are many reasons why we now know that this theory is incorrect. We know that a given state of physiological arousal is common to many emotions. For example, a person might feel tenseness in his or her body as a result of being nervous, scared, or even excited. How, then, is it possible that the identical physiological state could lead to the rich variety of emotions that we experience? Another common experience that conflicts with the logic of the James-Lange theory is cutting onions. The physiological response to cutting onions is crying; however, this physiological response does not make us sad.

The **Cannon-Bard theory** arose as a response to the James-Lange theory. The Cannon-Bard theory asserts that the physiological response to emotion and the experience of emotion occur simultaneously in response to emotion-provoking stimulus. For example, a tarantula, which acts as an emotion-provoking stimulus, would stimulate the thalamus. The thalamus would send simultaneous messages to both the autonomic nervous system and the cerebral cortex. Messages to the cortex produce the experience of emotion (fear) and messages to the autonomic nervous system produce physiological arousal (running, heart palpitations, etc.).

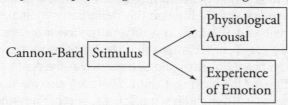

The **two factor-theory,** proposed by **Schachter and Singer,** adds a cognitive twist to the James-Lange theory. The first factor is physiological arousal; the second factor is how we cognitively label the experience of arousal. Central to this theory is the understanding that many emotional responses involve very similar physiological properties. The emotion that we experience, according to this theory, is the result of the label that we apply. For example, if we cry at a wedding, we interpret our emotion as happiness, but if we cry at a funeral, we interpret our emotion as sadness.

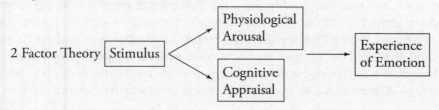

A: The drive reduction theory is based on the premise that physiological needs put demands on the body; the need to fulfill these demands is known as drive. Motivated action, according to this theory, is the result of trying to reduce drive.

A: Self-actualization is the act of creatively and meaningfully fulfilling one's own potential.

A: The James-Lange theory posits that environmental stimuli cause physiological changes and responses. The experience of emotion, according to this theory, is a result of the physiological change.

A: The Cannon-Bard theory arose as a response to the James-Lange theory and asserts that emotion is the result of neural activity, particularly in the thalamus.

A: Type-A personalities react quickly and aggressively to stress. Type-B personalities become stressed more slowly, and their stress levels do not seem to reach the levels seen in people with the Type-A pattern of behavior.

According to more recent studies by Zajonc, Le Doux, and Armony, some emotions are felt before being cognitively appraised. A scary sight travels through the eye to the thalamus, where it is then relayed to the amygdala before being labeled and evaluated by the cortex. According to these studies, the amygdala's position relative to the thalamus may account for the quick emotional response. There are several parts of the brain implicated in emotional processing. The main area of the brain responsible for emotions is the limbic system, which includes the amygdala. The amygdala is most active when processing negative emotions, particularly fear. Different sides of the brain also seem to be responsible for different emotional states. That is, the right brain is dominant in processing negative emotions, while the left brain seems to be more involved in processing positive emotions.

Although theorists have disagreed over time about how emotions are processed, there has been a great deal of agreement about the universality of emotions. A scientist and pioneer in the study of emotions, **Paul Ekman** observed facial expressions from a variety of cultures and pointed out that, regardless of where two persons were from, their expressions of that emotion were almost identical. In particular, Ekman identified six basic emotions that appeared across cultures: anger, fear, disgust, surprise, happiness, and sadness. These findings suggest that emotions and how they are expressed are innate parts of the human experience.

STRESS

A concept related to emotion is the feeling of stress. **Stress** causes a person to feel challenged or endangered. Although this definition may make you think of experiences such as being attacked, in reality, most **stressors** (events that cause stress) are everyday events or situations that challenge us in more subtle ways. Stressors can be significant life-changing events such as the death of a loved one, a divorce, a wedding, or the birth of a child. There are also many smaller, more manageable stressors, such as holidays, traffic jams, or other nuisances. Although these situations are varied, they share a common factor: They are all challenging for the person experiencing them.

As you may have inferred, the same situation may have different value as a stressor for different people. The perception of a stimulus as stressful may be more consequential than the actual nature of the stimulus itself. For example, some people find putting together children's toys or electronic items quite stressful; yet other people find relaxation in similar tasks, such as building models.

Some stressors are **transient**, meaning that they are temporary challenges. Others, such as those that lead to job-related stress, are **chronic** and can have a negative impact on health. The physiological response to stress is related to what is referred to as a **fight-or-flight response**, a concept developed by **Hans Selye** and enhanced by Walter Cannon into the **general adaptation syndrome**. The three stages of this response to prolonged stress are alarm, resistance, and exhaustion. **Alarm** refers to the arousal of the sympathetic nervous system, resulting in the release of various stimulatory hormones, including corticosterone, which is used as a physiological index of stress. In the alarm phase, the body is energized for immediate action, which is adaptive for transient, but not chronic, stressors. **Resistance** is the result of parasympathetic rebound. The body cannot be aroused forever, and the parasympathetic system starts to reduce the arousal state. If the stressor does not relent, however, the body does not reduce its arousal state to baseline. If the stressor persists for long periods of time, the stress response continues into the **exhaustion** phase. In this phase, the body's resources are exhausted, and tissue cannot be repaired. The immune system becomes impaired in its functioning, which is why we are more susceptible to illness during prolonged stress.

Richard Lazarus developed a cognitive theory of how we respond to stress. In this approach, the individual evaluates whether the event appears to be stressful. This is called primary appraisal. If the event is seen to be a threat, a secondary appraisal takes place, assessing whether the individual can handle the stress. Stress is minimized or maximized by the individual's ability to respond to the stressor.

Research into stress has revealed that people can be loosely divided into two different types of behavior patterns based on their responses to stress. The **Type-A** pattern of behavior is typified by competitiveness, a sense of time urgency, and elevated feelings of anger and hostility. The **Type-B** pattern of behavior is characterized by a low level of competitiveness, low preoccupation with time issues, and a generally easy-going attitude. People with Type-A patterns of behavior respond to stress quickly and aggressively. Type-A people also act in ways that tend to increase the likelihood that they will have stressful experiences. They seek jobs or tasks that put great demands on them. People with a Type-B pattern of behavior get stressed more slowly, and their stress levels do not seem to reach those heights seen in people with the Type-A pattern of behavior. There is some evidence that people with Type-A behavior patterns are more susceptible to stress-related diseases, including heart attacks, but may survive them more frequently than Type-Bs.

KEY TERMS

Biological Bases
motivation
primary drives
secondary drives
Olds and Milner
instinct theory
arousal theory
Yerkes-Dodson law
opponent process theory
drive-reduction theory
homeostasis
set point
ventromedial
    hypothalamus
lateral hypothalamus

Hunger, Thirst, and Sex
hypothalamus
leptin
blood glucose
glucostatic hypothesis
insulin
lipostatic hypothesis
anorexia nervosa
bulimia nervosa
body dysmorphia
pituitary gland
androgens
estrogens

Theories of Motivation
instinct
Abraham Maslow
self-actualization
intrinsic
extrinsic
overjustification effect
self-determination
self-efficacy

Henry Murray
need for affiliation
cognitive dissonance
Kurt Lewin
approach-approach
avoidance-avoidance
approach-avoidance
multiple approach-avoidance

Theories of Emotion
James-Lange theory
Cannon-Bard theory
two-factor theory
Schachter and Singer
Paul Ekman

Stress
stressors
transient
chronic
fight-or-flight response
Hans and Selye
general adaptation syndrome
alarm
corticosterone
resistance
exhaustion
Richard Lazarus
Type-A
Type-B

REVIEW QUESTIONS

See Chapter 18 for answers and explanations.

1. An example of a secondary drive is
   - (A) the satisfying of a basic need critical to one's survival
   - (B) an attempt to get food to maintain homeostatic equilibrium related to hunger
   - (C) an attempt to act only on instinct
   - (D) an effort to obtain something that has been shown to have reinforcing properties
   - (E) an effort to continue an optimal state of arousal

2. An example of the Yerkes-Dodson law is
   - (A) the need to remain calm and relaxed while taking an SAT
   - (B) performing at the highest level of arousal in order to obtain a primary reinforcer
   - (C) a task designed to restore the body to homeostasis
   - (D) the need to remain calm and peaceful while addressing envelopes for a charity event
   - (E) working at maximum arousal on a challenging project

3. A substance that can act directly on brain receptors to stimulate thirst is
   - (A) angiotensin
   - (B) endorphin
   - (C) thyroxin
   - (D) lipoprotein
   - (E) acetylcholine

4. Rhoni is a driven woman who feels the need to constantly excel in her career in order to help maintain the lifestyle her family has become accustomed to and in order to be seen as successful in her parent's eyes. The factors that motivate Rhoni's career behavior can be described as
   - (A) primarily intrinsic
   - (B) primarily extrinsic
   - (C) primarily hierarchical
   - (D) primarily self-determined
   - (E) primarily instinctual

5. Which of the following is less likely to be characteristic of a Type-A personality than of a Type-B personality?
   - (A) A constant sense of time urgency
   - (B) A tendency toward easier arousability
   - (C) A greater likelihood to anger slowly
   - (D) A higher rate of stress-related physical complaints
   - (E) A need to see situations as competitive

TEST BREAK #3: USING ALL THREE

Now, practice the first two smart-tester strategies (Ask It Like It Is and Answer Before You Answer) and then find the "credited response" from the choices given. If you're having trouble, use POE to get your answers into the right ballpark. Once you've crossed off what you can, take a smart guess! Answers are on pages 217–219.

15. Of the following variables, which typically requires a measurement that is more complex?

Ask It Like It Is.

Answer Before You Answer.

    (A) Categorical
    (B) Confounding
    (C) Extraneous
    (D) Independent
    (E) Dependent

35. Which of the following most accurately states the role of the iris?

Ask It Like It Is.

Answer Before You Answer.

    (A) To provide adaptive trait distinctions (eye color) within a species
    (B) To dilate or constrict the pupil in order to regulate the amount of light that enters the eye
    (C) To refract light that enters the eye, projecting it onto the retina
    (D) To house the aqueous humor and supply the eye with oxygen and nutrients
    (E) To transduce visual sensations into visual perceptions of color

42. The nature-nurture controversy concerns

Ask It Like It Is.

Answer Before You Answer.

    (A) the question of determinism versus free will
    (B) the degree to which the kinesthetic prowess of an individual overrides other aspects of intelligence
    (C) the degree to which inborn processes versus environmental factors determine behavior
    (D) the natural tendency of humans to nurture their young
    (E) the role of unconscious processes as a determinant of behavior

66. Prior to the fall of the Berlin wall, East Berlin schools de-emphasized the individuality of the student. As a result, many of the children from those schools tend to have a(n)

Ask It Like It Is.

Answer Before You Answer.

    (A)   optimistic explanatory style
    (B)   pessimistic explanatory style
    (C)   internal locus of control
    (D)   external locus of control
    (E)   indiscriminant set of expectancies

85. A prototypic example of a category is called a(n)

Ask It Like It Is.

Answer Before You Answer.

    (A)   expectancy
    (B)   defining feature
    (C)   concept
    (D)   phenotype
    (E)   exemplar

12

Developmental Psychology

LIFE-SPAN APPROACH

Q: What is the cross-sectional method?

The life-span approach to **developmental psychology** takes the view that development is not a process with a clear ending. For decades, development was thought to end with the onset of adolescence. Rather, it is now viewed as a process that continues from birth to death. From this perspective, developmental psychology can be defined as the study of the changes that occur in people's abilities and behaviors as they age. It is important to differentiate between **life-span psychologists** and **child psychologists**. Although both study development, the child psychologist has decided to focus on a particular earlier portion of the typical life span. The view that development occurs across an entire lifetime was first championed successfully by **Erik Erikson**.

RESEARCH METHODS

Q: What is the longitudinal method?

Research methods in developmental psychology vary according to the questions being asked by the researcher. Some developmental psychologists are interested in studying **normative development**, which is the typical sequence of developmental changes for a group of people. For example, some developmental psychologists talk about development occurring in a series of stages, universal to human development. Other developmental psychologists are more interested in individual development, or the individual pattern of development, including differences among individuals during development. Often the techniques and research methods useful for studying one type of development are not useful for studying other types of development.

Normative development is often studied using the **cross-sectional method**. The cross-sectional method seeks to compare groups of people of various ages on similar tasks. So, for example, a cross-sectional study might involve administering cognitive tests to a group of two-year-olds, a group of four-year-olds, and a group of six-year-olds, and then comparing the means of the groups. This approach can reveal the average age at which certain skills or abilities appear. However, the data collected in cross-sectional studies tell us little about the actual development of any single individual.

Q: What are the distinct phases of gestation?

To research the developmental process, many developmental psychologists use the **longitudinal method**. The longitudinal method involves following a small group of people over a long portion of their lives, assessing change at set intervals. As you might imagine, longitudinal research is more difficult and more expensive to conduct and, therefore, is conducted less frequently than is cross-sectional research. However, the longitudinal method does have some benefits because the study of individuals over time rules out the differences between subjects that other studies include. They also allow for the study of the temporal order of events.

DEVELOPMENTAL ISSUES

Developmental psychology, like most aspects of psychology, must deal with the so-called **nature-nurture debate**. **Maturationists** emphasize the role of genetically programmed growth and development on the body, and particularly on the nervous system. **Maturation** can best be defined as biological readiness. From their point of view, greater preprogrammed physiological development of the brain allows for more complex conceptualization and reasoning.

The opposing position is the learning perspective and adherents to this position are sometimes referred to as **environmentalists**. The extreme form can be found in **Locke's** *tabula rasa* idea, which states that all development is the direct result of learning—infants are born with a blank slate onto which experience etches its lessons. The organism develops more complex behaviors and cognition because it acquires more associations through learning.

There are other issues to be considered when studying development. One is whether development is **continuous** or **discontinuous**—gradual or stage-oriented. Evidence of growth spurts and leaps of cognition support the discontinuous approach, but other studies show gradual development, particularly in social skill building. A **critical period** refers to a time during which a skill or ability must develop; if the ability does not develop during that time, it probably will never develop or at the least will not develop as well. An example of this is language. Studies of feral children have shown that if they are not exposed to language by about age twelve, their ability to learn language disappears.

Culture also impacts development in important ways. The nature of one's culture, whether collectivist or individualist, can influence development in many ways. A **collectivist** culture is one in which the needs of society are placed before the needs of the individual. Conversely, **individualist** cultures promote personal needs above the needs of society. It is important to realize that a developing child's relationship with his environment and culture is bidirectional, meaning that just as a child's social environment plays a role in how he develops, he also contributes to the society in which he is born.

A: The cross-sectional method seeks at a given time to compare groups of people of various ages on similar tasks.

A: The longitudinal method involves following a small group of people over a portion of their lives, assessing change at set intervals.

A: Zygote, germinal stage, and embryonic stage.

DEVELOPMENTAL THEORIES

Developmental theories can be divided into two broad classes: those that conceptualize development as a single, continuous, unitary process and those that view it as occurring in discrete stages. **Stages** are patterns of behavior that occur in a fixed sequence. Each stage has a unique set of cognitive structures, or sets of mental abilities, that build on the cognitive structures established in the previous stage. Quite likely, some aspects of development may occur in stages at the same time that others occur along a continuum. Psychologists typically agree that the edges of stages are blurred and may overlap for various domains within a stage.

DIMENSIONS OF DEVELOPMENT

Development typically occurs within three realms: physical, cognitive, and social development.

PHYSICAL DEVELOPMENT

Physical development starts at conception. The **zygote**, or fertilized egg, goes through three distinct phases of gestation prior to birth. The first stage is the **germinal stage**, in which the zygote undergoes cell division, expanding to sixty-four cells, and implants itself in the uterine wall. This stage lasts about two weeks. The **embryonic stage** consists of organ formation and lasts until the beginning of the third month. In the **fetal stage**, sexual differentiation occurs and movement begins to develop. Growth is rapid in this stage. Various harmful environmental agents, known as **teratogens**, may affect fetal development. One such agent is alcohol. Some fetuses exposed to alcohol develop **fetal alcohol syndrome (FAS)**, resulting in physical abnormalities and cognitive deficiencies.

A newborn baby, or **neonate**, is nearly helpless, but is equipped with a few reflexes. The **sucking reflex** can be triggered by placing something in the baby's mouth. The **palmar reflex** is the automatic grabbing elicited by something being placed in one of the neonate's hands. Stroking the bottom of the foot causes the toes to splay out. This is known as the **Babinski reflex**. The **head-turning reflex** (also called the rooting reflex) is the response elicited by touching the baby's cheek, and the **Moro reflex** is the splaying out of the limbs when a loud noise occurs. Finally, neonates have an **orienting reflex**, which is activated when they orient themselves to sudden changes in their surroundings. For example, if there is a loud crash, infants will search for the origin of the noise to orient themselves. This reflex persists into adulthood. However, most of the reflexes mentioned above disappear months after birth as the child matures and develops.

Infants also seem to have innate likes and dislikes. Infants prefer to look at face-like patterns over other more or less complex patterns. Infants have a developed sense of taste. Neonates will make **stereotyped ingestive responses**, sucking and smacking their lips, if someone places a drop of sugar water in their mouths. If one uses lemon juice, the neonate will gape—allowing the fluid to come out of the mouth—will stick out the tongue, and will probably cry. This behavior makes evolutionary sense given that sour and bitter flavors are often associated with harmful bacteria that can make the baby ill.

Much of the research on the physical development of children focuses on the refinement of motor control and perceptual abilities. Both of these processes are dependent on neural development. There is evidence that the brain is still organizing itself in the months after birth. In fact, nervous system development continues into early adulthood. It is important to note that although perceptual and motor development depend on the development of the nervous system, the development of the nervous system depends on **environmental interaction** on the part of the child. It has been demonstrated that children raised in situations where their ability to crawl or walk is restricted (as occurs, for example, in some institutions in countries without regulation over childcare facilities) have impaired motor skills. Additionally, perceptual development can be retarded by lack of stimulation. A critical theme in developmental psychology is that of the

Q: What is the orienting reflex?

critical period—that for some parts of the brain, the phrase "use it or lose it" holds true. The most famous illustration of this idea is the case of "Genie," a girl who was deprived of language until the age of 13. No matter how much language she was exposed to after being discovered and educated, she was never able to develop language beyond expressing herself in two-word phrases. In contrast, another girl, "Isabelle," was able to develop language normally after not having any experience with language until the age of six.

The critical period is also evident in the brain. Experiments with animals have shown that depriving an eye of stimuli by covering it at the very beginning of life will lead to the underdevelopment of the part of the occipital lobe responsible for vision in that eye. As a result, that section of the brain will be allocated to another function. This plasticity, or changeability, of the brain is illustrated in an experiment in which a third eye was added to a frog. The occipital lobe flexibly responded by dividing the processing power of the occipital lobe into three eyes rather than two. This experiment only worked if the eye was introduced very close to birth, demonstrating the limited critical period during which some experience must occur for the brain to develop in a particular way.

This phenomenon is informative with regard to the nature-nurture issue. The child is not born as a blank slate: It has some innate reflexes. However, the physiological development of the child depends on its interactions with the environment. Nature and nurture play complementary roles in development.

A: The orienting reflex refers to orienting oneself to sudden changes in the surroundings.

Physical development, though most extensive through the pre- and neonatal periods, continues through childhood and adolescence. Specific markers achieved during childhood are the development of motor skills, both gross (enabling children to run or jump, for example) and fine (enabling them to draw or write).

Puberty is another landmark of physical development. Growth spurts in height and weight, development of secondary sex characteristics, and menstruation in girls or nocturnal emissions in boys characterize this stage. There are also social and cognitive changes that are discussed later in this section.

Most people peak physically in early adulthood. One just needs to look at sports heroes to recognize this fact. Adulthood is marked by gradual decrease of physical abilities, although a healthy lifestyle will slow this process. At approximately fifty years old, women experience menopause, a change in estrogen production causing menstruation to cease.

In the elderly population, the gradual diminution of adulthood reaches noticeable proportions. The senses lose much of their efficacy. For example, half of those over age eighty have lost their sense of smell. Diseases such as Alzheimer's can affect memory, cognition, and personality.

COGNITIVE DEVELOPMENT

Cognitive development refers to the development of learning, memory, reasoning, problem-solving, and related skills.

Piaget

Jean Piaget proposed an influential theory of the cognitive development of children. Piaget's developmental theory is based on the concept of **equilibration**. Equilibration is a child's attempt to reach a balance between what the child encounters in the environment and what cognitive structures the child brings to the situation. Children try to reach equilibration through **assimilation**, incorporating new ideas into existing schemas. For example, a child may develop a **schema**, or mental representational model, for animals after encountering dogs and cats. When he goes to the zoo and sees more exotic four-legged animals like elephants or giraffes, he must **assimilate** this new information into existing category of animals. However, when facing information that does not easily fit into an existing schema, the child must modify the schema to include the new information. This process is called **accommodation**. For example, if in developing the same schema for animals described above, the child's schema of animal might go through a process of accommodation if he encountered a kangaroo that hopped on two legs.

According to Piaget, children go through a series of developmental stages. Piaget believed that these stages occur in a fixed order, and that a child can only be in one stage at any given time. The following are the four stages Piaget proposed, first presented as a chart and then in more detail.

Each stage can be categorized by the presence/absence of schemas, the types of mental operations the child can perform, and the presence or absence of theoretical thought.

Stage	Explanation	Schemas	Mental Operations	Theoretical thinking
Sensorimotor	act on objects that are present and begin to develop schemas but incapable of operations			
Pre-operational	able to use schemas not present (symbolic thought) but lacks ability to perform mental operations	X		
Concrete Operational	able to access schemas and perform mental operations but still limited to experiences	X	X	
Formal Operational	able to use schemas, understand operations and apply both to theoretical questions not based on experiences	X	X	X

Sensorimotor Stage

This stage usually occurs during the first two years of life and is typified by reflexive reactions and then circular reactions, which are repeated behaviors by which the infant manipulates the environment. For example, if an infant kicks its legs and hits the mobile on its crib with its foot, stimulating movement, the infant is likely to repeat the action in the future. **Object permanence**, which develops during this stage, is the knowledge that objects continue to exist when they are outside the field of view. For example, if a ball rolls under a chair, the child will continue to look for it. At this age, the child lacks the ability to access mental schemas or solve problems through performing a mental operation, which is the ability to represent and manipulate information in a person's mind. Schemas are acquired in the preoperational stage, while mental operations become accessible during the concrete operational stage. Another hallmark of the sensorimotor stage is the development of goal-oriented behavior. For example, a very young child who is able to roll over at will, but not yet able to crawl, may consciously roll over multiple times to reach a favorite toy.

Preoperational Stage

The preoperational stage typically occurs from ages two to seven. Children generally begin this stage with the development of language. Language represents a shift to **symbolic thinking**, or the ability to use words to substitute for objects. Other characteristics of the stage are **egocentrism**, seeing the world only from one's own point of view, **artificialism**, believing that all things are human made, and **animism**, believing that all things are living.

Concrete Operational Stage

Typically occurring from ages seven to eleven, this is the stage when children develop the ability to perform a mental operation, then reverse their thinking back to a starting point, a concept called **reversibility**. Another important concept is **conservation**—the idea that the amount of a substance does not change just because it is arranged differently. For example, conservation of mass might be demonstrated by taking a large ball of clay and using it to create several smaller balls of clay. A child in the concrete operational stage will understand that the total amount of clay has not changed, while a child in the preoperational stage might think that there is more clay because there are more balls.

Formal Operational Stage

This stage begins at about age twelve. At this level, children are fully capable of understanding abstractions and symbolic relationships. They are also capable of **metacognition**, or the ability to recognize one's cognitive processes and change and adapt those processes if they aren't successful. The formal operational stage is also the point at which a child acquires hypothetical reasoning, which is the ability to figure out answers to problems with which a person does not have direct experience. For example, a child in the concrete operational stage would have great difficulty imagining how the world might change as a result of an alien invasion, while a 12-year-old could posit numerous theories on the issue.

Criticism of Piaget

Piaget's theory is not universally accepted. Other researchers find flaw in his research methods (because he studied his own three kids), and his underestimation of children's abilities especially at ages four to five. Critics attest that some children that age can take another's perspective and are not so egocentric. Other criticisms include the failure of Piaget to recognize the environmental factors pushing child development.

Theory of Mind (TOM) and the False Belief Task

Q: Define *conservation*.

A key cognitive ability that develops in childhood around the age of four is theory of mind. TOM allows children to understand that other people see the world differently than they do. It is the opposite of egocentrism. Psychologists test theory of mind through the "false belief task." For example, in this test, a child under the age of four opens a container that is labeled "pencils" and finds gumballs instead. The child is asked what another child, who is not present, would think is in the container. The correct answer is "pencils," but because a child under the age of four does not have TOM, that child will answer "gumballs." Psychologists now believe that the absence of theory of mind helps to explain the actions of people with autism, which is discussed in Chapter 15.

Vygotsky

Another influential theory of cognitive development was proposed by **Lev Vygotsky**. Piaget believed that biological maturation is the driving force in development. Vygotsky, on the other hand, stressed social factors as critical to the developmental process. Vygotsky believed that much of development occurs by **internalization**, the absorption of knowledge into the self from environmental and social contexts. Vygotsky also proposed the concept of a zone of proximal development, which is the range between the developed level of ability that a child displays and the potential level of ability of which the child is actually capable. These two levels are often referred to as the **actual development level** vs. the **potential development level**, respectively. Actual development rarely lives up to its potential because ability depends on input from the environment, and environmental input is rarely truly optimal. According to Vygotsky, the way by which a child realizes his potential is through the process of scaffolding. Scaffolding is the support system that allows a person to move across the zone of proximal development incrementally, with environmental supports, such as teachers and parents. If a person fails to advance, it might mean that the scaffolding steps are too high above the person's current abilities.

Q: Differentiate between fluid and crystallized intelligence.

Life-span psychologists have realized that cognitive development continues into adulthood. Childhood and early adulthood are times marked by relatively rapid neural growth. However, we lose a small percentage of brain weight between our early twenties and our eighties. In the later years, many adults show a decrease in **fluid intelligence**, that is, the ability to think in terms of abstract concepts and symbolic relationships. This decrease, however, is accompanied by increased **crystallized intelligence**, or specific knowledge of facts and information.

A related feature of adult cognitive development is **wisdom**. It is assumed in many cultures that older members of a society have a perspective or level of accumulated knowledge that gives them wisdom. Wisdom is a form of insight into life situations and conditions that results in good judgments about difficult life problems.

Q: Define *gender constancy*.

SOCIAL DEVELOPMENT

Social development is the development of the ability to interact with others and with the social structures in which we live. **Erik Erikson** tried to capture the complexities of social development in his psychosocial theory. This theory is important not only for its description of the developmental process as a series of stages marked by the resolution of specific developmental "tasks," but also because it was the first theory to assert that development is a life-span process. Erikson's stages of **psychosocial development** include the following:

Trust vs. Mistrust

This stage occurs during the first year of life. Infants decide whether the world is friendly or hostile, depending on whether or not they can trust that their basic needs will be met. Trust and hopefulness are the outcomes of positive resolutions of this stage.

Autonomy vs. Shame and Doubt

Between the ages of one and three, the child must develop a sense of control over bodily functions, as well as over the environment. Successful resolution of this stage involves mastery of toilet training, walking, and others skills related to control of the self.

Initiative vs. Guilt

This is the stage that occurs at about three to six years of age and often corresponds with a child's entry into a broader social world outside the home. Children at this stage must take initiative and learn to assert themselves socially, without overstepping their bounds. The successful resolution of this stage results in the development of a sense of purpose.

Industry vs. Inferiority

Children from ages six to twelve are in this stage. They are now in school and are becoming accustomed to receiving feedback for their work. Thus, they must gain a sense of accomplishment and pride in their work. They begin to understand what they are capable of doing. The successful resolution of this stage produces a sense of competence.

Identity vs. Role Confusion

This stage involves the adolescent search for identity. Adolescents question what type of person they are and begin to develop their own values at this stage. The resolution of this stage is **fidelity**, or truthfulness to one's self.

Intimacy vs. Isolation

This is the stage of early adulthood when we attempt to form loving, lasting relationships. The successful resolution of this stage results in one's learning how to love in a mature, giving way. If this stage is not successfully resolved, feelings of isolation or a lack of intimacy may result.

A: Conservation is the understanding that a change in one attribute does not involve a change in another attribute—for example, that a change in form or size does not require a change in area or amount.

A: Fluid intelligence is the ability to use abstract concepts and symbolic relationships. Crystallized intelligence is knowledge of specific facts and information.

A: Gender constancy is the knowledge that gender is a fixed, unchangeable characteristic.

Generativity vs. Stagnation

This stage occurs during middle adulthood and brings with it the struggle to be productive in both career and home and to contribute to the next generation with ideas and possibly with children. Being productive in these ways is called **generativity**. This is the stage where we try to leave our "mark" on the world. Failure to resolve this stage can result in feelings of **stagnation** or isolation.

Integrity vs. Despair

This stage occurs during old age and brings with it the struggle to come to terms with one's life, which involves accepting both successes and failures. The positive outcome of this stage is wisdom, whereas the failure to resolve this stage can lead to bitterness and despair.

Erikson's is not the only social development theory. In the 1950s, **Harry Harlow** demonstrated that rhesus monkey infants need comfort and security as much as food. Through the use of artificial, inanimate surrogate mothers, Harlow ascertained that these infants become more attached to soft "mothers" than to wire ones. **Attachment** is defined as the tendency to prefer specific familiar individuals over others. **John Bowlby** is considered the father of attachment theory. He devoted extensive research to the concept of attachment and pioneered the psychoanalytic view that early experiences in childhood have an important influence on development and behavior later in life. Bowlby believed that a close and loving relationship between a child and his caregiver is critical to the infant's healthy development and provides a model that the growing child will use to build mutually beneficial relationships in his or her life. In contrast, a lack of responsiveness and physical support on the part of the parent will hurt the child in the short-term and his or her relationships in the long-term. In the 1970s, **Mary Ainsworth** studied human infant attachment. Using the **"strange situation,"** where a parent or primary guardian leaves a child with a stranger and then returns, Ainsworth recognized four attachment patterns.

- **Secure**—the child uses the parent for support. This is the most common type of attachment.

- **Insecure**—the child is not sure whether the parent will be supportive and shows great discomfort in the arms of strangers. This type of attachment is relatively rare, affecting between 7–15 percent of the population.

- **Avoidant**—the child does not use the parent for support. Again, this is relatively rare.

- **Disorganized**—the child behaves erratically. It is this style of attachment that is associated with abuse.

Q: How does Gilligan's theory differ from Kohlbergs's?

Q: What is the Oedipal conflict?

On the flip-side of child attachment are the three types of parenting styles identified by **Diana Baumrind**.

- **Authoritarian**—Parents have high expectations for their child to comply with rules without debate or explanation. This style is the most likely to use corporal punishment (like spanking) for disobedience. Children of these parents are socially withdrawn, lack decision-making capabilities, and lack curiosity. Authoritarian parents will exert a high level of control and low level of warmth.

- **Authoritative**—Parents also expect compliance to rules but explain rules and encourage independence. Parents set limits, give out punishments, and forgive. Children of these parents have high self-esteem, are independent, and are articulate. Authoritative parents will exert a high level of control and high level of warmth.

- **Permissive**—Parents have few expectations and are warm and non-demanding. Children are rarely punished and parents consider themselves friends of the child. Children of these parents are not good at accepting responsibility, controlling their impulses, or being generous in social relationships. Permissive parents will exert a low level of control and high level of warmth.

A: Rather than focusing on the awareness and development of the concept of justice, as Kohlberg did, Gilligan focused on the development of caring relationships as central to moral development.

Another theory of social development concerns the stages of death and dying developed by **Elisabeth Kubler-Ross**. She identified the following ways people tend to come to terms with terminal illnesses—denial, anger, bargaining, depression, and acceptance. Later psychologists have acknowledged these as well as other emotions involved in grieving and shown that the stages are not necessarily ordered.

Moral Development

The most influential theory of **moral development** was advanced by **Lawrence Kohlberg**, who expanded on an early theory proposed by Piaget. Kohlberg's theory can be divided into levels, each of which has two distinct stages.

Kohlberg's Level I

Level I encompasses ages seven to ten and is the level of preconventional morality. **Preconventional morality** is a two-stage system of moral judgment. In the first stage, it is based on avoiding punishment and receiving rewards. In this stage, children often will mention a fear of being punished as a reason why rules should not be broken. As children age, preconventional morality changes slightly. The second stage of preconventional morality is characterized by a focus on individualism and exchange. Children work for their own interest at this stage, and while they will strike deals with others to satisfy the other person, their primary interest is a selfish one. In summary, in stage 1 of preconventional morality, children make judgments motivated by fear; in stage 2 they make judgments by evaluating the benefit for themselves.

A: The Oedipal conflict is the male child's sexual desire for the mother, which conflicts with his fear of his father.

Kohlberg's Level II

Level II typically occurs from about ages ten to sixteen and sometimes beyond. This is the stage of **conventional morality**. Conventional morality is the internalizing of society's rules and morals. The motivation to follow these rules is generated by the child's knowing that it is "right" to do so. The first stage of this level (stage 3) is typified by the child's trying to live up to what others, especially authority figures, expect of him or her. The child understands that the rules set forth by society are important, and the child tries to conform to these rules. The second stage of preconventional morality (stage 4) involves the development of conscience. Young teens at this stage obey rules and feel moral, societal obligations.

Kohlberg's Level III

Level III occurs from age sixteen and onwards. This is the level of **postconventional morality**. At this level, societal rules are still important, but an internal set of values has developed that may generate occasional conflict with societal values. The first stage of this level (stage 5) is characterized by a belief in individual rights and social contracts. Individual rights, such as those of life and liberty, may outweigh social contracts. In general, however, a balance must be maintained between individual interests and societal rules. The second stage of postconventional morality (stage 6) represents the highest stage of moral development in Kohlberg's model. This stage involves the belief in universal principles of justice. Universal principles of justice are universal rules of morality that typically do, but occasionally do not, agree with the rules of society. An individual at stage 6 believes that the universal principles of justice outweigh societal rules and acts accordingly. Few people reach this level, according to Kohlberg.

Although Kohlberg's theory is an important and influential one, it has been challenged as being inadequate for describing the moral development of people who live in non-Western culture and of women. **Carol Gilligan** has developed a revised version of Kohlberg's theory. Rather than focusing on the awareness and development of the concept of justice, as Kohlberg did, Gilligan's theory places the development of caring relationships as central to moral progress.

SEX ROLES, SEX DIFFERENCES

Psychosexual development is the development of an awareness of one's own sexuality, including the identification of the self with a particular gender. There are differences between the sexes at birth, and, although most observable sexual development occurs during adolescence, psychosexual development starts at a much younger age.

Children develop **gender identity**, the awareness that they are boys or girls, by age two or three. The acquisition of sex-related roles, called **gender typing**, also occurs very early, from the ages of two to seven. This age range is also when children come to understand that there is **gender constancy**, that is, that gender is a fixed, unchangeable characteristic. At this age, children begin to understand that gender is a characteristic of the individual and that items such as clothes or even behavior do not define the sex of the individual. **Androgyny** may develop as children begin to blur the lines between stereotypical male and female roles in society. For example, androgynous individuals can be assertive and aggressive when necessary, but also gentle and nurturing.

An influential theory of psychosexual development was offered by **Sigmund Freud**. Freud divided development into four major stages. The **oral stage**, which occurs during the first two years of life, is the stage when the primary source of pleasure for the infant comes from sucking. The **anal stage** occurs from ages two to four and is a time when the child derives pleasure from the process of elimination, particularly defecation. The **phallic stage** begins at four years of age and extends into middle childhood. In this stage the child discovers that genital stimulation is pleasurable. After the phallic stage there is a **latency period**, during which psychosexual issues are suppressed. The latency period is followed by the **genital stage**. The genital stage is the final stage of development and extends from adolescence through adulthood. According to Freud, this stage brings (for most people) the establishment and maintenance of standard heterosexual relationships.

Freud proposed that children could become fixated at any stage. **Fixation** is the inadequate resolution of a stage, which prevents an individual from progressing to the next stage. Fixation, in Freud's view, leads to psychological problems in adulthood that are related to the stage at which the fixation occurred. A stage of particular importance in Freud's theory is the phallic stage, which is the stage in which the **Oedipal conflict** occurs. The Oedipal conflict is the male child's sexual desire for the mother, which conflicts with the child's fear of the father. The **Electra conflict** is the roughly parallel situation in which girls desire their fathers while fearing their mothers. In Freud's view, inadequate resolution of these conflicts could lead to homosexuality.

Another theory of how sex roles develop has been proposed by **Albert Bandura**. Bandura felt that, like violent behavior, sexual roles could be acquired through social or vicarious learning. Young boys see older boys being rewarded for being masculine and punished for being feminine. This pattern creates a self-perpetuating cycle, according to Bandura, with each successive generation providing the model for the following generation. This view has been supported by research showing that parents reward independence and competition in boys, at the same time that they reward nurturing and caring behaviors in girls.

It is important to consider that biological, social, and cognitive factors all play a role in sexual development. Additionally, we must consider that, when discussing sexual development, there is much disagreement on what is "normal." Theories of sexual development are often products of the culture and time in which they were developed and do not always reflect what is considered normal in modern society.

KEY TERMS

Life-Span Approach
developmental psychology
life-span psychologists
child psychologists
Erik Erikson
normative development
cross-sectional method
longitudinal method

Developmental Issues
nature-nurture debate
maturation
environmentalists
tabula rasa
continuous
discontinuous
collectivist
individualist
critical period
culture

Developmental Theories
physical development
germinal stage
embryonic stage
fetal stage
zygote
embryo
fetus
teratogens
fetal alcohol syndrome (FAS)
neonate
sucking reflex
palmar reflex
Babinski reflex
head-turning reflex
Moro reflex
orienting reflex
stereotyped ingestive responses
environmental interaction

Cognitive Development
Jean Piaget
equilibration
schema
assimilation
accommodation
sensorimotor stage
pre-operational stage
concrete operational stage
formal operational stage

symbolic thinking
object permanence
egocentrism
artificialism
animism
conservation
metacognition
Lev Vygotsky
internalization
actual development level
potential development level
fluid intelligence
crystallized intelligence
wisdom
social development
psychsocial development
fidelity
stagnation
generativity
Harry Harlow
Mary Ainsworth
"strange situation"
child attachment patterns:
    secure, insecure,
    avoidant, disorganized
Diana Baumrind
parenting styles:
    authoritarian, authoritative,
    permissive
Elizabeth Kubler-Ross
moral development
Lawrence Kohlberg
preconventional morality
conventional morality
postconventional morality
Carol Gilligan
psychosexual development
gender identity
gender typing
gender constancy
androgyny
Sigmund Freud
stages of psychosexual development:
    oral, anal, phallic, latency period,
    genital
Oedipus complex
fixation
Elektra conflict
Albert Bandura

REVIEW QUESTIONS

See Chapter 18 for answers and explanations.

1. In neonates, the response to sudden loud noises that involves a splaying out of the limbs is called the

   (A) palmar reflex
   (B) Babinski reflex
   (C) orienting reflex
   (D) Moro reflex
   (E) rooting reflex

2. The belief that there is often a discrepancy between a child's outward cognitive abilities and his or her true cognitive abilities is most closely associated with which of the following theorists?

   (A) Jean Piaget
   (B) Lev Vygotsky
   (C) Leon Festinger
   (D) Sigmund Freud
   (E) Julian Rotter

3. According to Erik Erikson, the major developmental task of school age children before puberty is to develop

   (A) a sense of competence in their efforts
   (B) the ability to form stable intimate relationships
   (C) a feeling of trust that their basic needs will be met
   (D) control over basic bodily functions
   (E) a consistent self-view of identity and roles

4. Shyera, approaching the age of five, believes that all things, from people to animals to plants to objects, are alive, but she has trouble understanding circumstances from these other "living" things' points of view. Piaget's theory would place Shyera

   (A) at the sensorimotor stage
   (B) at the preoperational stage
   (C) at the concrete operational stage
   (D) at the formal operational stage
   (E) at the latency stage

5. Lawrence Kohlberg's theory of moral development posits that a child at the first stage of preconventional morality

   (A) is motivated primarily by the evaluation of self-benefit
   (B) is motivated primarily by the desire to live up to expectations
   (C) is motivated primarily by a belief in balancing individual rights with social contracts
   (D) is motivated primarily by the desire to maintain a "just world"
   (E) is motivated primarily by the desire to receive reward and avoid punishment

13

Personality

PERSONALITY THEORIES AND APPROACHES

Personality can be defined as a person's enduring general style of dealing with others and with the world around them. Personality theories can be divided into four broad categories: psychoanalytic, humanistic, social-cognitive, and trait theories.

PSYCHOANALYTIC THEORIES

Sigmund Freud and those who followed his basic beliefs and practices typify **psychoanalytic** theories of personality. The term **psychodynamic** means a psychological approach based on a marriage of Freudian concepts, such as the unconscious, with more modern ideas. Freud, the first and most influential personality psychologist, believed that the mind can be divided broadly into the conscious and the unconscious. The unconscious, according to Freud, plays a major role in behavior; however, the contents of the unconscious mind are not readily accessible. People's motivations and the source of their problems lie within the unconscious. Although the unconscious is typically not open to scrutiny, certain events, according to Freud, allow for glimpses into the unconscious mind. When people make slips of the tongue or reveal the latent content of dreams, they provide brief looks into their unconscious minds. Freud also discovered that free association is a way to get a glimpse of the unconscious mind. A popular metaphor of the mind is to imagine it as an iceberg with the "conscious" brain sitting above the water and the dark recesses of the "unconscious" lying below. In **free association**, a therapist simply listens, while the patient relaxes and reports anything that comes into his mind, no matter how absurd it might seem. The therapist then analyzes this seemingly random jumble of thoughts, looking for themes that may demonstrate some of what lies in the unconscious.

Freud was also a pioneer in the analysis of dreams, which he viewed as a window into the unconscious mind. Freud devised lists of **Freudian symbols**—items or events that appear in dreams, which actually represent other items or events in the unconscious. For example, knives, spears, and other sharp weapons were thought to symbolize male genitalia, and boxes and ships or other vessels symbolize the female reproductive organs.

Freud further described the mind as consisting of three distinct components: the id, the superego, and the ego. The **id** is the source of mental energy and drive. It encompasses all of the basic human needs and desires, including those for food and sex. The id operates on the **pleasure principle**, which is the desire to maximize pleasure while minimizing pain.

The **superego** is the internal representation of all of society's rules, morals, and obligations. The superego represents the polar opposite of the id.

The **ego**, according to Freud, is the part of the mind that allows a person to function in the environment and to be logical. It operates on the **reality principle**, which is that set of desires that can be satisfied only if the means to satisfy them exists and is available. The ego works as an intermediary between the id and the superego. The ego is most involved in conscious thought and attempts to balance the interaction with the environment along with the opposing forces of the id and superego.

Freud hypothesized that the ego deals with the anxiety produced by the id-superego conflict using various defense mechanisms. Defense mechanisms often serve a useful purpose in helping the individual reduce tension and maintain a healthy outlook, even if it means using self-deception. Repression is one of these defense mechanisms. **Repression** is the process by which memories or desires that provoke too much anxiety to deal with are pushed into the unconscious. For example, some people involved in terrible accidents have no memory of the accidents at all. The memory, according to Freudian theory, has been repressed.

Displacement is a defense mechanism that directs anger away from the source of the anger to a less threatening person or object. A boy who is angry with his father may not want to show hostility directly to his father; instead, he may yell at a friend or stuffed animal, thereby displaying his rage but in a way that does not make his situation worse.

Reaction formation is another defense mechanism by which the ego reverses the direction of a disturbing desire to make that desire safer or more socially acceptable. For example, a person who unconsciously hates the poor might consciously experience this feeling as a strong desire to help the homeless. Other defense mechanisms include the following:

- **Compensation**—making up for failures in one area by success in others

- **Rationalization**—creating logical excuses for emotional or irrational behavior

- **Regression**—reverting to childish behaviors

- **Denial**—the refusal to acknowledge or accept unwanted beliefs or actions

- **Sublimation**—the channeling or redirecting of sexual or aggressive feelings into a more socially acceptable outlet

Freud's theory paved the way for a variety of **psychodynamic** theories, many of which were developed in direct response to Freud's own. **Karen Horney**, for example, pointed out the inherent male bias in Freud's work. She developed a theory of personality based on the need for security. According to Horney's theory, **basic anxiety**, or the feeling of being alone in an unfamiliar or hostile world, is a central theme in childhood. The interactions between the child and the parent, as the child deals with this anxiety, form the basis for adult personality. Children who find security in their relationships with their parents will find security in other adult relationships. Children who lack security in their relationships with their parents and their surroundings will grow up insecure and distrusting, and are likely to end up with various unhealthy personality styles.

Carl Jung formulated another theory of personality that was, in part, a response to Freud's theory. Jung believed that the mind comprises pairs of opposing forces. For example, each person has a **persona**, the mask the person presents to the outside world, and a **shadow**, the deep, passionate, inner person (including the person's "dark side"). Interestingly, Jung also proposed that we each have an

anima and an **animus**, a female and male side to our personality. Jung believed that all of the opposing forces and desires of the mind were balanced by a force called the **Self**. Jung also divided the unconscious differently than Freud. Jung proposed that each of us has a **personal unconsciousness** comprised of repressed memories and clusters of thought, and a **collective unconscious** of behavior and memory common to all humans and passed down from our ancient and common ancestors. **Archetypes** are the behaviors and memories in the collective unconscious. Reverence for motherhood is an example of an archetype.

Alfred Adler, like other psychoanalytic psychologists, believed that childhood is the crucial formative period. He also thought, however, that all children develop feelings of inferiority because of their size and level of competence. He speculated that people spend the rest of their lives trying to overcome this inferiority and develop lifestyles suited to this purpose. Adler thought the best way to overcome inferiority is to develop a lifestyle of social interest, that is, one of contribution to society. Failure to make these accommodations may result in the development of an **inferiority complex**. Adler also saw personality as a product of birth order.

HUMANISTIC THEORIES

Humanistic theories of personality emphasize the uniqueness and richness of being human. These theories arose partially in response to behaviorism (see Chapter 4). As a result, they focus on subjective reality and subjective mental events. In contrast to behaviorism's attempts to reduce behavior to its smallest components, humanistic theories take a holistic view. They view people as unitary, not separable into learned reactions, and certainly not divisible into compartments such as the ego, superego, etc. The final and most important concept in humanistic theories is the concept of self-actualization. **Self-actualization** is becoming, in a creative way, the person you are capable of being. According to humanistic theories, self-actualization is the ultimate purpose for existence.

Two humanistic theorists whose work typifies this school of thought are **Abraham Maslow** (discussed in Chapter 11) and **Carl Rogers**.

Rogers believed that the self constitutes the most important aspect of personality. Our **self-concept** is our mental representation of who we feel we truly are. Internal conflicts arise when we experience **incongruence**, or discrepancies between our self-concept and our actual thoughts and behavior, as well as from feedback from our surroundings. Rogers believed that **conditions of worth**, that is, other people's evaluations of our worth, distort our self-concept. Parents and teachers play a critical role in child development, Rogers hypothesized, and should not impose conditions of worth on children. Instead, people should be treated with **unconditional positive regard**. This means that people, particularly children, should be loved despite failures. Saying, for example, "I only love you when you're good," creates poor self-concept.

SOCIAL-COGNITIVE THEORIES

Social-cognitive theories of personality are based on the assumption that cognitive constructs are the basis for personality. We bring constructs such as expectations to every social situation. These constructs are developed and modified through learning in social environments.

A representative example of a social-cognitive theory of personality was developed by **Albert Bandura**. Bandura focuses on the concept of self-efficacy as central to personality. **Self-efficacy** refers to a person's beliefs about his or her own abilities in a given situation. Basically, the belief that you can do a particular task greatly increases the chances that you actually can do it. Bandura has proposed that this theory has implications for education. Emphasizing accomplishments rather than failures should, according to self-efficacy theory, increase the likelihood of future successes. People have different **explanatory styles,** or ways in which people explain themselves or react in different situations. Explanatory styles can be either positive or negative.

Another important social-cognitive theory is the **locus of control theory**. **Julian Rotter** proposed that the extent to which people believe that their successes or failures are due to their own efforts plays a major role in personality. People who have an **internal locus of control** believe that successes or failures are a direct result of their efforts, whereas people with an **external locus of control** are more likely to attribute success or failure to luck or chance.

TRAIT THEORIES

Trait theories of personality provide quantitative systems for describing and comparing traits or stable predispositions to behave in a certain way. A particular trait theory stipulates that certain traits are part of the person and are not typically environmentally dependent. Additionally, we each have traits in some degree or another. Trait theorists generally believe that traits are largely inherited, rather than acquired through experience. Trait theorists are divided over how to categorize traits. A relatively recent and influential theory focuses on the **Big Five** personality traits, which are introversion-extroversion, neuroticism-stability, agreeableness-antagonism, conscientiousness-undirectedness, and openness-nonopenness.

Two ways of researching traits are by **nomothetic** and **idiographic** analysis. Nomothetic traits such as the Big Five are thought to be universal. Idiographic traits are those that are unique to the individual, such as openness, or curiosity. **Gordon Allport**, a trait theorist, identified three types of traits: cardinal (traits that override a person's whole being), central (the primary characteristics of the person), and secondary (traits that constitute interests). **Raymond Cattell** saw traits differently because he believed that sixteen source traits were the basis of personality. Source traits are the person's underlying characteristics. They give rise to clusters of surface traits, those readily seen in the individual. **Walter Mischel** recognized that traits are not necessarily consistent across various situations but often vary depending upon the circumstances.

EVALUATION OF THE VARIOUS PERSONALITY THEORIES

Each of the personality theories provides some insight into the formation of personality, but each also has its flaws. The main problem with the psychoanalytic theory is that it was not developed through empirical testing, although recent psychologists have subjected Freud's theories to the scientific method. Testing supported some of his theories but not others. The humanistic theories also suffer from lack of empirical evidence, in addition to what some believe is an overly optimistic outlook on life. Nevertheless, they are frequently the basis of counseling today. Cognitive theories, also popular in today's world, describe personality as a function of environmental perception and rational thought. However, critics suggest that this approach does not take into account the breadth of humanness. Trait theories face criticism that they are unable to explain the origin of personality.

ASSESSMENT TECHNIQUES

Techniques used for assessing personality vary. The psychoanalytic approach has traditionally involved the classic one-on-one therapist and patient relationship. In this situation, the therapist's role is to use various techniques, such as free association and dream recall, to gain access to the unconscious.

The humanistic theorists fall short in the area of assessment. Maslow described the characteristics of self-actualizing people, but the characteristics were chosen by Maslow himself, and are not necessarily quantifiable or useful for assessment. The very personal nature of the self makes it nearly impossible for a test or assessment tool to measure the levels at which someone is being true to his or her self. Rogers and others relied primarily on interviews.

Social-cognitive theorists have the benefit of questionnaire-type assessment tools. Rotter developed a locus-of-control questionnaire, versions of which are still used in psychological assessment today. There are also a number of scales or questionnaires designed to evaluate people's level of self-efficacy. These measures have been used to look at the validity of Maslow's hypothesis by computing correlations between people's levels of self-efficacy and their actual performance levels.

TRAIT THEORY ASSESSMENTS

If there were a competition among the various kinds of theorists as to who had the most complete tools for assessment, the trait theorists would win hands down. **Hans Eysenck** developed the **Eysenck Personality Inventory**, a questionnaire designed to examine people's personalities, based on their traits. Raymond Cattell also developed a questionnaire to quantify traits. Cattell named his assessment tool the **16 PF (Personality Factor) Questionnaire**, signifying the 16 traits or personality factors it measures. These are just two of a number of questionnaires designed to evaluate personality traits.

Perhaps the most widely used assessment tool that measures traits is the **MMPI-2**, (Minnesota Multiphasic Personality Inventory, second edition). This test is frequently used as a prepackaged assessment tool, measuring everything from traits to mental disorders.

SELF-CONCEPT, SELF-ESTEEM

Self-concept refers to how we view ourselves, whereas **self-esteem** refers to how much we value ourselves. Self-understanding can be divided into two parts: the **me** and the **I**.

The *me* is comprised of the following:

- **The physical self**—our body, our name, etc.

- **The active self**—how we behave

- **The social self**—how we interact with others

- **The psychological self**—comprises our feelings and personalities

The self-knower, the *I*, is responsible for the coordination and interpretation of the four parts of the *me*. The *I* is responsible for how we perceive ourselves as consistent over time, as individuals, and as having free will. The *I* allows us to reflect on ourselves and to have a self-concept.

Self-esteem develops and differentiates as we age. As children, we are able only to make judgments about ourselves in the general domains of cognitive, physical, social, and behavioral competence. Young children also make errors of self-evaluation due to the **halo effect**, which refers to the error by which we generalize a high self-evaluation from one domain to another. (It also applies to evaluations of others, such as when one assumes a successful athlete would also be articulate.) Domains continue to emerge as we age and are faced with increasingly differentiated areas in which to test ourselves. By the time we reach adulthood, self-esteem can be broken into eleven domains of competency within which we evaluate ourselves. These domains are morality, sociability, intimacy, athleticism, intelligence, sense of humor, nurturance, job competence, adequacy as a provider, physical appearance, and household management. Low self-esteem can result in reluctance to try new tasks and to persist at tasks already started. Self-esteem is also related to whom we compare ourselves to, which is posited by Leon Festinger in his "social comparison theory." People can also inflate their self-esteem by basking in reflective glory, which is when someone takes pride in the accomplishments of an individual or group that the person strongly affiliates with in his or her life.

TEMPERAMENT

Temperament is the early-appearing set of individual differences in reaction and regulation that form the "nucleus" of personality. For a trait to be considered part of temperament, it must be early-appearing, stable, and constitutionally-based, meaning that it is rooted in the physiology of the child. According to developmental psychologist **Mary Rothbart**, temperament is generally assessed on three scales: surgency (amount of positive affect and activity level), negative affect (amount of frustration and sadness), and effortful control (ability of a child to self-regulate moods and behavior). **Jerome Kagan's** work on the physiology of young children showed that children classified as low in effortful control were more likely to have higher baseline heart rates, more muscle tension, and greater pupil dilation. The stability of temperament is also quite remarkable, with surgency at 21 months correlating with the person's behavior at 18 years old.

KEY TERMS

Theories and Approaches

psychoanalytic
humanistic
social-cognitive trait
psychodynamic
free association
personality
Sigmund Freud
id
ego
superego
pleasure principle
reality principle
repression
displacement
reaction formation
compensation
rationalization
regression
denial
sublimation
defense mechanisms
Karen Horney
basis anxiety
Carl Jung
persona
shadow
personal unconscious
collective unconscious
anima
animus
archetypes
Alfred Adler
inferiority complex
self-actualization
Abraham Maslow
Carl Rogers
self-concept
incongruence
conditions of worth
unconditional positive regard

Albert Bandura
self-efficacy
explanatory styles
locus of control theory
Julian Rotter
internal locus of control
external locus of control
Big Five
nomothetic analysis
idiographic analysis
Gordon Allport
Raymond Cattell
Walter Mischel

Assessment Techniques

Hans Eysenck
Eysenck Personality
    Inventory
16PF (Personality Factor) Ques-
    tionnaire
MMPI-2

Self-concept, Self-esteem

self-concept
self-esteem
physical self
active self
social self
psychological self
halo effect

Temperament

temperament
Mary Rothbart
Jerome Kagan

REVIEW QUESTIONS

See Chapter 18 for answers and explanations.

1. According to Freudian theory, which part of the mind operates according to the reality principle?

   (A) The superego
   (B) The ego
   (C) The id
   (D) The archetype
   (E) The shadow

2. The defense mechanism of reaction formation is defined as

   (A) directing angry feelings away from the source of the anger to a less threatening object
   (B) reverting to behaviors more characteristic of childhood
   (C) attempting to make up for failures in certain areas by overcompensating efforts in other areas
   (D) creating excuses for irrational feelings or behaviors that sound logical
   (E) reversing the direction of a disturbing feeling or desire to make it safer or more socially acceptable

3. All of the following personality theorists can be considered psychodynamic in approach EXCEPT

   (A) Karen Horney
   (B) Carl Jung
   (C) Alfred Adler
   (D) Albert Bandura
   (E) Erik Erikson

4. In Rogerian theory, the process by which human beings attain their full creativity and potential is termed

   (A) self-esteem
   (B) self-amplification
   (C) self-efficacy
   (D) self-actualization
   (E) self-reflection

5. A psychologist interested in demarcating and measuring traits would most likely use which of following:

   (A) the 16 PF Questionnaire
   (B) the WAIS
   (C) the DSM-IV
   (D) the ANOVA
   (E) the WISC

14

Testing and Individual Differences

STANDARDIZATION AND NORMS

Q: What is a standardization sample, and why is it used?

When we use tests designed to measure psychological characteristics, we need to know what the scores mean. For example, if a tester measures your IQ, and you score a 125 on this IQ test, how do you know what your IQ is relative to the rest of the world? To determine such relative standing, tests are standardized. Standardization is accomplished by administering the test to a **standardization sample,** a group of people who represent the entire population. The data collected from the standardization sample is compared against **norms**, which are standards of performance against which anyone who takes a given test can be compared. Tests need to be restandardized when a new, different population takes the test. The **Flynn effect** supports the need to restandardize because the data indicate that the population has gotten smarter over the past 50 years. Thus, an IQ of 100 may mean different things in different years, depending on the standardization sample.

RELIABILITY AND VALIDITY

Q: Define *reliability*.

Tests used to measure any psychological trait or ability must be both reliable and valid. **Reliability** is a measure of how consistent a test is in the measurements it provides. In other words, reliability refers to the likelihood that the same individual would get a similar score if tested with the same test on separate occasions (disallowing for practice effects or effects due to familiarity with the test items from the first testing). In fact, reliability is often assessed by giving participants a test and later—preferably after they have forgotten the specific items—administering the same test again. The two sets of scores are compared and a correlation coefficient is computed between them. This is called the **test-retest** method. Other methods of testing reliability include **split-half**, in which one group takes half the test (perhaps only the odd-numbered questions) and another group takes the other half, and **equivalent form**, in which different but similar tests covering the same concepts are given to different groups. Tests that are perfectly reliable have a reliability coefficient of one. Reliabilities apply only to groups, however, so that even though a given test is highly reliable, a given individual may show substantial fluctuations in scores.

Q: Define *validity*.

Validity refers to the extent that a test measures what it intends to measure. Validity is calculated by comparing how well the results from a test correlate with other measures that assess what the test is supposed to predict. So, for example, if you just developed a new IQ test, and you wanted to know if it was valid, you might compare your results to those that the same participants had achieved on other IQ measures. Even better, you might correlate the IQ test scores with school grades, on the notion that IQ test scores should predict school grades. It is possible to have a test that is reliable but not valid. Such a test consistently measures something, but not what it is intended to measure. However, it is impossible to have a test that is valid but not reliable. If individuals' scores fluctuate wildly, then they cannot consistently correlate with others' scores, whatever these other scores may be. **Internal validity** is the degree to which the subject's results are due to the questions being asked and not another variable. **External validity** is true validity—that is, the degree to which results from the test can be generalized to the "real world." In this case, a test would be externally valid if it does, in fact, measure intelligence.

TYPES OF TESTS

Tests used in psychology can be **projective** tests, in which ambiguous stimuli, open to interpretation, are presented, or **inventory-type** tests, in which participants answer a standard series of questions.

Two popular projective tests are the **Rorschach Inkblot Test** and the **Thematic Apperception Test (TAT)**. The Rorschach is a sequence of ten inkblots, each of which the participant is asked to observe and then characterize. For example, a participant might see one inkblot as a bat or another as two people staring at each other. Sometimes, people see multiple images in a single inkblot. Different aspects of the participant's descriptions, such as form and movement of objects, are scored to yield an evaluation of the individual's personality.

The TAT is a series of pictures of people in ambiguous relationships with other people. The participant's task is to generate a story to accompany the picture. The story includes both what led up to the scene in the picture and what will occur next. Again, the participant's responses are used to make judgments about his/her personality. Both of these tests are used by followers of the psychoanalytic view of personality. The major criticism of projective personality tests is that the assessment of the responses can be too subjective.

Inventory-type tests contain fixed answers to questions. They typically do not allow free responses. A classic example is the MMPI-2, mentioned in Chapter 13. This test presents the participant with a variety of statements. The participant's task is to answer "true," "false," or "can't say." This test, too, yields a characterization of personality. It is often used to diagnose abnormalities.

There are many other types of tests. **Power tests** gauge abilities in certain areas. These are usually extremely difficult tests where it is unlikely that a person could answer all the questions correctly. At the other end of the spectrum are **speed tests**. These have very easy items, but the test is timed, making completion difficult. **Achievement tests** assess knowledge gained; the Advanced Placement exams are of this type. In contrast to these are **aptitude tests**, which evaluate a person's abilities. A road test before getting a driver's license is an example of an aptitude test.

INTELLIGENCE

Intelligence can be defined as goal-directed adaptive thinking. Such thinking is difficult to measure on a standardized test. In fact, the nature of intelligence itself is an issue of contention among psychologists. Few psychologists would claim that the popular "intelligence" tests measure all aspects of intelligence. **Alfred Binet** was a French psychologist who first began to measure children's intelligence for the French government. Binet's test measured the "mental age" of school-age children so that children needing extra help could be placed in special classrooms. An American psychologist and Stanford University professor named

A: A standardization sample is a group of people who represent the entire population against which a particular group is to be compared. The standardization sample is used to set the norms.

A: Reliability is a measure of how consistent a test is in its measurements. In other words, reliability refers to the likelihood that the same individual would get a similar score if tested with the same test, on separate occasions.

A: Validity refers to the extent to which a test truly measures what it was intended to measure.

Q : What types of tests are the
Rorschach and the TAT?

Lewis Terman modified Binet's test to create a test commonly referred to as the **Stanford-Binet** test. The Stanford-Binet became the first widely-administered intelligence test during World War I when the United States Army used it to rank recruits. Most modern psychologists measure an aspect of intelligence, called the IQ or **intelligence quotient**. This quotient originally was conceived of as a ratio of mental age over chronological (physical) age, multiplied by 100. Mental age is a measure of performance based on comparing the participant's performance to that of an "average" person of a given age. Therefore, if you take a test and your score is comparable to that of an average ten-year-old, then your mental age is 10. IQ scores are normally distributed, with a mean, median, and mode of about 100, and a standard deviation of 15 or 16 points. Today, IQs are rarely computed as quotients but rather are computed on the basis of the extent to which a person's score is above or below the average.

The most common intelligence tests given to children today are the **Stanford-Binet Intelligence Scale** and the **Wechsler Intelligence Scale for Children** (WISC-R). There is also a version of the Wechsler specifically geared toward adults, the **Wechsler Adult Intelligence Scale** (WAIS). The WISC-R and WAIS generally have six types of questions: information (how many wings does a bird have?), comprehension (what is the advantage of keeping money in a bank?), arithmetic (if 3 pencils cost $1, what will be the cost of 15 pencils?), similarities (in what ways are seals and sea lions alike?), vocabulary (what does "retain" mean?), and digit span questions by which subjects are asked to hold information in short-term memory.

There has been an ongoing debate as to whether intelligence is one specific set of abilities or many different sets of abilities. In the early part of the twentieth century, **Charles Spearman** proposed that there was a general intelligence (or **g factor**) that was the basis of all other intelligence. The g factor is the intelligence applied across mental activities, which is close to the standard definition for "intelligence." The s factor is the breakdown of this intelligence into specific component, such as one's ability to process math equations or linguistic puns. Spearman used **factor analysis**, a statistical measure for analyzing test data. **Robert Sternberg** proposed that intelligence could be more broadly defined as having three major components: **analytical, practical, and creative intelligence**. **Louis Thurstone**, a researcher in the field of intelligence, posited that we need to think of intelligence more broadly, because intelligence can come in many different forms. The most famous proponent of the idea of multiple intelligences is **Howard Gardner** of Harvard University. Gardner has identified the following types of intelligence: verbal and mathematical (these are the two traditionally measured by IQ tests) as well as musical, spatial, kinesthetic, environmental, interpersonal (people perceptive) and intrapersonal (insightful, self-awareness). **Daniel Goleman**, a psychologist at Rutgers, has done recent work on the importance of **emotional intelligence** (being able to recognize people's intents and motivations) and has created programs for enhancing one's emotional intelligence.

HEREDITY/ENVIRONMENT AND INTELLIGENCE

Nature and nurture interact in the formation of human intelligence. One way to measure the influence of inheritance on IQ is through a **heritability coefficient**. This coefficient, which ranges from 0 to 1, is a rough measure of the proportion of variation among individuals that can be attributed to genetic effects. Heritability is sometimes computed by comparing the IQs of identical twins who were raised separately. The assumption is that because the identical twins have identical genes, all variation in identical twins reared apart must be due to environment. Of course, the assumption is rarely completely met because identical twins are usually not separated at birth and even if they are, they still have shared the intrauterine environment of the mother. This type of analysis typically yields heritability quotients of about 0.6–0.8 (on a scale of 0–1.0). The percentage not due to heritability can be contributed to the environmentality of a particular trait. When psychologists compare the IQs of identical twins raised together to those of fraternal twins raised together, the resulting heritability quotient is about 0.75. This analysis assumes that families and people outside families treat identical and fraternal twins in the same way, an assumption that seems questionable. Many psychologists believe that the true heritability quotient for IQ is about 0.5. Thus, half of the variation among people is due to heredity, half to environment. It is important to realize that the heritability of a trait has nothing to do with its modifiability. For example, height is highly heritable, but heights have been increasing over the past several generations, especially in certain Asian countries such as Japan, as a result of changing diet. Here's a helpful analogy to illustrate modifiability of intelligence and the interplay of nature and nurture: Think of nature as the soil in which intelligence can grow and the degree of care for the crop as nurture.

A: These tests are projective tests, which use ambiguous stimuli open to alternative interpretations.

HUMAN DIVERSITY

As previously stated, IQs are roughly normally distributed. As a result, the large majority of people will have an IQ near 100. However, in a normal distribution, there will also be a small number of people at the high and low ends of the IQ range.

Very high IQs are one basis for considering people to be intellectually gifted. Sometimes, an IQ in the 99th percentile (higher than about 135) is considered to be "gifted," although there is no set standard. Moreover, other measures beside IQ should be used in assigning a label of "gifted." Louis Terman conducted a study of gifted children, following them into adulthood. Many of the sample went on to be very successful; however, part of their success may have been due to the socioeconomic status of their parents. Other factors unrelated to IQ may also have influenced the ability of the participants to succeed.

Mental retardation refers to low levels of intelligence and adaptive behavior. Low IQ alone does not signify mental retardation. To be classified as retarded, a person must also demonstrate a low level of adaptive competence, or ability to get along in the world. Mental retardation can be categorized by severity ranging from mild retardation, with an IQ range of 50–70, down to profound retardation, characterized by an IQ lower than 25.

ETHICS IN TESTING

Those who are involved in **psychometrics**, or psychological testing, must be sure that they follow certain guidelines. Confidentiality must be protected. The purposes of the test must be clear to those administering and those taking the test. Questions should be asked and answered concerning who will see the results of the test and how the scores will be used. Furthermore, the impact of the scores should be ascertained before the test is given.

KEY TERMS

Standardization
> standardization sample
> norms
> Flynn effect

Reliablity and Validity
> equivalent-form reliability
> split-half reliability
> test-retest reliability
> internal validity
> external validity
> predictive validity

Types of Tests
> projective tests
> inventory-type tests
> Rorschach Inkblot Test
> Thematic Apperception Test
> power tests
> speed tests
> achievement tests
> aptitude tests

Intelligence
> Alfred Binet
> Louis Terman
> intelligence quotient (IQ)
> emotional intelligence
> Stanford-Binet Intelligence Scale
> Wechsler Adult Intelligence Scale
> Charles Spearman
> g factor
> factor analysis
> analytical intelligence
> practical intelligence
> creative intelligence
> Robert Sternberg
> Howard Gardner
> Daniel Goleman
> heritability coefficient
> psychometrics

REVIEW QUESTIONS

See Chapter 18 for answers and explanations.

1. In the context of psychometric testing, content validity is defined as

   (A) the extent to which the test actually measures what it is purported to measure

   (B) the degree to which there is a correlation between results on the test and future performance on another measure

   (C) the degree to which the test will yield similar results across administrations

   (D) the extent to which scores on two versions of the test are highly correlated

   (E) the degree to which scores on two sections of the same test are consistent with each other

2. Which of the following is an example of a projective test?

   (A) The Stanford Binet Intelligence Scale

   (B) The Thematic Apperception Test (TAT)

   (C) The Minnesota Multiphasic Personality Inventory (MMPI)

   (D) The Strong Vocational Interest Blank

   (E) The F-scale

3. On a normal score distribution, an IQ score of 85 would be located

   (A) approximately one standard deviation above the mean

   (B) approximately one standard deviation below the mean

   (C) approximately two standard deviations above the mean

   (D) approximately two standard deviations below the mean

   (E) in a variable position—it would depend on the age of the respondent

4. Test standardization is accomplished by

   (A) administering the test to a sample chosen to reflect the characteristics of the population in question

   (B) administering different parts of the test to different samples meant to reflect different populations

   (C) correlating the results on the test with results on other tests that claim to measure the same dimension

   (D) correlating the consistency of scores given by different sets of graders

   (E) equilibrating the number of times each answer choice appears

5. Which of the following is NOT a dimension of intelligence in Howard Gardner's theory of multiple intelligences?

   (A) Environmental

   (B) Mathematical

   (C) Spatial

   (D) Musical

   (E) Emotional

TEST BREAK #4: ESSAY DRILL

Before you can write a smart essay, you need to Work Over the Question, then Chart It, Count It, and Sketch It. Practice your smart essay steps on the following essay question. You don't need to write the full essay now, but, if you feel like taking it all the way, go "write" ahead! Before you do, be sure to compare your smart steps with ours on page 223.

1. One of the major approaches to learning is classical conditioning.

   A. Explain the process of classical conditioning, defining and illustrating all necessary terms. Show how classical conditioning could be used to

   (1) Condition a monkey to "appreciate" only the works of certain artists

   (2) Teach a group of students a mathematical concept

   B. Explain how both extinction and spontaneous recovery transpire. Use one of the above examples to illustrate.

15

Abnormal Psychology

DEFINITIONS OF ABNORMALITY

Q: What is the *DSM-IV-TR*?

When is behavior abnormal? The definition of **abnormal behavior** is composed of four components. First, abnormal behavior is unusual—it deviates statistically from typical behavior. Second, abnormal behavior is maladaptive, that is, it interferes with a person's ability to function in a particular situation. Third, abnormal behavior is labeled as abnormal by the society in which it occurs. Finally, abnormal behavior is characterized by perceptual or cognitive dysfunction. In order for behavior to be abnormal, it should meet all of these criteria. Behavior must be compared to the behavior of the society in which it occurs. So, for example, self-mutilation in this country is behavior that stands apart from what society considers normal. In other parts of the world, however, scarring is an important part of certain rituals.

THEORIES OF PSYCHOPATHOLOGY

Different schools of psychology have attempted to understand the causes of abnormal behavior in different ways. Sigmund Freud engaged in careful observation and analysis of people with varying degrees of behavioral abnormalities. Freud and the **psychoanalytic** school hypothesized that the interactions among the id, the ego, and the superego were responsible for a great deal of abnormal behavior. The power of unconscious motives drives behavior. To protect the ego, painful or threatening impulses are repressed into the unconscious. The source of this repression stems from issues that arose during childhood. Generally speaking, if intrapsychic conflicts are not resolved, they may lead us to act abnormally. Much of Freud's writing described his analyses of maladaptive behavior.

Q: What is OCD?

The **humanistic** school of psychology suggests that abnormal behavior is, in part, a result of people being too sensitive to the criticisms and judgments of others. This tendency is related to people being unable to accept their own nature and having low self-esteem. This lack of acceptance may result, according to the humanistic view, from feelings of isolation due to a lack of positive regard received as a child.

The **cognitive** perspective views abnormal behavior as the result of faulty or illogical thoughts. Distortions in the cognitive process, according to this point of view, lead to misperceptions and misinterpretations of the world, which in turn lead to abnormal behavior. The cognitive approach to treatment involves changing the contents of thought or changing the ways in which those contents are processed.

Q: What is a phobia?

The **behavioral** approach to abnormal behavior is based on the notion that all behavior, including abnormal behavior, is learned. Abnormal behavior has, at some point, been rewarded or reinforced, and has now been established as a pattern of behavior. Treatment involves the unlearning of the maladaptive behavior, or the modification of the learned responses to certain stimuli.

The **biological** view of abnormal behavior, which is a popular one in the United States at the present time, views abnormal behavior as a manifestation of abnormal brain function, due to either structural or chemical abnormalities in the brain. This point of view supports medication as providing appropriate treatments for various types of abnormal behavior.

The **sociocultural** approach holds that society and culture help define what is acceptable behavior.

There are commonalities among theories on psychopathology, though. Psychologists of all perspectives realize that disorders have multiple causes. One part of explaining a disorder is to look at the predisposing causes, which are the environmental or genetic influences that exist before the disorder begins and makes people vulnerable to the disorder. The next set of factors to consider is the precipitating causes, which are the triggering events that bring about the disorder. Lastly, psychologists consider the maintaining causes, which are the factors that make the disorder more likely to continue.

A: *The Diagnostic and Statistical Manual (DSM-IV-TR)* is the American Psychiatric Association's handbook for the identification and classification of behavioral abnormalities.

Causes of Disorder					
Psychoanalytic	**Humanistic**	**Cognitive**	**Behavioral**	**Biological**	**Sociocultural**
Negative, early childhood experiences or a conflict between the superego and id	Low self-esteem or negative self-regard	Maladaptive thought processes	Reinforcement of depressive behavior	Neurons or neurotransmitters	Cultural and environmental influences

DIAGNOSIS OF PSYCHOPATHOLOGY

The Diagnostic and Statistical Manual (DSM-IV-TR) is the American Psychiatric Association's handbook for the identification and classification of behavioral abnormalities. The *DSM-IV-TR* contains the diagnostic criteria, background, and prevalence of disorders that are used to classify behavior across five dimensions, or axes.

Axis I is concerned with the major disorders, such as schizophrenia and mood disorders. It also includes delirium and dementia, which are states of perceptual and cognitive disruption, as well as eating disorders, such as anorexia and bulimia, sleeping disorders like narcolepsy and somnambulism, and substance-related disorders.

Axis II includes personality disorders, such as avoidant and dependant personalities, and mental retardation.

Axis III is concerned with physical disorders that have an impact on behavior. These physical disorders are not limited to disorders of the brain, but include any physical disorder that might interact with behavioral abnormality.

Axis IV assesses the level of psychosocial and environmental stress the person is experiencing.

Axis V represents an overall assessment of the person's level of functioning.

The five-axes system is used to try to provide an accurate description and diagnosis of the abnormal behavior. Despite the level of measurement involved, the *DSM-IV-TR* cannot describe every possible symptom and diagnosis. It serves as a guide to psychologists as they attempt to classify abnormal behavior patterns.

A: Obsessive-compulsive disorder (OCD) is an anxiety disorder characterized by persistent thoughts or obsessions, as well as by compulsions.

A: Phobias are persistent, irrational fears of common events or objects.

The major criticism of the *DSM-IV-TR* is that it is overly reliant on the medical aspect for understanding the nature of psychologically disordered behavior. Another criticism of the *DSM* is that it labels behaviors as disordered and because labeling is not an exact science, it can have adverse effects on how a person is judged. The dangers of labeling are best illustrated in the research of **David Rosenhan** (1973). Rosenhan and seven of his colleagues went to a mental hospital and reported that they were "hearing voices." Even though their responses to questions showed no evidence of pathology, they were diagnosed as mentally ill.

Q: What are the symptoms of major depression?

ANXIETY DISORDERS

Anxiety disorders are characterized by feelings of tension and nervousness and sometimes by panic attacks, during which the individual feels an overwhelming sense of panic, fear, and the desire to escape. While panic attacks last only a few minutes, they are debilitating. They are accompanied by sweating, increased heart rate, and a general feeling of being paralyzed with fright.

Panic disorder is an anxiety disorder characterized by recurring panic attacks, as well as the constant worry of another panic attack occurring.

Generalized anxiety disorder (GAD) is an anxiety disorder characterized by an almost constant state of autonomic nervous system arousal and feelings of dread and worry.

Obsessive-compulsive disorder (OCD) is another anxiety disorder, characterized by involuntary persistent thoughts or **obsessions**, as well as by **compulsions**, or repetitive behaviors that are time consuming and maladaptive. A classic example of obsessive-compulsive disorder is the person who is obsessed with germs and so compulsively washes his or her hands. The handwashing might take up significant portions of the person's time, while the obsession with germs comprises a significant portion of the person's thoughts.

Q: What symptoms are common to all types of schizophrenia?

Q: Distinguish between retrograde and anterograde amnesia.

Post-traumatic stress disorder is caused by exposure to trauma, such as war or violence, which leads to recurring thoughts and anxiety linked to the trauma. These symptoms in turn lead to a decreased ability to function as well as to a general detachment from reality.

Phobias, or persistent, irrational fears of common events or objects, are also anxiety disorders. Phobias include fear of objects, such as snakes, and fear of situations. Agoraphobia, for example, is the fear of being in open spaces or public places or other places from which escape is perceived to be difficult.

Q: What is fugue?

SOMATOFORM DISORDERS

Somatoform disorders are psychological disorders characterized by physical symptoms without any actual physical causes. **Conversion disorder** is a somatoform disorder in which a psychological problem manifests itself as a deficit in physiological function. Freud, for example, described cases of people with paralysis or blindness with no known physiological cause. Freud believed that these symptoms were caused by psychological conflicts, whose resolution resulted in the resolution of the physical problem. Freud referred to the physiological manifestation as **hysteria**, a term rarely used by modern psychologists.

Another somatoform disorder is **hypochondriasis**, in which the person is irrationally concerned with having serious disease. Frequently, the person imagines symptoms and seeks treatment. The person is genuinely convinced that he or she is ill. This concern occasionally may result in **factitious disorders**, in which the person inflicts injury or ingests toxins in order to produce symptoms.

MOOD DISORDERS

Mood disorders are extreme disturbances of emotional balance. There are two major types of mood disorders: major depression and bipolar disorder.

Major depression is characterized by depressed mood, general lack of interest in things that were once enjoyable, low sense of self-worth, low energy, and possibly by thoughts of death or suicide. These symptoms must last for two or more weeks to qualify for a diagnosis of major depression. Major depression is often linked to situational factors, such as the death of a close friend or relative, as well as biological factors. It has been found that those suffering from major depression have low levels of the neurotransmitter serotonin. If the symptoms of major depression persist for longer than two years, the diagnosis becomes dysthymic disorder.

Bipolar disorder can appear in a number of forms. The most common form exhibits severe depression similar to unipolar or major depression but with infrequent manic episodes. The second type is one that is primarily manic—in other words, characterized by extreme talkativeness, increased self-esteem, excessive pleasure seeking, and lack of sleep. This form is quite rare. A third form cycles from normal to manic to depressive. Bipolar depression appears to have some genesis in biology, as it affects men and women in similar numbers and seems to run in families.

Seasonal affective disorder is a mood disorder that affects people mostly during winter, when the daylight hours are short. Low levels of light make some people susceptible to depression.

SCHIZOPHRENIC DISORDERS

Schizophrenia refers to a family of disorders of thought and behavior, which share the common features of delusions, hallucinations, and disturbed or inappropriate emotional responses to environmental stimuli.

There are many suggested causes of schizophrenia including the **dopamine hypothesis**, a theory that suggests that schizophrenics have an excess number of dopamine receptors in the brain, which may account for many of the positive symptoms of schizophrenia. Other causes may include abnormal brain tissue, a smaller than normal thalamus, exposure to prenatal viruses, and a genetic link showing that if one identical twin has schizophrenia, the other twin has a 50 percent chance of being similarly diagnosed.

Schizophrenia can be subdivided into five main types. **Disorganized schizophrenia** is characterized by incoherent speech and flat or inappropriate emotional

A: Major depression is characterized by depressed mood, a general lack of interest in things that a person usually enjoys, possible thoughts of death or suicide, low sense of self-worth, and low energy.

A: Delusions, hallucinations, and disturbed or inappropriate emotional responses to environmental stimuli are common to all types of schizophrenia.

A: Anterograde amnesia refers to the loss of memories occurring after a traumatic event, and retrograde amnesia to the loss of memories from before a traumatic event.

A: Fugue is the sudden and complete loss of identity, sometimes caused by severe stress, followed by the assumption of a new identity.

affect. **Catatonic schizophrenia** is marked by stupor and rigid body postures for extended periods of time. **Paranoid** schizophrenia is characterized by auditory hallucinations and feelings of persecution. Afflicted individuals may feel as though there are secret or coded messages hidden in everyday items or occurrences. The paranoid schizophrenic often has delusions of grandeur or persecution. **Undifferentiated schizophrenia** is used as a category for schizophrenics who exhibit multiple symptoms that are not easily categorized into the other afflictions. Finally, **residual schizophrenia** is the term for people currently displaying some schizoid tendencies or traits, but who are not currently profoundly schizophrenic. This diagnosis is usually applied to people who have had one or more psychotic episodes in their lifetime.

ORGANIC DISORDERS

Organic disorders are those caused by damage to brain tissue. Most organic disorders are the result of disease or chemicals. Dementia, Alzheimer's disease, and certain forms of drug/alcohol dependence fit into this category of brain dysfunction.

PERSONALITY DISORDERS

Personality disorders are characterized by the pervasive expression of extreme, abnormal personality constructs which interfere with normal social functioning.

- **Paranoid personality disorder** is characterized by extreme distrust and suspicion of others.

- **Antisocial personality disorder** is marked by disregard for the rights or interests of others.

- **Narcissistic personality disorder** is characterized by self-preoccupation and the need for others to focus on oneself.

- **Dependent personality disorder** is characterized by a need to be cared for.

- **Histrionic personality disorder** is characterized by excessive emotional reactions and excitability, as well as by the need for attention.

DISSOCIATIVE DISORDERS

The **dissociative disorders** are those that involve dysfunction of memory or an altered sense of identity. There are three main types of dissociative disorders: amnesia, fugue, and identity disorder.

Amnesia is the sudden loss of memory, usually precipitated by a traumatic event. Amnesia can be separated into **anterograde amnesia**, the loss of memories occurring after the traumatic event, and **retrograde amnesia**, the loss of memories from before the traumatic event.

Fugue is the sudden and complete loss of identity, sometimes caused by severe stress, followed by the assumption of a new identity. People in a fugue state often leave their homes and find their new identity elsewhere.

Dissociative identity disorder (DID), formerly multiple personality disorder, is the appearance of two or more distinct identities in one individual. The identities may or may not be aware of each other, and the personality that manifests itself may depend on the environmental or social context. There is some question as to whether this syndrome actually exists.

ATTENTION DEFICIT AND DISRUPTIVE BEHAVIOR DISORDERS

A classification of disorders revolving around attention issues has been more deeply explored in the past few years. **Attention deficit hyperactivity disorder (ADHD)** is a condition in which there is evidence of inattentiveness, which includes difficulty paying attention in class, trouble listening, difficulties in organization, forgetfulness and distractibility. Fidgeting, constant movement, and the constant need for attention characterize hyperactivity and impulsivity. Other related disorders are **conduct disorder** and **oppositional defiance disorder,** both of which affect student performance at home and at school.

Autism is a complex disorder that has been increasingly diagnosed in children over the last decade. Autistic symptoms can lessen with time or remain prevalent across a person's life. Autism is defined by four factors: deficits in social interactions; impairment in communication; restrictive or repetitive patterns of behavior, interests or activities; and the appearance of abnormal functioning by the age of three. Autism is a spectrum disorder, meaning that some people have less severe symptoms (these people are classified as being affected by **Asperger syndrome**) and others suffer from extreme autism, which can appear alongside retardation. Autistic children tend to prefer to be alone and can be either over or under sensitive to sensory stimuli. Autistic children prefer routine and show little to no eye contact. Symptoms tend to become less severe with age but most people suffering from autism never live independently. Roughly 10 percent of people suffering from autism have savant skills, which are islands of exceptional talent expressed by a person who otherwise has extreme difficulty acting normally. An autistic savant might have a very low IQ and be unable to interact with others, but also possess the ability to play any song on guitar after hearing it only once. Leading theories on the cause of autism posit that autistics lack theory of mind (the ability to understand other's intentions and perspectives) and poor executive function (the ability to shift from one task to another).

KEY TERMS

Psychopathology
abnormal behavior
psychoanalytic
humanistic
cognitive
behavioral
biological
sociocultural
DSM-IV-TR
Axis I–V
David Rosenhan

Anxiety Disorders
panic disorder
generalized anxiety disorder
    (GAD)
obsessive-compulsive disorder
    (OCD)
post-traumatic stress disorder
    (PTSD)
phobia

Somatoform Disorders
conversion disorder
hysteria
factitious disorders
hypochondriasis

Mood Disorders
major depression
bipolar disorder
seasonal affective disorder

Schizophrenic Disorders
schizophrenia
dopamine hypothesis
disorganized schizophrenia
catatonic schizophrenia
paranoid schizophrenia
undifferentiated schizophrenia
residual schizophrenia

Personality Disorders
paranoid personality disorder
antisocial personality disorder
narcissistic personality disorder
dependent personality disorder
histrionic personality disorder

Dissociative Disorders
anterograde amnesia
retrograde amnesia
fugue
dissociative identity disorder
    (DID)

Behavior Disorders
attention deficit hyperactivity
    disorder (ADHD)
oppositional defiance disorder
autism
Asperger syndrome

REVIEW QUESTIONS

See Chapter 18 for answers and explanations.

1. A physical condition, such as vitamin B-12 deficiency or exposure to a neurotoxin, that can have effects on the brain, the nervous system, or behavior, would most likely be noted on which axis of the *DSM-IV-TR* during a psychosocial evaluation?

   (A) Axis I
   (B) Axis II
   (C) Axis III
   (D) Axis IV
   (E) Axis V

2. The term used by most contemporary psychologists to refer to psychological difficulties that manifest themselves as physical symptoms is

   (A) bipolar disorder
   (B) conversion disorder
   (C) organic disorder
   (D) undifferentiated disorder
   (E) paranoid disorder

3. Which of the following are most characteristic of a dissociative disorder?

   (A) A persistent, irrational fear of objects or situations
   (B) Difficulties in forming lasting personal relationships
   (C) Involuntary and persistent thoughts that interfere with daily activity
   (D) Auditory and tactile hallucinations
   (E) Memory dysfunction and/or altered perceptions of identity

4. Depression has been associated with low levels of the neurotransmitter

   (A) acetylcholine
   (B) GABA
   (C) serotonin
   (D) chlorpromazine
   (E) dopamine

5. Which of the following is NOT characterized by the *DSM-IV-TR* as an anxiety disorder?

   (A) Post-traumatic stress disorder
   (B) Panic disorder
   (C) Agoraphobia
   (D) Seasonal affective disorder
   (E) Obsessive-compulsive disorder

16

Treatment of Psychological Disorders

TREATMENT APPROACHES

The various psychological disorders described in the previous chapter can be viewed from varying perspectives. Often insight into the true nature of a disorder can be derived from examining the strategy that is most effective in treating the disorder.

INSIGHT THERAPIES: PSYCHOANALYTIC AND HUMANISTIC APPROACHES

The psychoanalytic approach to the treatment of abnormal behavior is rooted in the concept of **insight**. Insight into the cause of the problem, according to this theory, is the primary key to eliminating the problem. The primary way in which a patient gains insight is through psychoanalysis.

Psychoanalysis

Psychoanalysis, or psychoanalytic therapy, as it is sometimes called, was developed by Freud and focuses on probing past defense mechanisms of repression and rationalization to understand the unconscious cause of a problem. A primary tool for revealing the contents of the unconscious is **free association**, in which the patient reports any and all conscious thoughts and ideas, sometimes while under **hypnosis**. Within the pattern of free associations are hints to the nature of the unconscious conflict. The insight process does not occur quickly, however, as patients exhibit resistance to the uncovering of repressed thoughts and feelings.

According to psychoanalytic theory, another window into the unconscious is provided by dreams. Freud believed that the images and occurrences in dreams—the **manifest content** of dreams—are actually symbols representing the **latent**, or truly meaningful, content of dreams. Freud developed catalogues of what he thought certain items in dreams truly represented.

In psychoanalytic therapy, the therapist strives to remain detached from the patient, resisting emotional or personal involvement. This detachment is intended to encourage **transference**, which occurs when the patient shifts thoughts and feelings about certain people or events onto the therapist. This process is thought to help reveal the nature of the patient's conflicts. However, the risk of **countertransference** exists. Countertransference occurs when the therapist transfers his or her own feelings onto the patient. In order to avoid countertransference, psychotherapists have typically undergone analysis themselves, and many continue to do so while practicing therapy.

Humanistic

The humanistic school of psychology takes a related, yet different approach to the treatment of abnormal behavior. Rather than treating the person seeking help as a patient, the humanistic approach treats the individual as a client. **Client-centered therapy** was invented by **Carl Rogers** and involves the assumption that clients can only be understood in terms of their own reality. This approach differs from the Freudian approach, in its focus on the client's present perception of reality, rather than the past and in its analysis of conscious, instead of unconscious, motives. The goal of the therapy is to help the client realize full potential through self-actualization. In order to accomplish this, the client-centered therapist takes a somewhat different approach from that of the Freudian. Rather than remaining detached, the therapist is open, honest, and expressive of feelings with the client (an active listener). Rogers referred to this way of relating to the client as **genuineness**.

The next key for successful client-centered therapy, according to Rogers, is **unconditional positive regard**. You may recall from previous chapters that Rogers believed that unconditional positive regard for the child by the parent was critical for healthy development. Typically, however, clients are not raised in this way. The therapist provides this unconditional positive regard to help the client reach a state of unconditional self-worth.

The final key to successful therapy is **accurate empathic understanding**. Rogers used this term to describe the therapist's ability to view the world from the eyes of the client. This empathy is critical to successful communication between the therapist and client.

A different type of approach toward treatment is **Gestalt therapy**, which combines both physical and mental therapies. **Fritz Perls** developed this approach to blend an awareness of unconscious tensions with the belief that one must become aware of and deal with those tensions by taking personal responsibility. Clients may be asked to physically "act out" psychological conflicts in order to make them aware of the interaction between mind and body.

BEHAVIORAL THERAPY

Behavioral therapy stands in dramatic contrast to the insight therapies. First, behavioral therapy is a short-term process, whereas the insight approaches are extended over long periods of time, typically spanning years. Secondly, behavior therapy treats symptoms because, in this school of thought, there is no deep underlying cause of the problem. The abnormal behavior itself is both problem and symptom. To change behavior, behavioral therapists use specific techniques with clearly defined methods of application and clear ways to evaluate their efficacy.

Counterconditioning is a technique in which a response to a given stimulus is replaced by a different response. For example, if a patient seeks behavioral therapy to stop drinking alcohol, the therapist must take the learned responses, the positive feelings generated by drinking alcohol, and replace them with a new reaction, namely, negative feelings concerning alcohol.

Counterconditioning can be accomplished in a few ways. One is to use **aversion therapy**, in which an aversive stimulus is repeatedly paired with the behavior that the client wishes to stop. So, to use our alcohol example, the therapist might administer a punishment to the patient each time the patient drinks alcohol. This approach is sometimes used in treating alcoholism. Patients are administered a drug called Antabuse, which makes them violently ill if they consume alcohol.

Another method used for counterconditioning is **systematic desensitization**. This technique involves replacing one response, such as anxiety, with another response, such as relaxation. In order to achieve this goal, a therapist constructs, with the help of the client, a hierarchical set of mental images related to the stressful stimulus. These mental images are laid out in an order such that each one is slightly more anxiety-inducing than the next. The patient then learns a deep-relaxation technique. Next, the therapist asks the patient to bring to mind the least stressful of the mental images. As the client imagines the scene, he or she may become anxious. The client is instructed to practice the relaxation technique the moment the feelings of anxiety begin, and to continue using the relaxation technique until he or she feels fully relaxed while imagining the scene. The therapist, over time, systematically helps the client work up the hierarchy until he or she is able to imagine the most stressful scene in the hierarchy without experiencing anxiety. This technique relies on learning mechanisms to associate the formerly anxiety-provoking stimuli with relaxation. A variation on this technique can occur when a therapist introduces the client to increasingly more anxiety-inducing stimuli instead of relying solely on his or her imagination.

Other forms of behavioral therapy involve **extinction procedures**, which are designed to weaken maladaptive responses. One way of trying to extinguish a behavior is called **flooding**. Flooding involves exposing a client to the stimulus that causes the undesirable response. If, for example, a client has come to a therapist to try to overcome a fear of spiders, the therapist will actually expose the client to spiders. Of course, the client will have a high anxiety level, but after a few minutes of being near the spider without any negative consequences, the client will presumably realize that the situation is not dangerous.

Implosion is a similar technique, where the client imagines the disruptive stimuli rather than actually confronting them.

Operant conditioning is a behavior-control technique that we discussed in the chapter on learning. A related approach is **behavioral contracting**, in which the therapist and the client draw up a contract to which they both agree to abide. The client must, according to the contract, act in certain ways, such as not exhibiting undesirable behaviors; meanwhile, the therapist must provide stated rewards if the client holds up his or her end of the bargain.

Modeling is a therapeutic approach based on Bandura's social learning theory. This technique is based on the principle of vicarious learning. Clients watch someone act in a certain way and then receive a reward. Presumably, the client will then be disposed to imitate that behavior.

COGNITIVE THERAPY

Cognitive approaches to the treatment of abnormal behavior rely on changing cognitions, or the ways people think about situations, in order to change behavior. One such approach is **rational-emotive behavior therapy (REBT)** (sometimes called simply **RET**, for **rational-emotive therapy**), formulated by **Albert Ellis**. REBT is based on the idea that when confronted with situations, people recite statements to themselves that express maladaptive thoughts. The maladaptive thoughts result in maladaptive emotional responses. The goal of REBT is to change the maladaptive thoughts and emotional response by confronting the irrational thoughts directly. Incorrect thoughts are changed in a simple way: The patient is told that he or she is incorrect and why. An example of a maladaptive thought is, "I always have to be perfect in everything I do" or "Other people's opinions are crucial to my happiness."

Another cognitive approach is **cognitive therapy,** formulated by **Aaron Beck,** in which the focus is on maladaptive schemas. These schemas cause the client to experience cognitive distortions, which in turn lead them to feel worthless or incompetent. Beck asserted that there is a **negative triad** of depression that involves a negative view of self, of the world, and of the future. This view is learned through experiences and then becomes a cycle of response that needs to be addressed through cognitive therapy. Maladaptive schemas include **arbitrary inference**, in which a person draws conclusions without evidence, and **dichotomous thinking**, which involves all-or-none conceptions of situations. An example might be that of a person, faced with the stress of a job interview, who thinks, "If I don't get this job, I'll be a complete failure." The goal of cognitive therapy is to eliminate or modify the individual's maladaptive schemas.

BIOLOGICAL THERAPIES

Biological therapies are medical approaches to behavioral problems. Biological therapies are typically used in conjunction with one of the previously mentioned forms of treatment.

Electroconvulsive therapy (ECT) is a form of treatment in which fairly high voltages of electricity are passed across a patient's head. This treatment causes temporary amnesia and can result in seizures. It has been successful in the treatment of major depression, but today is used only when all other means of treating depression have failed because of the risks involved with memory loss.

Another form of biological treatment is **psychosurgery**. Perhaps the most well-known form of psychosurgery is the **prefrontal lobotomy**, in which parts of the frontal lobes are cut off from the rest of the brain. This surgery was a popular treatment for violent patients from the 1930s to the 1950s. It frequently left patients in a zombie-like or catatonic state. Its use marked a controversial chapter in the history of psychotherapy.

Psychopharmacology is the treatment of psychological and behavioral maladaptations with drugs. There are four broad classes of **psychotropic**, or psychologically active drugs: antipsychotics, antidepressants, anxiolytics, and lithium salts.

Antipsychotics like Clozapine, Thorazine, and Haldol reduce the symptoms of schizophrenia by blocking the neural receptors for dopamine. You may recall that dopamine is implicated in schizophrenia and in movement disorder. Unfortunately, jerky movements, tremors, and muscle stiffness are among the side effects of these drugs. The clinician must decide which is worse—the psychological disorder being treated or the side effects of the drugs.

Antidepressant drugs can be grouped into three types: the monoamine oxidase (MAO) inhibitors, the tricyclics, and the selective reuptake inhibitors. **MAO inhibitors** like Eutron work by increasing the amount of serotonin and norepinephrine in the synaptic cleft. They produce this increase by blocking monoamine oxidase, which is responsible for the breakdown of many neurotransmitters. These drugs are effective but toxic and require special dietary modifications. The **tricyclics** like Norpramin are used more frequently. Amitriptyline and imipramine are tricyclics that increase the amount of serotonin and norepinephrine.

The third class of antidepressants, the **selective reuptake inhibitors** (often called the selective serotonin reuptake inhibitors, or SSRIs, for the neurotransmitter most affected by them), also work by increasing the amount of neurotransmitter at the synaptic cleft, in this case by blocking the reuptake mechanism of the cell that released the neurotransmitters. Prozac (fluoxetine) is one example of such a drug. The indirect mechanism of action of these drugs means that they have fewer side effects.

Anxiolytics depress the central nervous system and reduce anxiety while increasing feelings of well-being and reducing insomnia. A commonly prescribed anti-anxiety medication is Xanax. Anxiolytics also include the barbiturates, which are rarely used because of their potential for addiction and their danger when mixed with other drugs. **Benzodiazepines**, such as Valium (diazepam) and Librium (chlordiazepoxide), cause muscle relaxation and a feeling of tranquillity.

Lithium carbonate, a salt, is effective in the treatment of bipolar disorder. The mechanism of action is not known, however.

MODES OF THERAPY

Not all forms of therapy involve an individual client seeing a therapist. **Group therapy**, where clients meet together with a therapist as an interactive group, has some advantages over individual therapy. It is less expensive, and the group dynamic may be therapeutic in and of itself. Of course, the psychological effect of the therapist also may be diluted across the members of the group because attention is focused on the group rather than on a specific individual. One area in which group therapy has gained popularity is in the treatment of substance abuse. **Twelve-step programs** are one form of group therapy, although they are usually not moderated by professional psychotherapists. These programs, modeled after Alcoholics Anonymous, are a combination of spirituality and group therapy. The twelve-step programs focus on a strong social support system of people who are experiencing or who have experienced addictions or other types of maladaptive adjustments to life.

Another therapy in which there is more than a single client is **couples** or **family therapy**. This type of treatment arose out of the simple observation that some dysfunctional behavior affects the afflicted person's loved ones. Couples therapy approaches the couple dyad as a system that involves complex interactions. Family therapy has distinct advantages in that it allows family members to express their feelings to each other and to the therapist simultaneously. This behavior in turn encourages family members to listen to each other in a way that might not occur in other settings.

KEY TERMS

Treatment Approaches
insight
psychoanalysis
free association
hypnosis
manifest content
latent content
transference
countertransference
client-centered therapy
Carl Rogers
genuineness
unconditional positive regard
accurate empathetic
    understanding
Gestalt therapy
Fritz Perls
behavioral therapy
counterconditioning
aversion therapy
systematic desensitization
extinction procedures
flooding
implosion
operant conditioning
behavioral contracting
modeling
cognitive therapy
rational-emotive behavior
    therapy

Albert Ellis
Aaron Beck
negative triad
arbitrary inference
dichotomous thinking
electroconvulsive therapy (ECT)
psychosurgery
prefrontal lobotomy
psychopharmacology
psychotropic drugs
antipsychotics
antidepressants
MAO inhibitors
tricyclics
selective reuptake inhibitors
anxiolytics
benzodiazepines
lithium carbonate

Modes of Therapy
family therapy
group therapy
twelve-step programs

REVIEW QUESTIONS

See Chapter 18 for answers and explanations.

1. The concept of *accurate empathic understanding* is most closely associated with which of the following therapeutic approaches?

   (A) Psychoanalytic therapy
   (B) Inductive therapy
   (C) Client-centered therapy
   (D) Implosion therapy
   (E) Reductionist therapy

2. Behavioral therapeutic approaches, such as systematic desensitization, have been most often used with those experiencing or diagnosed with

   (A) fugue
   (B) dementia
   (C) dissociative disorder
   (D) schizophrenia
   (E) phobia

3. A psychoanalytically oriented therapist would most likely be in accord with which of the following criticisms regarding behaviorally oriented therapies?

   (A) Behaviorally oriented therapies often take years to complete and create an onerous financial burden for the patient.
   (B) Behaviorally oriented therapies are concerned solely with the modification of troubling behavioral symptoms and do not address the underlying problems which may have produced those symptoms.
   (C) Behaviorally oriented therapies can be performed only by therapists who have had the longest and most rigorous training and, as a result, can never impact as many people as can other treatment approaches.
   (D) Behaviorally oriented therapies are relatively uninterested in the development of an egalitarian client-therapist relationship and miss opportunities to promote emotional growth and empowerment.
   (E) Behaviorally oriented therapies avoid the technique of role-playing and may not be suitable for group or family therapy situations.

4. The cognitively oriented therapeutic approach known as rational-emotive behavior therapy is most closely associated with

   (A) Julian Rotter
   (B) Albert Ellis
   (C) Abraham Maslow
   (D) Raymond Cattell
   (E) Rollo May

5. Which of the following is not a major class of drugs used for psychotherapeutic effect?

   (A) Anticoagulants
   (B) Anxiolytics
   (C) Monoamine oxidase inhibitors
   (D) Lithium salts
   (E) Selective reuptake inhibitors

TEST BREAK #5

You are going to read an awful lot of wrong answer choices while working on Section I of the AP Psychology Exam. And, believe it or not, a lot of those choices are not only wrong, but also just plain stupid. Using your knowledge of psychology, plus the information in the question itself, examine each of the following sets of answer choices to determine which is the best answer to the question. Remember, if it's stupid, extreme, or fallacious, it cannot be the answer to any question. Check your POE smarts on page 226 when you're finished.

4. Blah, Blah, Blah?

   (A) Obese people have fewer but larger fat cells than average-weight people.
   (B) Obese people have many more fat cells than average-weight people.

27. Connectionist approaches blah, blah

   (A) are carried out by individual segments of the brain
   (B) occur simultaneously through the action of multiple networks

47. Blah, blah, chunking?

   (A) Christina remembers two new phone numbers by recognizing that each has a familiar exchange, and that the second half of each represents a familiar date in history.
   (B) Chelsea learns her times tables by methodically practicing one set each night, then reviewing with flashcards.

85. Blah, blah, person-centered psychotherapy blah

   (A) suppresses negative feelings that arise within the client
   (B) uses a didactic approach to teach the client to correct maladaptive behavior
   (C) accepts the client unconditionally so that his or her desire for healing will grow

92. Blah, blah, blah, blah, blah

   (A) repressing the client's deviant feelings
   (B) slowly altering the contingencies of reinforcement for the client
   (C) removing the underlying causes of a client's problems for the client

17
Social Psychology

Social psychology is the study of people in interaction with each other.

GROUP DYNAMICS

Group dynamics is a general term for some of the phenomena we observe when people interact. For example, **social facilitation** is an increase in performance on a task that occurs when that task is performed in the presence of others. You may have experienced this effect if you play sports. The opposite effect is called **social inhibition**, which occurs when the presence of others makes performance worse. Many people experience social inhibition when they give a speech. People experience social facilitation when they find a task to be easy or well-practiced, and suffer from social inhibition when a task is overly difficult or novel.

Another effect that occurs when people interact in groups is **social loafing**, or the reduced effort group members put into a task as a result of the size of the group. For example, if you are lifting a large box, it takes great effort, but if you are one of four people lifting, you may tend to put in less effort than your share in the hope that other members of the group will not realize that you are slacking off. People are prone to social loafing when they believe their performance is not being assessed or monitored.

Another interesting effect of being in groups is the exaggeration of our initial attitudes. This effect is known as **group polarization**. Group polarization occurs when a judgment or decision of a group is more extreme than what individual members of the group would have reached on their own. For example, if people with negative racial attitudes are placed into a group and told to discuss racial issues, those who started off the experiment with high prejudice often end up with an even higher prejudice after the discussion.

Research has been conducted on the resolution of conflicts within groups. The most effective method to resolve a conflict between two groups is to have them cooperate towards a superordinate goal. For example, in the Robbers Cave experiment, campers who had been feuding for weeks were able to overcome their differences when they cooperated to solve problems, such as a water leak that threatened the whole camp. Another effective technique is **GRIT (Graduated and Reciprocated Initiatives in Tension-Reduction)**. This approach encourages groups to announce intent to reduce tensions and show small, conciliatory behaviors, as long as these reduced tensions and behaviors are reciprocated.

Another interesting phenomenon that may occur when people are in groups is what **Irving Janis** has referred to as "groupthink." **Groupthink** occurs when members of a group are so driven to reach unanimous decisions that they no longer truly evaluate the repercussions or implications of their decisions. Group-think occurs when the groups making decisions are isolated and homogeneous, when there is a lack of impartial leadership inside or outside the group, and when there is a high level of pressure for a decision to be made. Often groups experiencing groupthink start to acquire feelings of invulnerability and omnipotence. They do not believe they can make a mistake and as a result, often do. A **mindguard** in the group may take on the responsibility of criticizing or even ostracizing members of the group who do not agree with the rest. The groupthink hypothesis has been applied to understand political situations, such as how political leaders can make decisions that seem, in retrospect, so obviously bad to people outside of the group.

ATTRIBUTION

Attribution refers to how people assign responsibility for certain outcomes. Typically, attribution falls into two categories—dispositional (or person) and situational. **Dispositional attribution** assumes that the cause of a behavior or outcome is internal. **Situational attribution** assigns the cause to the environment or external conditions. When students fail a test, they might attribute that failure to their own poor work habits or lack of intellectual abilities (a dispositional attribute) or they could attribute their failure to some external factor such as that they had bad instruction (a situational attribute).

A **self-serving bias** sees the cause of actions as internal (or dispositional) when the outcomes are positive or external (or situational) when the results are negative. When a teacher's class fails a test, that teacher blames the students for their lack of initiative and motivation. However, when the class does very well, the teacher attributes the students' success to his or her superior teaching and motivational ability. A related concept is the **fundamental attribution error**. In this process of judging the behavior of others, people are more likely to overestimate the role of dispositional attributes and to underestimate the role of the situation. For example, if you are waiting for your friend to meet you at the movies and she is so late that the movie has already started, you would be more likely to blame your friend's lateness on her laziness or procrastination than on a traffic jam or car accident. Your judgment exemplifies a fundamental attribution error.

Some attributions actually affect the outcome of the behavior, as in the case of the **self-fulfilling prophecy**. Because Person A expects Person B to achieve or fail, Person B is likely to do just that. This is especially true in education and is known as the **Rosenthal Effect**. When teachers are told that certain children are expected to achieve in the following year, those children tend to do better than others, even when there is actually no difference in ability levels.

INTERPERSONAL PERCEPTION

Psychologists have studied **interpersonal attraction**, the tendency to positively evaluate a person and then to gravitate to that person. Interpersonal attraction is obviously based on characteristics of the person to whom we are attracted, but also may be subject to environmental and social influences as well. Factors leading to interpersonal attraction include positive evaluation, shared opinions, good physical appearance, familiarity, and proximity of the individuals to each other. **Positive evaluation** refers to the fact that we all like to be positively evaluated, and therefore, we tend to prefer the company of people who think highly of us. **Shared opinions** as a basis for interpersonal attraction are typically thought of as a form of social reinforcement. If we are praised and rewarded by a person for our opinions, then we tend to prefer their company. It is important to note that similarity across other factors, such as age and race, also tends to be a good predictor of interpersonal attraction. The variability of proximity is an interesting factor. It has been shown that people are more likely to be attracted to those in close physical proximity to them. Studies have shown that apartment building residents are much more likely to have friends who live on their floor than they are to have friends who live on other floors. This is an example of the **mere exposure effect**, which states that people tend to prefer people and experiences that are familiar.

CONFORMITY, COMPLIANCE, OBEDIENCE

Conformity is the modification of behavior to make it agree with that of a group. **Solomon Asch** performed studies on the nature of conformity. In these studies, participants thought that they were being evaluated on their perceptual judgments. Small groups of people sitting together were shown stimuli, such as lines of differing lengths. Each member of the group was to report which of several comparison lines matched a standard line in length. Each individual in the group was asked to respond orally in turn. The participants did not know that the other members of a given group were not naïve participants, but rather, were confederates of the experimenter. The correct answers in the experiment were obvious. However, the confederates, pretending to be naïve participants, would purposely respond incorrectly. Asch found that, in general, the naïve participants agreed with the other members of the group, even though the answer they gave was obviously incorrect. Furthermore, Asch demonstrated that the participants knew that the answers they gave were wrong, but said them anyway.

Factors influencing conformity include group size, the cohesiveness of the group opinion, gender, social status, culture, and the appearance of unanimity. Generally speaking, three or more members of a group are sufficient for conformity effects to occur. The desire to conform seems higher if the participants see themselves as members of a cohesive group. In general, women are more likely to conform than are men. People who view themselves as being of medium or low social status are more likely to conform than are those who perceive themselves as being of high social status. The cultural influence on conformity is interesting; people in more collective societies tend to conform more than do those in individualistic societies. Finally, unanimity is important. A participant is much less likely to conform if even one other person in the group did not conform.

Compliance is the propensity to accede to the requests of others, even at the expense of your own interests. One method of eliciting compliance is justification, in which you present reasons why a person should comply. Another method is reciprocity, which involves creating the appearance that you are giving someone something in order to induce that individual to comply with your wishes. Sales people have perfected the **foot-in-the-door phenomenon**, which involves making requests in small steps at first (to gain compliance), in order to work up to big requests. The likelihood of compliance to a particular request also depends on our regard for the person making the request. Generally speaking, the more highly we regard the person making the request, the more likely we are to comply with the person's request. In general, there are two reasons why people will resist compliance. One reason is because people have been exposed to a weak version of an argument and are, therefore, inoculated to further attempts to get them to comply. This theory is known as the "inoculation hypothesis." Another reason people resist is because they feel that they are being forced against their will to comply, which is known as "psychological reactance."

Obedience was studied by **Stanley Milgram** in a series of famous experiments. The basic paradigm was as follows. Participants were led to believe that their job was to administer shocks of increasing intensity to another participant if that participant performed poorly on a given learning task. The other participant was actually a confederate, intentionally performing badly, so that the real participant would be obliged to administer shock. The confederate also acted as if the shocks were painful, pleading with the participant to stop. (In fact, no shocks were given.) The participant was instructed by the experimenter to continue the shocks, despite the obvious pain the "other participant" was enduring. You might think that you would not administer painful shocks in this paradigm, but a very high percentage of people did just that. Through additional studies, Milgram found that several factors were critical to whether or not the person would obey. The first was the perceived authority of the test administrator. For example, when the person overseeing the experiment introduced himself as a graduate student instead of as a scientist, the subject was much less likely to comply. Another factor was physical distance. If the subject was forced to sit in the room with the person receiving the shocks, his level of obedience dropped; the subject was also less likely to obey if the experimenter communicated the commands by phone instead of in person. Obedience also tended to go down if the subject was told that he was responsible for the outcome; if the subject witnessed someone else disobeying the experimenter; and if the experimenter instructed the subject to immediately apply a high level of voltage to the "learner." The major conclusion from this study was that people tended to be obedient to a figure of authority, but only if certain criteria were met. It also demonstrated that people are much less likely to obey when they feel that they have an ally in standing up to the pressure.

ATTITUDES AND ATTITUDE CHANGE

Attitudes are combinations of affective (emotional) and cognitive (perceptual) reactions to different stimuli. The affective component is the emotional response an item or issue arouses, whereas the cognitive component is what we think about the item or issue. Attitudes are acquired, in part, by vicarious conditioning. If, for example, we observe a person being bitten by a dog, we form an attitude about that dog. In this case, the affective component might be fear, and the cognitive component might be the understanding that this particular dog bites.

Persuasion is the process by which a person or group can influence the attitudes of others. The efficacy of persuasion derives in part from the characteristics of the persuader. People who have positions of authority or who appear to be experts on a given topic are more likely to be viewed as persuasive. The motive of the persuader is also critical. If an author tries to convince you that authors are poor, and that you should donate five dollars to the poor authors' fund, you probably would not believe the author. Your disbelief would stem from your confidence that the author's motive is selfish. However, if an author asks for five dollars for disaster relief, you might be more likely to be persuaded because the motive seems more altruistic.

An additional factor affecting persuasive ability is interpersonal attractiveness. More attractive, likeable, trustworthy, and knowledgeable people are viewed as more persuasive. Most people are also swayed by the presentation of facts. Market researchers refer to the use of facts as the **central route to persuasion**.

Another factor influencing the persuasion process is the nature of the message. Repetition is an effective technique for achieving persuasion, which is why the same advertisements run so frequently. Fear is another motivator of attitudinal change. A prime example of the use of fear in persuasive attempts is the practice of putting cars wrecked in DWI (driving-while-intoxicated) accidents on display. The idea is that the fear of such an accident will induce an attitudinal change about drunk driving.

Finally, some people can be influenced to change their attitudes more easily than others. In general, people with high self-esteem are less easily persuaded than are those with low self-esteem. Thus, many hate groups recruit people who are considered outsiders or who have few friends. These people with low self-esteem are susceptible to having their attitudes on issues, such as race, changed to match those of the hate group.

Cognitive dissonance occurs when attitudes and behaviors contradict each other. Generally, such tension is not pleasant, and people tend to change in order to achieve cognitive consistency. **Leon Festinger** studied this phenomenon and came to the conclusion that people are likely to alter their attitude to fit their behavior. For example, law-abiding citizens speed frequently. A cognitive conflict exists. Which is going to change—their attitude toward the law or their over-the-limit driving? Generally, people adjust their attitudes and continue their behavior. Cognitive dissonance tends to occur only when the person feels that he has a choice in the matter. If someone feels that he is being forced to speed, his attitude will remain intact.

ALTRUISM AND HELPING BEHAVIOR

Some psychologists are interested in **altruism** and **helping behavior**. Research into these topics emerged in part as a result of the case of Kitty Genovese, a woman who was murdered in her apartment complex. Thirty-eight neighbors saw or heard what was happening but nobody intervened or even called the police. Psychologists refer to this indifference as the **bystander effect**. It occurs as a result of **diffusion of responsibility**. Simply put, each person assumes that someone else will (or should) help or call the police.

Altruism can help reduce the tendency toward the bystander effect. Altruism is selfless sacrifice, and it occurs more frequently than it might appear. Altruism has been explained in terms of an empathic response to the plight of others. People place themselves in the position of others in distress, and act toward the others as they would wish those others to act toward them.

ORGANIZATIONAL PSYCHOLOGY

This area of social psychology deals primarily with the workplace. The **equity theory** proposes a view whereby workers evaluate their efforts versus their rewards. Job satisfaction is often based on this concept. **Human factors** research deals with the interaction of person and machine. Many job-related accidents are caused by design flaws in equipment related to the expectancy of the worker. The **Hawthorne effect** indicates that workers being monitored for any reason work more efficiently and productively. This was demonstrated in an experiment that took place in a Western Electric plant. The study was intended to test whether levels of light increased or decreased worker productivity. The outcome, however, showed that worker productivity increased at all levels of light simply because of the presence of the monitors.

AGGRESSION/ANTISOCIAL BEHAVIOR

Antisocial behavior, behavior that is harmful to society or others, can be divided roughly into two kinds: **prejudice** and **aggression**.

Prejudice is a negative attitude toward members of a particular group without evidentiary backing. Quite literally, prejudice is the result of prejudging members of a group. Discrimination is behavioral; that is, acting on the attitude and treating members of that group differently from members of other groups.

People tend to categorize things into groups based on common attributes. One theory of this phenomenon is that classification occurs when people compare new stimuli or people to preexisting prototypes in order to determine the group to which the novel stimuli belong. **Stereotypes** are prototypes of people. Although stereotypes can be useful for categorization, they can be harmful by leading us from incorrect assumptions to incorrect conclusions. One assumption we tend to make is **outgroup homogeneity**, that is, that every member of a group other than our own is similar. A false conclusion is **illusory correlation**, in which we tend to see relationships where they don't actually exist. For example, illusory correlation is noticing that people of a certain ethnic group are apprehended for crimes while ignoring that people of the same ethnic group also do positive things for the society.

Attempts to understand how to reduce prejudice and stereotyping have included the **contact hypothesis**, which posits that groups with stereotypes about each other would lose these stereotypes if the groups were exposed to each other. This hypothesis has not been supported by data because contact can also serve merely to reinforce existing stereotypes. Factors such as the different social status of the two groups or a lack of common interests may stand in the way of groups reducing stereotypes through contact. These factors are also illustrated in the robbers' cave experiment, discussed previously.

Aggression is behavior directed toward another, with the intention of causing harm. Aggression occurs for multiple reasons. **Hostile aggression** is emotional and impulsive, and it is typically induced by pain or stress. **Instrumental aggression**, in contrast, is aggression committed to gain something of value. For example, a child pushing another child on a playground to get a prized toy is an example of instrumental aggression.

Biological factors play a role in aggression in all species, including humans. Aggression is sensitive to hormonal fluctuations, particularly fluctuations of the androgen, testosterone, which increases aggressive tendencies. Steroid abusers, who use large quantities of synthetic hormones, may experience uncontrollable aggression.

As Albert Bandura's work has demonstrated, aggression has a strong learned component. If children see adults rewarded for aggression, it is likely that they will learn that aggression is an effective strategy for coping with problems. Additionally, pornography frequently depicts violence toward women. Again, vicarious learning theory tells us that watching pornographic films can lead to learning that might result in violence at a later time.

Environmental factors also can lead to aggression. Experiencing pain and being surrounded by aggressive behavior, discomfort, and frustration have all been shown to be possible causes of aggressive behavior. Additionally, we have the ability to view the victims of violence as somehow less than human, a process called **dehumanization**. This phenomenon was demonstrated in a study by **Phil Zimbardo** in which some randomly selected participants were "jailed" while others were randomly selected to act as guards. The prisoners had numbers, not names. The guards wore uniforms and mirrored glasses. Within a short period of time, the participants in each group began to act as though they hated the participants in the other group. The two groups, when stripped of their individual identity, turned to mob identity and violence. In effect, what started out as role-playing became serious identification with the roles. The experiment got out of hand and had to be stopped prematurely to preserve the participants' well-being.

Research on reducing aggression has identified some successful techniques. Punishment, which is frequently used as a treatment for aggression, is not particularly effective in reducing aggression. Rather, the observation of nonaggressive models of conflict resolution, or the diffusion of aggression with humor or empathy, are more effective at disrupting violent behavior.

KEY TERMS

Group Dynamics
social facilitation
social inhibition
social loafing
group polarization
GRIT (Graduated and
    Reciprocated Initiatives in
    Tension-Reduction)
Irving Janis
groupthink
mindguard

Attribution
dispositional attribution
situational attribution
self-serving bias
fundamental attribution error
self-fulfilling prophecy
Rosenthal Effect

Interpersonal Perception
interpersonal attraction
positive evaluation
shared opinions
mere exposure effect

Conformity, Compliance, Obedience
Solomon Asch
compliance
conformity
obedience
foot-in-the-door phenomenon
Stanley Milgram

Attitudes and Attitude Change
attitude
persuasion
central route to persuasion
cognitive dissonance
Leon Festinger

Altruism
altruism
helping behavior
bystander effect
diffusion of responsibility

Organizational Psychology
equity theory
human factors
Hawthorne effect

Aggression and Antisocial Behavior
aggression
prejudice
stereotype
outgroup homogeneity
illusory correlation
contact hypothesis
hostile aggression
instrumental aggression
dehumanization
Phil Zimbardo

REVIEW QUESTIONS

See Chapter 18 for answers and explanations.

1. The "fundamental attribution error" phenomenon can best be seen in the following example:

(A) John blames his failure to get a job on his lack of appropriate skills and ill-preparedness.

(B) Phyllis doesn't get the lead in the school play and blames her drama teacher for this failure.

(C) Jane blames herself for forgetting that she has a term paper due in two days.

(D) Bill doesn't hire John, because John was a half-hour late for his interview and Bill believes that John's lateness is a result of his laziness and lack of respect for the job. In reality, John was late because he got a flat tire on the way to the interview.

(E) Karen understands that her friend is late because she was caught in rush-hour traffic.

2. In the Asch conformity experiments, which of these was NOT a consistent factor influencing the degree to which conformity to the group answer would be shown by the experimental subject?

(A) Unanimity of group opinion

(B) Size of the group

(C) The subject's perception of his/her social status compared to that of group members

(D) Age of the subject

(E) Gender of the subject

3. Students are randomly designated by experimenters as likely to experience significant jumps in academic test scores in the coming semester, and this designation is communicated to their teachers. When actual test scores are examined at the end of the semester, it is found that these randomly designated students did indeed tend to experience jumps in performance. This phenomenon is known as

(A) the Hawthorne effect

(B) the Kandel effect

(C) cognitive dissonance

(D) the self-fulfilling prophecy

(E) the Ainsworth effect

4. An old woman carrying a number of packages has tripped and fallen on a busy urban sidewalk and is having trouble getting back up. The fact that few people are likely to stop and offer her help is referred to by social psychologists as an example of

(A) illusory correlation

(B) diffusion of responsibility

(C) cognitive dissonance

(D) altruistic orientation

(E) just-world bias

5. Which of the following would illustrate the "foot-in-the-door" technique of facilitating compliance with a request?

(A) A professional fundraiser, needing to get $10,000 from a foundation, first requests four times that amount, expecting to be turned down so that she can then ask for the lesser amount.

(B) A teenager, wanting to extend his curfew from 10:00 P.M. to midnight, first asks if it can be extended to 11:00 P.M. for a specific "special" occasion; he then plans to ask for the further extension at a later date after pointing out to his parents he was able to handle the 11:00 P.M. curfew.

(C) A mother wishing to get her twins to do their homework each day upon coming home from school and before other activities tells each of them separately that the other twin has agreed to do just that.

(D) An interviewee desperately needing to get a new job researches the mode of dress in each company he lands an interview with and always shows up at the meeting in that exact mode of dress.

(E) A teacher wishing all her students to get their assignments in on time promises her class extra grading points for turning them in early.

18

Answers and Explanations

CHAPTER 2

Ask It Like It Is Drill (Page 13)

3. What's a scientist who's into the physical basis of psychological phenomena called?

10. One of the <u>primary tools</u> of the school of was

18. Binocular cues help you see depth because

35. What type of effect is this: person only remembers words from the beginning and end of a list?

47. The theory asserts that we categorize objects by breaking them down into their component parts and then

   We break stuff down and then do what?

56. The fact that V. can ignore the crowd is called what?

70. Which of the following was <u>true</u> of Stanley ?

88. In their discussions of the <u>process of development</u>, the advocates of in the <u>nature-nurture controversy</u> emphasize which of the following?

   Nurture emphasizes what?

EASY QUESTIONS DRILL (PAGES 19–20)

1. Ask It Like It Is:
   Answer Before You Answer:
   Answer:

   Freud = which perspective?
   Psychoanalytic
   (B) Easy enough.

2. Ask It Like It Is:

   Answer Before You Answer:
   Answer:

   When you stop using a drug, you go through what?
   Withdrawal
   (C) Be careful not to rush through and accidentally pick another, like (A).

3. Ask It Like It Is:

   Answer Before You Answer:
   Answer:

   Conditioning: when the dog salivates at what?
   The light without the food
   (B) Watch for (A) and (C). Both are wrong, but close enough to trip up someone who is rushing. If you picked (D) or (E), better hit the books.

4. Ask It Like It Is:

   Answer Before You Answer:
   Answer:

   Circle *basic unit* and underline *nervous system*
   Neuron
   (D) Watch out for the others— all parts of the neuron.

5. Ask It Like It Is:

   Answer Before You Answer:
   Answer:

   Circle *methods of research* and underline *central to behaviorist*.
   Experimenting
   (E) Again, if you don't know, start reviewing. POE should easily get rid of (B), (C), and (D).

Medium Questions Drill (Pages 20–21)

33. Ask It Like It Is:

    Answer Before You Answer:

    Answer:

    What regulates hunger and thirst?

    I'm not sure, but I know what it's not (use POE).

    (C) Using POE, you should have been able to get rid of at least (D) and (E), and most likely (A) (review Chapter 6).

34. Ask It Like It Is:

    Answer Before You Answer:

    Answer:

    Which psychologists were into viewing things as part of a whole?

    Don't remember but I know all the main perspectives well (use POE).

    (D) If you know your perspectives well, you could easily have gotten rid of at least (A), (B), and (C). Cognitive social-ist doesn't make sense, so the answer must be (D).

35. Ask It Like It Is:

    Answer Before You Answer:
    Answer:

    What's wrong with the study: Survey comp sci class to find out who in the school has computers.

    The sample is biased.
    (B) It's the closest answer to yours. POE the rest.

36. Ask It Like It Is:

    Answer Before You Answer:
    Answer:

    Looking out the window stimulates which two parts of the brain?

    Occipital and another (use POE)
    (E) Knowing occipital gets it down to two answer choices. If you don't know it from there, guess and move on (review Chapter 6).

37.	Ask It Like It Is:	Circle *behaviorism* and underline *true of*.
	Answer Before You Answer:	Experimenting, everything is learned, consequences
	Answer:	**(C)** It's the closest answer to yours. (A) is psychodynamic, (B) is sort of cognitive behaviorism, (D) is wrong, and (E) is stupid.

CHAPTER 3

FINAL ESSAY QUESTION (PAGE 37)

Our Sample Essay

Stress can have serious psychological and physiological consequences. Although one cannot completely avoid stress, it is essential to our health and well-being that we learn effective coping strategies to better manage stress. Many things in our lives are very stress-inducing. These stressors can range from major life-changing events such as marriage, divorce, moving, or the death of a loved one to simple daily hassles like traffic or family arguments.

From a physiological standpoint, when an individual is stressed, the sympathetic nervous system responds with readiness for "fight or flight." In normal circumstances, this elevated level of stimulation abates when the perceived danger disappears. But what if it doesn't disappear? Then, the body does allow some systems to return to normal—breathing, heart rate—but other systems remain at the ready—elevated levels of sugar and adrenaline in the blood, for example. The greatest danger of prolonged exposure to stress, according to Hans Seyle's General Adaptation Syndrome, is that the strain placed on the body, coupled with elevated hormone levels caused by stress reactions, can lead to cardiovascular disease and can weaken a person's immunity to disease.

From a psychological standpoint, stress represents a challenge to the way that we think and the way that we behave. It is very easy, when struggling with major and minor stresses, to feel defeated or overwhelmed by what it might take to overcome the challenge. Stress is more than just the occurrence of a stressful event. It is also an individual's vulnerability to stress and, according to Richard Lazarus, the importance of the stressful event to the individual. For example, the death of a grandparent can be a highly stressful occurrence. However, if the death occurs after a long illness, it may be more of a relief.

There are three main types of events that contribute to stress in an individual's life: daily hassles, life events, and catastrophes. Daily hassles typically have a low level of personal importance, yet individuals may still react strongly to these minor stressors if they are, at the time, highly vulnerable to stress. If a person already endured a great deal of stress that day, new stress becomes, in a sense, cumulative, serving to increase already present physiological stress responses.

A life event is any event that requires change and adaptation. Again, the level of importance and the vulnerability of the person will impact the amount of stress the person experiences. Many people experience extreme physiological reactions to life events such as the death of a spouse. They may be unable to eat or sleep, most likely because the body is in this state of pseudo-alertness.

Finally, catastrophes—rare, unexpected disasters such as earthquakes or floods—can lead to physiological stress responses such as post-traumatic stress disorder (nightmares, flashbacks, etc., about a past catastrophe). Most individuals tend to experience some degree of stress response to catastrophes, because the events are often so extreme and overwhelming.

To deal with a stressful event such as a catastrophe, many people unconsciously employ a coping strategy such as denial or repression. Denial, not accepting that a catastrophe has actually occurred, is one way that individuals stave off the full impact of what has just happened. Some theorize that having the knowledge of an event such as a catastrophe and denying it allows the body to gradually process the stress that it could not handle all at once.

Repression, the ability of the mind to keep anxiety-producing thoughts in the subconscious, allows individuals to attempt to deal with a catastrophic situation without thinking through the many horrifying ramifications. As a means of coping, repression often allows individuals to function, whereas full awareness might impede their ability to respond as needed.

In conclusion, the body and mind are an amazing team—working together they are able to cope with difficult and stressful situations while still functioning. However, in a society wrought with stress, it is possible that individuals may lose this adaptive strength, breaking down under the "stress" of a constant need to cope with stress.

CHAPTER 4

REVIEW QUESTIONS (PAGE 48)

1. **D** A cognitive psychologist is primarily interested in thought processes and products, and (D), involving word association, is most directly connected to such processes and products. (A) is more the province of biological psychologists, (B) that of humanistic psychotherapists, (C) of clinical psychotherapists or behaviorists, and (E) is more of interest to developmental psychologists.

2. **C** The idea of *tabula rasa* is most closely associated with the philosopher John Locke. David Hume (A) is a philosopher who speculated on the nature of knowledge and perception, Charles Darwin (B) is more closely identified with the theory of natural selection and evolution of species; Sigmund Freud (D) was the founder of psychoanalytic theory, and Erich Fromm (E) was one of the theorists influenced by Freud.

3. **B** The concept of dualism refers to the division of the world and all things in it into two parts: body and spirit. (C) refers to two ways of conceptualizing the structure and function of the mind; (E) to two different types of experimental variables.

4. **D** Humanistic psychologists are primarily concerned with the impact of free will on behavior. The stress on childhood experiences (A) is emphasized in the psychoanalytic approach. The importance of biological predispositions (B) refers to either the biological/medical model or the behavioral-genetics approach. The cognitive approach focuses on how maladaptive thoughts (C) can influence behavior, and the social-cognitive approach centers on the interaction of culture and behavior (E).

5. **C** Proponents of the psychoanalytic or psychodynamic approach believe that the source of all current trauma can be traced back to childhood repressed memories. The cognitive approach (A) stresses the importance of thought processes and schemas in evaluating behaviors. The behaviorists (B), such as Skinner and Watson, believe in the power of learning and other environmental influences on behavior. The social cultural perspective (D) focuses instead on the culture of individuals and how it shapes them into who they are; the biological/medical approach (E) seeks physiological answers in brain and body chemistry to explain behavior.

CHAPTER 5

REVIEW QUESTIONS (PAGES 59–60)

1. **D** By definition, a double-blind experimental design is one in which neither the researchers nor the experimental subjects know whether the subjects have been assigned to an experimental group or a control group; this is done to minimize the chance that either the researchers or the subjects will influence the results through their own expectations (researchers) or by trying to act in accordance with what is thought to be desired (subjects). (B) describes a single-blind experimental design; (E) is completely nonsensical.

2. **B** In a normal statistical curve, about 68 percent of all scores will fall within one standard deviation of the mean; this includes scores both above and below the mean. (A) is the percentage that would occur between the mean and one standard deviation above it only; (C) is the percentage that would occur within two standard deviations of the mean.

3. **B**   This is the definition of a Type II error—concluding there is no difference when in fact there is a difference. (A) is the definition of a Type I error. (E) is an erroneous conclusion drawn when, in fact, a Type I error has been made.

4. **C**   All of the other answers are standard tenets for designing and carrying out ethically acceptable research. (C) has nothing to do with ethics, though it would not be very good for the research design in another way—if both the subjects and the researchers knew which of the former would be part of the experimental group, there would be a great likelihood of expectancy effects confounding the study.

5. **B**   A correlation of –0.84 implies that as one variable increases, the other is likely to decrease—positive correlations indicate that two variables vary directly, while negative correlations indicate that two variables vary inversely. Remember the famous research statement, "correlation does not imply causation," and you'll know that neither (D) nor (E) is correct.

CHAPTER 6

REVIEW QUESTIONS (PAGE 72)

1. **B**   Damage to the Broca's Area, which is on the left side on the frontal lobe of the cortex, controls the muscles of speech. Repetition of the speech of others (A) is often referred to as echolalia. The loss of the ability to visually integrate information (C), or prospagnosia, is often the result of damage to the occipital lobe. The loss of the ability to comprehend speech (D) refers to damage in the Wernicke's Area of the temporal lobe, and the inability to solve verbal problems (E) stems from some kind of damage to the left hemisphere.

2. **D**   The dendrites are attached to the cell body and their purpose is to receive signals and information from other neurons, usually by receiving neurotransmitters; these signals will determine whether or not the neuron will "fire." (A) is the function of the terminal buttons; (B) is that of the myelin sheaths; (C) is that of the cell body, and (E) is that of the axon hillock.

3. **C**   The cerebellum is the part of the brain most involved with maintaining balance and muscular strength and tone. (A) is the part of the brain that controls heart rate, swallowing, breathing, and digestion; (B) is the part, in most people, that is specialized for spatial and intuitive processing; (D) are involved in processing visual input; and (E) is the brain's primary relay station for sensory information.

4. **C** GABA is the neurotransmitter most associated with inhibitory neural processes; the others generally act to excite neurons further.

5. **A** The phenotype is the actual observable trait or behavior that results from a specific genetic combination. Due to dominant and recessive trait expressions, the phenotype can represent more than one specific possible genotype, or genetic contribution, which (E) is talking about. (C) is the definition of a gene itself.

6. **C** The hypothalamus, part of the limbic system, controls motivated behaviors such as hunger, thirst, and sex. The thalamus (A) routes sensory information to the sensory areas of the brain; the pons (B) connects the lower brain regions with the higher functioning areas of the brain. The amygdala (D) in the limbic system controls fear and aggression, and the association areas (E) of the brain match existing information with incoming information already stored in the brain.

CHAPTER 7

Review Questions (Page 89)

1. **D** Opponent process refers to a theory of color vision/processing that is thought to occur at the thalamic cellular level. The other answers are all monocular (one eye) depth perception cues that come into play at "higher" brain levels of visual processing.

2. **B** This is the only choice that contains the five basic taste sensations—bitter, salty, sweet, sour, and umami; relative combinations of these result in the full range of taste sensations. (C) refers to types of touch sensations, and (D), to the five basic food groups!

3. **D** Know your retinal receptor cells; the rods are sensitive to low light conditions and to movement, while the cones are responsible for color vision and work best at higher illumination levels. (A) contains two other types of cells found in the retina, but not the ones that make the distinction noted here. The same is true of the ganglion cells of (B), and osmoreceptors sense thirst, anyway. The mechanoreceptors of (E) sense physical touch, and ossicles are bones of the middle ear.

4. **C** Among the Gestalt principles of perception, continuity refers to our tendency to perceive fluid or continuous forms preferentially, rather than jagged or irregular ones—we would tend to see two lines that "cross" at a point in that way, rather than as two angles sharing a vertex. (A) and (D) are two other Gestalt perceptual principles—proximity and similarity, respectively, and (E) refers to binocular disparity, a depth perception cue.

5. **A** Weber's law relates to the issue of thresholds in sensation and perception. The law states that stimuli need to vary by a constant proportion if we are to distinguish among the stimuli. Recognition of an imperceptible amount of perfume (B) relates to the issue of absolute threshold. People not attending to more than one stimuli at a time (C) focuses on selective attention. The ability to tell the difference between 20 and 100 watt bulbs 50 percent of the time refers again to the absolute threshold. All auditory stimuli being the same above a certain frequency (E) negates frequency theory in audition.

TEST BREAK #1 (PAGE 90)

7. Psychoanalytic vs. behaviorist: How are they different?

22. What technology should you use to look at different regions of the brain?

39. The __ is the __ area of the __

58. To know what a picture is, the info. has to get to which part of the brain?
    (Answer: occipital lobe)

78. What's it called when someone doesn't give false positives—if there is no sound, there is no report?

89. The <u>lower</u> the __ of a study, the __

    Lower p-value means what?

CHAPTER 8

REVIEW QUESTIONS (PAGE 100)

1. **B** The specific pattern of brain waves known as sleep spindles is characteristic of stage 2 sleep, and is associated with a relaxation of the skeletal musculature. Stage 1 sleep and REM sleep characteristically show the smaller, less regular theta waves, and stage 3 and 4 sleep are both more likely to show the longer, slower delta waves.

2. **B** Subliminal information is presented just below the threshold. This information is often referred to as imperceptible, yet it is believed to influence behavior. Immediate recognition of the stimuli (A) refers to the absolute threshold. The inability of the stimuli to be subject to the tip-of-the-tongue phenomenon (C) is another kind of preconscious processing, but the inability of a stimulus to be on the tip of the tongue would not be an indication of its presence. There is no evidence that there is proactive interference (D) or that it is slower in a matched pairs trial (E).

3. **C** Though the natural day/night cycle of humans and most other organisms matches the 24-hour cycle of earth and sun, if all cues (such as the sun) are removed, humans and many other organisms tend to follow a "free-running" rhythm that cycles approximately every 25 hours, which can be demonstrated through varying body temperature and hormonal levels.

4. **E** There is no evidence that there is any distinction between what kinds of concerns give rise to nightmares versus night terrors. The hypothesis that one of the functions of dreams is to express conscious or unconscious concerns has its roots in Freudian or psychoanalytic theory, and is only one of a number of competing theories of dream function, none of which has yet proven conclusive. (A), (B), (C), and (D) all represent characteristic differences between nightmares and night terrors.

5. **E** Cocaine is a strong stimulant, not a narcotic. Narcotics, such as those mentioned in (A), (B), (C), and (D), are derived originally from the opium poppy and tend to have analgesic and relaxation effects that depress the central nervous system.

CHAPTER 9

REVIEW QUESTIONS (PAGE 110)

1. **B** The fact that the dog is now exhibiting a fear response to any moving, wheeled vehicle represents a stimulus generalization. (A) is the opposite process; if the dog was originally struck by a blue van of a certain make, for example, and did not show a fear response to any vehicle but that type of blue van. (C) refers to the process whereby a conditioned response was made extinct by removing a conditioned stimulus, but might be elicited by a presentation of that stimulus at a later time. Backward conditioning (D) occurs when an unconditioned stimulus is presented before a conditioned one and has nothing to do with this situation.

2. **D** Second-order conditioning occurs when a previously conditioned stimulus—originally neutral, but now response-eliciting—acts as an unconditioned stimulus and is paired with a new neutral stimulus to be conditioned; eventually, this second stimulus is successful at eliciting a conditioned response. In (D), the rabbit was conditioned to fear the musical tone; then the musical tone was paired with a flashed light; and eventually the flashed light elicited fear even in the absence of the tone. (A) is an example of conditioned taste aversion; (B) is a simple classic conditioning paradigm; and (C) is stimulus generalization.

3. **C** A variable ratio reinforcement schedule is one in which the ratio of responses to reward is variable and therefore unpredictable. Although the original conditioning may take longer, the response is quite resistant to extinction. In a fixed ratio schedule (A), rewards always come after a certain number of correct responses; learning is quick but so is extinction, as it is easy to determine when the reinforcement schedule is no longer operative. This can also be said for (E), a continuous schedule. Fixed interval schedules (B), with rewards presented after a set time period, have a similar learning/extinction profile to fixed ratio schedules. Variable interval schedules (D), with rewards presented at variable time periods, are more resistant to extinction than fixed interval schedules but not as resistant as variable ratio schedules.

4. **A** The number of neurons does not increase with learning; in fact, the number of neurons is at its highest for most animals at birth—neurons do not reproduce under normal circumstances. However, they do grow in size and number of connections, alter the strength of already existing connections, and produce higher levels of neurotransmitters as a response to learning. Neurons that wire together, fire together.

5. **A** Though there are many social or observational learning situations that involve rewards or punishments, Bandura's experiments showed that such learning can occur even if there were no rewards or punishments—that is, consequences—to the observed behaviors. According to Bandura, attention to the behavior, retention of it, the ability to reproduce it, and the motivation to reproduce it as some point are what is necessary for observational learning.

Test Break #2 (Page 111)

5. How will Thomas learn to make a big meal using the stuff he knows?

   He can link together what he knows (called chaining, if you remember that).

22. What does the endocrine system do?

   It secretes hormones into the body.

35. What big thing did behaviorists give to psych?

   Experimentation

45. Why do taste buds need to be able to replace themselves?

   Otherwise, if you burned your mouth, you would lose your sense of taste forever.

72. What technology should you use to study brain waves?

   Electrosomething…(Electroencephalogram or EEG if you remember)

CHAPTER 10

Review Questions (Page 123)

1. **B** Visual sensory memory is referred to as *iconic* and auditory sensory memory is called *echoic*. Iconic memory has a shorter duration than auditory memory, making (A) inaccurate. Visual and auditory memory have approximately the same capacity before encoding (C). The phone number read out loud (echoic) should have a longer duration than visually presented information (D). If both auditory and visual information are presented at the same time (E), auditory information is more likely to be transferred to long term memory.

2. **D** The principle of encoding specificity states that information is more likely to be recalled if the attempt to retrieve it occurs in a situation similar to the situation in which it was first encoded. (A) refers to the process of new information pushing old information out of short-term memory; (B) to the grouping of items of information in order to better hold them in short-term memory; (C) to organizing short-term memory items in order to transfer them to long-term memory; and (E) to the memory for motoric skills and habits.

3. **E**   Prosody is the term given to the tones and inflections added to language that elaborate meaning with no word alterations. (A), syntax, refers to the set of rules in a language for arranging meaningful sounds into words; (B) is one step further up from syntax—the rules that govern the arrangement and formation of words into meaningful phrases and sentences; and (C) indicates the smallest units of speech sounds in a language that are still distinct from one another.

4. **C**   Telegraphic speech is a common occurrence in toddlers combining words for the first time; it consists of two or three word utterances that are composed mostly of salient nouns, verbs, and adjectives with an absence of articles, conjunctions, prepositions, and limited use of pronouns. All of the answers except (C) involve two- or three-word utterances that fit that definition; (C) is an example of a holophrase—a single-word utterance of younger children that has a broad meaning.

5. **A**   Divergent thinking is the name we give to the problem-solving process used when there are many possible solutions. In contrast, (B) is the process used when the problem only has one solution, such as is the case with most math equations. The intelligence quotient of (C) was originally conceived of as a ratio of mental age over chronological age, multiplied by 100; this was determined by comparing performance to that of others over a range of problem-solving tasks, which might involve both divergent and convergent abilities.

CHAPTER 11

REVIEW QUESTIONS (PAGE 135)

1. **D**   Secondary drives, like secondary reinforcers, are learned by association with primary drives and primary reinforcers. Satisfying basic needs (A) is a primary drive, as is the attempt to maintain homeostatic equilibrium (B). Instinct (C) refers to unlearned behaviors and optimal arousal (E) refers to biological theory.

2. **A**   The Yerkes-Dodson law relates levels of arousal and task difficulty. Here, a high-difficulty task (SAT) requires low levels of arousal (calm and relaxed). Arousal and obtaining a primary reinforcer (B) is an inaccurate comparison for this theory. Tasks related to homeostasis (C) involve drive-reduction theory. Remaining calm and addressing envelopes (D) is a low-arousal and low-difficulty task.

3. **A** Angiotensin is a chemical messenger released when the volumetric receptors that monitor extracellular body levels, particularly in the circulatory system, sense low fluid levels, and it acts directly on brain receptors to stimulate thirst. (B) is an opiate-like brain chemical that binds to neural receptor sites, but has nothing to do with thirst; neither does the neurotransmitter acetylcholine of (E); and (C) is a thyroid, not thirst, hormone.

4. **B** An extrinsic factor is one that motivates behavior but does not originate within the individual performing the behavior; it instead originates from the outside world. In Rhoni's case, feeling the need to excel at her career in order to keep up her family's lifestyle and her parents' opinion of her qualifies as being primarily from outside of her (though she may enjoy the lifestyle herself). (A) would be a factor that originated within the individual displaying the behavior; (D) and (E) would also describe such internal factors.

5. **C** As compared to Type-B personalities, Type-A's have a greater arousal response overall to stress and a greater tendency to seek it out, as in (B); they also tend to be more competitive (E), more prone to stress-related physical conditions (D), and to feel a greater sense of being pressed for time (A). Type-A's also tend to anger more quickly (part of being easier to arouse), so they would not be less likely to anger slowly.

Test Break #3 (Pages 136–137)

15. Of the following, which typically requires more complex measurement?

Ask It Like It Is:	Which variable requires more complex measurement?
Answer Before You Answer:	The complex one—not categorical.
Answer:	**(B) continuous.** (A) is out, (C) doesn't make sense, and (D) and (E) aren't those kinds of variables.

35. Which of the following most accurately states the role of the ?

Ask It Like It Is: *What does the iris do?*

Answer Before You Answer: *Opens and closes pupil (controls amount of light, if you remember)*

Answer: **(B) because it says to open and close the iris and regulate the entrance of light.** (A) is way off. Be careful of (C)—the iris does not project light onto the retina. (D) and (E) are not true and not close to your answer.

42. The controversy concerns

Ask It Like It Is: *Which is more important: genes or environment?*

Answer Before You Answer: *Inborn and external processes determine behavior.*

Answer: **(C) since it's the closest to yours: "inborn processes" (genes) and "external stimu-li" environment.** Be careful of (A): similar idea, but not the same. (B) is way off base, (D) is a silly trap answer (using the words *natural* and *nurture* to lure you, and (E) doesn't answer the question at all.

66. Prior to the fall of the Berlin wall, East Berlin schools de-emphasized the individuality of the student. As a result, many of the children from those schools tend to have a(n)

Ask It Like It Is: *What happens if kids are taught to not be individuals?*

Answer Before You Answer: *They depend on others for their self-identity and self-esteem.*

Answer: **(D) they have an external locus of control—looking to others for their self-esteem and self-identity.** (A) and (B) are not close to yours (no optimism, pessimism). (C) is the opposite of what you want and (E) is just filler.

85. A of a <u>category</u> is called a(n)

Ask It Like It Is:

Answer Before You Answer:

Answer:

A major example of something is called what?

I don't know—a major example.

(E) exemplar—a major example. (A) does not mean a major example. (B) is only a feature, not an example of the whole category. (C) is weak. Don't pick (D)! It's a verbal trap.

CHAPTER 12

REVIEW QUESTIONS (PAGE 153)

1. **D** The Moro reflex in newborns is the startle response that involves the splaying of limbs when a sudden loud noise is heard. (A) is the neonatal reflex of grabbing anything placed in the hand; (B) the Babinski reflex is produced when stroking the bottom of the neonate's foot results in a splaying out of the toes; and (E) is the reflex that causes a newborn to turn in the direction of a touch on the cheek. While the orienting reflex of (C) may be elicited to a loud noise, it occurs whenever there is any other sudden change in the environment as well.

2. **B** The cognitive theory of Vygotsky stresses social and environmental, not just biological/maturational, factors as critical to development; he proposed the concept of a zone of proximal development, which is the range between the developed level of ability a child displays and the potential, or latent, level of ability a child is actually capable of. He further theorized that this latent level is hard to elicit due to a lack of optimal environmental circumstances. Jean Piaget (A) and Sigmund Freud (D) created alternate theories of development; Leon Festinger (C) is most closely identified with the theory of cognitive dissonance (see Chapter 17), and Juliann Rotter (E) with the concept of locus of control (Chapter 13).

3. **A** Erik Erikson's psychosocial theory of development describes a series of "conflicts" or "tasks" at each stage of life, from infancy to old age. In his theory, the successful resolution of each developmental task results in the development of a certain ability or belief, which serves as the foundation for the resolution of the next "task." The developmental task for school-age children is termed "industry vs. inferiority," and the resolution of this stage produces a sense of competence in one's own efforts and work. (B) is the resolution of the task of early adulthood—"intimacy vs. isolation"; (C) is the resolution of the task of infancy—"trust vs. mistrust"; (D) is the resolution of the task of toddlerhood—"autonomy vs. shame/doubt"; and (E) is the resolution of the task of adolescence—"identity vs. role confusion."

4. **B** According to the developmental theory of Jean Piaget, a child of about five would generally be at the preoperational stage, characterized by both animism—the belief that all things are alive—and egocentrism—the ability to see the world only from one's own point of view. (A), (C), and (D) are other stages of Piaget's developmental model. (E) is a developmental stage in Sigmund Freud's theory.

5. **E** The theory of moral development elaborated by Lawrence Kohlberg divides such development into three levels—preconventional, conventional, and postconventional—each subdivided into two stages. At the first stage of preconventional morality, generally the first stage young children progress through, moral concerns are primarily motivated by the need to avoid punishment and to receive rewards. (A) characterizes the next stage of the preconventional level; (B) the first stage of the conventional level; and (C) the first stage of the postconventional level.

CHAPTER 13

REVIEW QUESTIONS (PAGE 163)

1. **B** In Freudian theory, the ego is the part of the mind that mediates between the wants/demands of the part of the mind known as the id; the internal representation of rules, morals, and social obligations known as the superego; and the realities of the outside world. The ego involves conscious thought and choice and attempts to find acceptable ways to satisfy desires. (D) and (E) are not parts of the mind in Freudian theory; they are concepts from Jungian theory.

2. **E** Reaction formation is the psychodynamic defense mechanism that involves the ego reversing the direction of a disturbing or unacceptable desire to make that desire safer and more acceptable, as when a person who unconsciously hates children might feel the need to volunteer at a day-care center. The other answers are all definitions of other defense mechanisms; (A) is displacement; (B) is regression; (C) is compensation; and (D) is rationalization.

3. **D** Albert Bandura is identified with a social-cognitive, rather than psychodynamic, theory of personality; his theory does not concern itself very much with unconscious desires and mechanisms, as psychodynamic theories do, but rather focuses on an individual's concepts and beliefs. Horney, Jung, Adler, and Erikson are all psychodynamic theorists who expanded on or modified Freud's original conception of personality.

4. **D** In the personality and therapeutic theories of Carl Rogers, self-actualization refers to the process by which an individual modifies and grows over time in ways that allow him/her to reach full potential and ability. To humanistic theorists like Rogers, self-actualization is the ultimate purpose of human existence. (A) refers to the value we place on ourselves—often a product of self-actualization, but not the actual process. Self-efficacy (C) refers to a person's belief in his/her own competence in a give situation.

5. **A** The 16PF (Personality Factor) Questionnaire, designed by Raymond Cattell, is designed specifically for investigating the traits, or primarily inherited, enduring, and situationally stable tendencies that govern individual personality (Cattell theorized there were 16 basic traits, which his instrument purported to measure.) (B) and (E) are intelligence tests—the Weschler Adult Intelligence Scale and the Weschler Intelligence Scale for Children, respectively; (C) is the Diagnostic and Statistical Manual, Version Four, currently in use for identification and classification of mental/behavioral abnormalities, and (D) is analysis of variance, a statistical technique.

CHAPTER 14

REVIEW QUESTIONS (PAGE 171)

1. **A** Content validity is a measure of the degree to which material on the test is balanced and is measuring what it is said to measure. (B) refers to another type of validity—predictive validity. (C), (D), and (E) refer not to measures of test validity, but to measures of test reliability—equivalent form and split-half reliability, respectively.

2. **B** A projective test is one in which ambiguous stimuli which are open to various kinds of interpretation are presented, in contrast to the more common inventory-type tests in which participants answer a standard series of questions. The Thematic Apperception Test (TAT) is a well-known projective test; it involves a series of pictures of people in ambiguous relationships with other people, and the respondent's task is to generate a story for each picture, including what led up to the scene in the picture, what is happening now, and what might occur next. All of the other choices are inventory-style tests in which participants are faced with standardized answer choices.

3. **B** IQ scores over a population are distributed along a normal curve, with the mean, median, and modal scores at 100 and a standard deviation of roughly 15 to 16 points; therefore, a score of 85 would be located approximately one standard deviation below the mean. (E) is deceptive, as the original definition of IQ as mental age divided by physical age multiplied by 100 makes it attractive; but physical age would have no effect on where an IQ score is located relative to established means, medians, modes, or standard deviations.

4. **A** Test standardization is used to set the norms for a given population of subjects; these norms can then be used to compare the test results of groups or individuals with specific characteristics to the whole population. In order to set these norms, the test is administered to a (usually fairly large) standardization sample which, as much as is feasible, possesses characteristics reflective of the entire population. (C) actually refers to the measurement of validity, and (D) is actually more of a way of ensuring reliability on tests where scoring is not computerized.

5. **E** Howard Gardner's theory of multiple intelligences—not just verbal and mathematical, the dimensions measured by most intelligence tests—posits that there are measurable intelligences in all of the dimensions listed except for (E), which is a dimension added by two other theorists, Peter Salovey and John Mayer.

Test Break #4 (Page 172)

Here Is Our Work It, Chart It, Count It, and Sketch It:

1. One of the major approaches to learning is classical conditioning.

    A. the <u>process of classical conditioning</u>,

      all necessary terms. Show how

    classical conditioning could be used to

      (1)   Condition a monkey to "appreciate" only the works of certain artists

      (2)   Teach a group of students a mathematical concept

    B. Explain how both and <u>transpire</u>. Use of the above examples to illustrate.

CHAPTER 15

REVIEW QUESTIONS (PAGE 181)

1. **C** In the *Diagnostic and Statistical Manual, version IV-TR (DSM-IV-TR)*, the handbook of the American Psychiatric Association for identification and classification of behavioral abnormalities, Axis III is concerned with physical disorders with behavioral impact, such as vitamin deficiency, toxic exposure, etc. Axis I (A) is concerned with the major "psychotic" disorders, such as schizophrenia, other states of major cognitive or perceptual dysfunction, and sleeping/eating disorders; Axis II (B) is concerned with personality disorders and mental retardation; Axis IV (D) with levels of psychosocial and environmental stress; and Axis V (E) with assessment of overall functionality.

2. **B** Conversion disorder occurs when a psychological difficulty manifests itself as a deficit in physiological function and there is no actual discernable physical problem. (A), bipolar disorder, is characterized by alternating periods of depression and mania, and (E), paranoid disorder, by extreme mistrust and suspicion, often with feelings of persecution. An organic disorder (C) would be linked to an actual physical deficit, usually of the brain or nervous system.

3. **E** Dissociative disorders, such as amnesia, fugue, or multiple personality disorder, are characterized by dysfunction of memory and disruption in the sense of identity. (A) is more characteristic of phobias; (C) of obsessive disorders; and (D) of certain types of schizophrenia. (B) might be descriptive of some individuals with dissociative disorders, but it is not a diagnostic criterion of or a widely seen characteristic of the disorder (many with such disorders have quite extensive social networks).

4. **C** Serotonin is a neurotransmitter that influences mood and seems to be present at lower-than-usual levels in many of those diagnosed with depression (at least, unipolar depression). (A), acetylcholine, has, at least in some studies, been associated with the expression of bipolar behavior when present in greater-than-average amounts. Dopamine (E) deficits have been implicated in Parkinson's disease, and may be implicated in certain instances of schizophrenia.

5. **D** By *DSM-IV-TR* definition, anxiety disorders are characterized by feelings of tension, nervousness, fear, and sometimes panic. All of the choices here qualify except for seasonal affective disorder, which is characterized by greater susceptibility to lethargy and depression during times of year when the daylight hours are short; it is thought that low light levels may exacerbate natural "hibernation" tendencies in those who are biochemically susceptible.

CHAPTER 16

REVIEW QUESTIONS (PAGE 190)

1. **C** Client-centered therapy, as an outgrowth of the humanistic school of psychology, is very concerned with trying to understand the client's view of the world and how it affects him or her, in order to facilitate the client's own tendencies toward growth and fulfillment. Therapists utilizing this approach see accurate empathic understanding—the therapist's ability to view the world through the eyes of the client—as critical to successful communication between client and therapist. While psychoanalytic therapy (A) also considers communication and understanding the client's view of the world important, it tends to discourage emotional or personal involvement with the patient through such empathy. Psychoanalytic therapists believe a stance of detachment is best for the encouragement of transference, which helps to reveal the nature of the patient's conflicts. Implosion therapy (D) is a behavioral approach with little emphasis on the kind of client-therapist relationship considered essential to client-centered therapy.

2. **E** Behavioral approaches to therapy are concerned with treating maladaptive or troubling symptoms, rather than underlying causes, as in this school of thought, there are no hidden, "deep" underlying causes—the abnormal behavior itself is the problem. As such, behavioral therapies have been most often used with those who seek to change specific behaviors, such as those who suffer from phobias. While behavioral approaches might be tried for individuals with some of the other conditions listed, the more symptom-oriented behavioral techniques are usually not the treatment of choice with conditions that involve more than just a specific maladaptive behavior and/or altered mental states.

3. **B** Psychoanalytic therapy focuses on probing past defense mechanisms to understand the unconscious roots of problems; indeed, its practitioners believe that troubling behaviors or symptoms cannot possibly cease until a patient gains insight into such unconscious roots. In this approach, treating just symptoms through behavioral methods without addressing the underlying hidden causes will not result in lasting "cure" and may indeed result in symptoms returning or new ones manifesting. (A) and (C) are not generally criticisms leveled at behavioral therapy by psychoanalysts; indeed, for those it's the other way around—these are criticisms of psychoanalytic approaches often made by behaviorists. The criticism in (D) would more likely be made by humanistic or client-centered therapists.

4. **B** Rational-emotive behavioral therapy, or simply rational-emotive therapy, is primarily associated with Albert Ellis, who formulated this cognitive approach, which concentrates on modifying incorrect thoughts or cognitions that lead to maladaptive emotional and behavioral responses. Julian Rotter (A) is associated with the concept of locus of control; Abraham Maslow (C) with the concepts of hierarchy of needs and self-actualization; Raymond Cattell (D) with a trait theory of personality and the 16PF Questionnaire; and Rollo May (E) with the existential approach to psychotherapy.

5. **A** Anticoagulants are not drugs used for psychotherapeutic purposes; they are instead used to modulate the ability of the blood to clot and form vessel blockages. Both (C) and (E) are classes of drugs that belong to the larger family of antidepressants; anxiolytics (B), as the name implies, are used primarily for the reduction of anxiety; and lithium salts (E) are useful in the treatment of some cases of bipolar disorder.

TEST BREAK #5 (PAGE 191)

4. **B** Can obese people have *fewer* fat cells than average-weight people?

27. **B** Your clue from the question is "connectionist approaches." Would connectionists think things occurred in individual segments or in a bunch of networks simultaneously?

47. **A** Your clue is "chunking." Even if you don't remember this memory technique, (A) sounds more like chunking than (B).

85. **C** Your clue is "person-centered psychotherapy." Even without that clue, suppressing negative feelings of a client or using a didactic approach are not typically the chosen methods of most psychotherapists.

92. **B** Even without a clue, it's understood in the field of psychology that counselors do not do either (A) or (C) for clients.

CHAPTER 17

Review Questions (Pages 202–203)

1. **D** The fundamental attribution error is defined as the tendency of people to overestimate a person's personal disposition and to underestimate the situational circumstances when evaluating another person's behavior. Both (A) and (C) are examples of an internal locus of control. Blaming a teacher for one's failures (B) is an example of an external attribution. In evaluating her friend's behavior, Karen (E) is balancing personal and situational attributes.

2. **D** In the Asch conformity experiments, many factors influenced the degree to which an experimental subject would show conformity to the obviously wrong group opinion, but the subject's age did not show a consistent effect in this regard. (A) certainly did—unanimity was very important; only one dissenting opinion drastically reduced the tendency of the subject to go along with the rest of the group; size of the group (B) has an influence in that it seems to take a group of at least three members for such conformity to be shown consistently; the subject's perception of his/her own social status vs. that of the group (C) was important—subjects who perceived themselves as of low/medium status were much more likely to conform than those who perceived themselves as of high status, and gender (E) was an influencing factor, with females more likely to conform than males.

3. **D** The self-fulfilling prophecy refers to the scenario in the question—students randomly labeled as likely to experience significant jumps in academic test scores in the coming semester did indeed seem to perform to those expectations on those tests at the end of the semester. The Hawthorne effect in (A) refers to the observation that students or workers who know they are being monitored tend to perform better, even if they do not know why they are being monitored. Kandel (B) is associated with research into learning and neurophysiology in sea slugs, cognitive dissonance theory (C) refers to the discomfort that comes from two conflicting thoughts, and Ainsworth (E) with studies of attachment in human infants.

4. **B** Diffusion of responsibility, also sometimes referred to as the bystander effect, occurs when every person in a crowded social situation defers to another to make the effort to mount a response to the situation. It can also occur when members of a group perform negative behaviors that no specific individual or individuals will take responsibility for. An altruistic orientation (D) usually refers to the decision-making paradigm in which individuals wish to maximize the outcome for others, but it could also be applied to this situation as a countervailing force to the diffusion of responsibility. Illusory correlation (A) refers to the false presumption that certain groups are associated with certain stereotypes or behaviors, and the just-world hypothesis (E) is the belief that since the world is basically fair, people deserve whatever befalls them, positive or negative.

5. **B** The "foot-in-the-door" technique involves making requests in small increments that people are more likely to initially comply with, and then working from those up to bigger requests; the incremental approach seems to work better than "going for the whole ball of wax all at once." This is what the teenager is trying to do in getting his curfew extended in small increments until he gets the curfew he actually wants. (A) is an example of the "door-in-the-face" technique, in which one asks for much more than what one actually wants, expecting to be turned down; one can then ask for the smaller, "more reasonable" request, which is more likely to be granted. People also tend to be more likely to comply with or be persuaded by those they feel they are similar to, as in (D), or by those they will receive a desired reward from (hardly a surprise), as in (E).

PART III

The Princeton Review AP Psychology Practice Tests

Congratulations! You made it through the book and to the practice tests. Although you have done much to improve your AP Psychology knowledge, there is one critical thing left to do: a few trial runs. Just as you would not walk out onto the basketball court or the theater stage without a scrimmage or a dress rehearsal, you should not even think about taking the AP Psychology Exam before you have done a few timed practice tests.

In this section you will find two complete practice tests with answers and explanations. We also strongly recommend you order a copy of a past AP Psychology Exam from the College Board (see page 8). We recommend you use these tests in the following way:

- Use Practice Test 1 for timed drills and practice.

- Take Practice Test 2 under timed conditions, then review your work.

- Take the College Board released exam under exact timing conditions.

Note: If you do not order a College Board exam, use *both* tests in this book as timed exams rather than using Practice Test 1 for drills.

PRACTICE TEST 1

TIMED SPRINTS

Although you must eventually take a complete, timed practice test, it is also useful to begin by doing what we call "timed sprints." First, get ready to answer the first ten easy questions. Before you begin, jot down your start time. Once you finish the ten questions, jot down the time you finished. Then, check your answers for accuracy. If you made more than one mistake on the easiest questions of the test, chances are you were rushing. Repeat the drill on the next ten questions.

Next, do the same drill, but on ten medium questions (begin at number 34). These questions should take you a little longer, but don't sacrifice accuracy for speed. Once you have done a few sets of medium questions, you can probably tell what your *efficient and effective pace* is. This is the pace at which you will work to score your personal best.

SMART STRATEGY DRILL

Another option for Practice Test 1 is to practice certain techniques. For example, choose a set of five to ten questions and practice Asking It Like It Is and Answering Before You Answer, and actually write down what you come up with. Then, after completing those two steps for all of the questions in the set, go back and only use your notes to use POE to get rid of answer choices. That way you can determine if you are doing enough work at the beginning of the question to get to the answer.

PRACTICE TEST 2 AND THE COLLEGE BOARD TEST

Use Practice Test 2, and preferably the test from the College Board as well, to take "the real thing." Set aside two hours in which you will not be interrupted. Turn off the TV, computer, stereo, and telephone, and create true testing conditions. Then, set a stopwatch to 70 minutes and begin Section I. When time runs out, stop working. Set the watch for 50 minutes and begin Section II. Once you are completely finished, check your performance against the answer key and calculate your score.

> **Note:** The time allotted for each section changed in 1999 to its current 70 minutes for Section I and 50 minutes for Section II. Any practice tests you order from the College Board that were given prior to 1999 will indicate 75 minutes for Section I and 45 minutes for Section II. You should ignore those directions and use the current time constraints even when practicing older exams, because the number of questions has remained constant.

DON'T STOP THERE

After you complete Practice Test 2, don't simply check off which answers were right and which were wrong. This test is part of your learning experience. Look up the explanations for all the questions you missed and even for questions that you got right but had trouble with. Review the areas of psychology that gave you trouble. Use this test as a tool to improve your score before you take a second timed exam. There is no point in jumping into another timed test if you didn't learn from the errors you made on the first one.

Don't forget to use the bubble sheet in the back of this book! It will get you in the habit of writing your answers not on the actual test but on another piece of paper. Remember to be careful to skip a line of bubbles when you skip a question!

ONE LAST THING

When you get to Practice Tests 1 and 2, you will first see a page of instructions. These are nearly identical to the instructions you will see at the start of your real AP exam. We put these instructions at the beginning of the test so that you will be familiar with them and can subsequently ignore them on test day. Feel free to read through them so that you are familiar with what they say.

YOUR PERSONAL BEST

Use the strategies you know, and you will achieve your personal best score. Here is a quick review of Section I and Section II strategies. Good luck!

SECTION I: SMART STRATEGIES

How to Score Your Personal Best on Section I

- Get almost all easy questions right.

- Get most medium questions right.

- *Do the Right Thing* on hard questions.

Smart-Tester Strategy Review

Strategy #1: Ask It Like It Is	Read the question and put it into your own words.
Strategy #2: Answer Before You Answer	Come up with your own answer to the question (exact or ballpark).
Strategy #3: Process of Elimination (POE)	Cross off each answer that is not close to yours. Pick the best match.

Section II: Smart Strategies

Essay-Writing Guidelines

- Write an introductory sentence that is *not* a repeat of the question.

- Use psychology terms and proper names of theories, theorists, etc.

- Define all terms.

- Support everything with an example or study, preferably from your course work (*not* an example from your own personal life).

- Clearly state the purpose of the example (support or contrast).

- Be clear, concise, and direct.

Essay-Writing Guidelines

Essay Smart-Tester Strategies #1–4	Total Time: 7–10 minutes
#1 Work It	1–2 minutes
#2 Chart It	3–5 minutes
#3 Count It	1 minute
#4 Sketch It	1–2 minutes
#5 Write It	10–15 minutes

Keep track of your own time. Finish the essay before time is called.

19

Practice Test 1

The Exam

AP® Psychology Exam

SECTION I: Multiple-Choice Questions

DO NOT OPEN THIS BOOKLET UNTIL YOU ARE TOLD TO DO SO.

Instructions

Section I of this exam contains 100 multiple-choice questions. Fill in only the ovals for numbers 1 through 100 on your answer sheet.

Indicate all of your answers to the multiple-choice questions on the answer sheet. No credit will be given for anything written in this exam booklet, but you may use the booklet for notes or scratch work. After you have decided which of the suggested answers is best, completely fill in the corresponding oval on the answer sheet. Give only one answer to each question. If you change an answer, be sure that the previous mark is erased completely. Here is a sample question and answer.

At a Glance

Total Time
1 hour and ten minutes
Number of Questions
100
Percent of Total Grade
66 2/3%
Writing Instrument
Pen required

Sample Question

Sample Answer

Omaha is a

(A) ● (C) (D) (E)

(A) state
(B) city
(C) country
(D) continent
(E) village

Use your time effectively, working as quickly as you can without losing accuracy. Do not spend too much time on any one question. Go on to other questions and come back to the ones you have not answered if you have time. It is not expected that everyone will know the answers to all of the multiple-choice questions.

About Guessing

Many candidates wonder whether or not to guess the answers to questions about which they are not certain. Multiple-choice scores are based on the number of questions answered correctly. Points are not deducted for incorrect answers, and no points are awarded for unanswered questions. Because points are not deducted for incorrect answers, you are encouraged to answer all multiple-choice questions. On any questions you do not know the answer to, you should eliminate as many choices as you can, and then select the best answer among the remaining choices.

This page intentionally left blank.

PSYCHOLOGY
SECTION I
Time—1 hour and 10 minutes
100 Questions

Directions: Each of the questions or incomplete statements below is followed by five answer choices. Select the one that is best in each case and then completely fill in the corresponding oval on the answer sheet.

1. Areas of the brain that are damaged are referred to as having

   (A) brain lesions
   (B) hemispheres
   (C) brain lobes
   (D) cortical adhesions
   (E) corpus collosum

2. The scientific investigation of mental processes and behavior is called

   (A) biology
   (B) psychology
   (C) cognition
   (D) scientific method
   (E) research

3. Which of the following types of scientists were the first to contend that an individual's ways of thinking are shaped primarily by cultural values and ideas?

   (A) Structuralists
   (B) Ethologists
   (C) Sociobiologists
   (D) Behaviorists
   (E) Anthropologists

4. Which of the following is the best example of an attribute that is culturally based rather than primarily psychologically based?

   (A) Caring for one's children
   (B) Arriving on time for work
   (C) Having the desire to reproduce
   (D) Seeking food and water
   (E) Smiling

5. Every time you buy ice cream from the Yellow Brick Road ice cream parlor, you get your over-the-rainbow card stamped. Once you purchase ten items, you get your next item free. The Yellow Brick Road ice cream parlor has you on which of the following reinforcement schedules?

   (A) Variable-ratio
   (B) Variable-interval
   (C) Fixed-ratio
   (D) Fixed-interval
   (E) Continuous

6. Which of the following neurotransmitters is most explicitly associated with the experience of pleasure?

   (A) GABA
   (B) Acetylcholine
   (C) Serotonin
   (D) Dopamine
   (E) Adrenaline

7. A psychologist, wishing to study the behavior of prisoners, arranges to dress as a prison guard so that he can stand in the recreation area and study unobtrusively the actions and interactions of the inmates. The psychologist is employing which of the following research tools?

   (A) Quasi-experimental
   (B) Naturalistic observation
   (C) Correlational research
   (D) Random sampling
   (E) Case study

GO ON TO THE NEXT PAGE.

8. An educational psychologist is administering a basic skills exam to second-graders of two different schools in order to compare the students' performance. The researcher administers the exam to the students of the Antrim School on a Wednesday morning, and then administers the same exam in exactly the same fashion on that same Wednesday afternoon to the second-graders of the Barton School. Which of the following best identifies a confounding variable in the psychologist's research?

   (A) The psychologist is comparing two different schools.
   (B) The psychologist is comparing the same grade in each school.
   (C) The psychologist is testing the students in the two schools at two different times.
   (D) The psychologist is testing the students in the two schools on the same day.
   (E) The psychologist is administering a basic skills exam.

9. The primary research method used by developmental psychologists is

   (A) case study
   (B) cross-sectional research
   (C) naturalistic observation
   (D) experimentation
   (E) correlational research

10. Narcotics work because they are chemically very similar to

   (A) endorphins
   (B) hormones
   (C) secretions
   (D) GABA
   (E) acetylcholine

11. Research indicates that a test participant exposed to a list of positive words and then asked to recall the words from that list a week later will be more likely to remember those words if

   (A) he is tested by a researcher who deliberately exhibits a positive attitude
   (B) he is in a positive mood when initially exposed to the words
   (C) he considers himself a "positive" person, regardless of his mood during the experience
   (D) he considers the initial testing experience positive
   (E) he perceives the list of words as positive, regardless of the true meaning of the words

12. The minimum amount of physical energy needed for a person to notice a stimulus is called a(n)

   (A) JND
   (B) difference threshold
   (C) absolute threshold
   (D) median difference
   (E) hit threshold

13. An individual with brain lesions in the hippocampus will most likely experience impairment to her

   (A) emotional regulation
   (B) motor coordination
   (C) speech production
   (D) learning
   (E) perception

14. A person who sustains major injuries that involve the destruction of the medulla oblongata will

   (A) be paralyzed
   (B) fall into a coma
   (C) suffer severe speech impairment
   (D) experience total loss of vision
   (E) die

15. In an emergency, the adrenal glands of the body secrete "emergency" hormones, while the body prepares for fight-or-flight, directed by

   (A) the central nervous system
   (B) the somatic nervous system
   (C) the sensorimotor nervous system
   (D) the sympathetic nervous system
   (E) the parasympathetic nervous system

GO ON TO THE NEXT PAGE.

16. In the Harlow study of emotional attachment, infant monkeys were placed in a cage and given both a "wire" mother and a "cloth" mother. Researchers then moved a bottle of milk from one mother to the other while introducing various stimuli to see if the monkeys would form an attachment to either of the "mothers." In this experiment, the independent variable is

    (A) with which "mother" the bottle of milk is placed
    (B) the "wire" mother versus the "cloth" mother
    (C) the preference of the infants for the source of milk
    (D) the preference of the infants for the "wire" mother
    (E) the preference of the infants for the "cloth" mother

17. As an experiment, a group of newborn kittens was allowed to see through only one eye at a time. Each day one of the eyes would be covered, switching between the two eyes on subsequent days. Which of the following best describes the visual limitations experienced by these cats as adults?

    (A) They were unable to make use of interposition depth perception.
    (B) They were unable to maintain perceptual constancy.
    (C) They were unable to distinguish left from right monocular cues.
    (D) They were unable to use binocular cues for depth perception.
    (E) They were unable to extinguish their visual blind spot.

Questions 18-19 refer to the situation described below.

A researcher wished to study the impact of classical music on memory in children. She therefore randomly selected two groups of children: One group was asked to read and later to recall lists of words while soft classical music played in the background. The second group was asked to read and recall lists of words with no background music playing.

18. The control group in this experiment is the group that

    (A) the researcher expected to demonstrate greater memory
    (B) demonstrated greater memory through recalling more words
    (C) demonstrated lesser memory through recalling fewer words
    (D) read the lists of words while classical music played in the background
    (E) read the lists of words with no background music playing

19. The dependent variable in this experiment is the

    (A) number of words recalled by the children
    (B) amount of time each child needs to recall the words
    (C) amount of music each child can recall
    (D) classical music playing in the background
    (E) lack of classical music playing in the background

20. Students diagnosed with attention deficit hyperactivity disorder (ADHD) are four to nine times more likely to be

    (A) females than males
    (B) males than females
    (C) children than adults
    (D) Caucasian children than African American children
    (E) urban area children than rural area children

GO ON TO THE NEXT PAGE.

21. Which of the following best summarizes the psychoanalytic perspective's view of behavior?

    (A) Behavior is motivated by inner, unconscious forces.
    (B) Behavior is a response to external reward and punishment.
    (C) Behavior is a product of genetic programming and evolution.
    (D) Behavior is a compilation of the ways in which people think and interact.
    (E) Behavior is each person's striving to reach his or her full potential.

22. Which of the following is the best example of a categorical variable?

    (A) Intelligence
    (B) Disposition
    (C) Optimism
    (D) Gender
    (E) Personality

23. Donia was soaked by an unexpected cloudburst while walking to her car from the office. The fact that she failed to realize that the newspaper she was carrying would have made a great makeshift umbrella is an example of

    (A) confirmation bias
    (B) limited visualization
    (C) functional fixedness
    (D) conceptual constriction
    (E) negative variation

24. Elise wanted to call the local coffee house to see what the entertainment would be for that evening. After looking up the phone number in the phone book, she repeated the number to herself several times as she walked over to the telephone. Elise was using which of the following to remember the phone number?

    (A) Iconic memory
    (B) Elaborative rehearsal
    (C) Chunking
    (D) Maintenance rehearsal
    (E) Retrieval

25. A participant in a single-trial free-recall task is presented with a list of words, one at a time, in the following order: house, flower, dog, table, license, water, computer, salad. In accord with the serial position curve, which of the following words is the participant most likely to forget?

    (A) House
    (B) Computer
    (C) Flower
    (D) Salad
    (E) License

26. The smallest units of meaning in a language are

    (A) phonemes
    (B) phenotypes
    (C) semantics
    (D) morphemes
    (E) syntactical rules

27. Which of the following psychological disorders is characterized by an abnormally elevated or expansive mood?

    (A) Depression
    (B) Schizophrenia
    (C) Euphoria
    (D) Dysthymia
    (E) Mania

28. During periods of darkness, the pineal gland in the middle of the brain produces which of the following hormones that is essential to sleep regulation?

    (A) Estrogen
    (B) Adrenaline
    (C) Testosterone
    (D) Melatonin
    (E) Dopamine

GO ON TO THE NEXT PAGE.

29. Jacob cries uncontrollably every time his mother takes him down the candy isle in the supermarket and refuses to let him buy anything. Eventually, Jacob's mother gives in and lets him choose one candy item to buy if he stops crying. Jacob's crying behavior is _____ by his mother.

    (A) punished
    (B) positively reinforced
    (C) negatively reinforced
    (D) extinguished
    (E) shaped

30. Which of the following scientists was among the first to study the relationship between reinforcement and learning?

    (A) Sigmund Freud
    (B) B. F. Skinner
    (C) Carl Rogers
    (D) Mary Ainsworth
    (E) Charles Darwin

31. Jonathan's IQ score is in the 97th percentile. Of the following, which score is most likely his?

    (A)   85
    (B)   100
    (C)   130
    (D)   150
    (E)   170

32. Which one of the following best states Ivan Pavlov's accidental discovery?

    (A) While experimenting with rats, Pavlov discovered that if he repeatedly placed pellets of food in one side of a "T-maze," the rats would automatically run to that side of the maze.
    (B) While experimenting with dogs, Pavlov discovered that once his dogs became accustomed to seeing and hearing the attendant who brought them food at mealtime, they would salivate in response to the sight and sound of the attendant.
    (C) While experimenting with cats, Pavlov discovered that if he placed a hungry cat inside a box and food outside the box, the cat could "learn" to press a lever to open the door of the box.
    (D) While experimenting with pigeons, Pavlov discovered that if he placed a pigeon in a box, he could condition it to recognize that if it pecked at a particular key, it would receive a food pellet.
    (E) While experimenting with dogs, Pavlov discovered that if he fed the dogs the same type of food each day, the dogs would salivate whenever they ate that type of food.

33. The parenting style that produces children with high degrees of self-esteem and self-efficacy is

    (A) authoritarian parenting
    (B) authoritative parenting
    (C) rejecting-neglecting parenting
    (D) permissive parenting
    (E) avoidant parenting

34. Which of the following best summarizes why people tend to stay in a slightly elevated state of arousal after a crisis has occurred?

    (A) Their neurons remain in a state of graded potentiality even after they have fired.
    (B) Their neurons continue to keep the body in an alert state.
    (C) Their adrenal glands continue to secrete epinephrine even after the crisis is over.
    (D) Their parasympathetic nervous system remains in a state of fight or flight.
    (E) Their bloodstream continues to contain elevated levels of adrenaline.

GO ON TO THE NEXT PAGE.

35. Which of the following subsystems of the autonomic nervous system help the body return to "business-as-usual" after an emergency?

(A) Somatic nervous system
(B) Peripheral nervous system
(C) Sympathetic nervous system
(D) Parasympathetic nervous system
(E) Central nervous system

36. Tina is a very good student: Her grades are high, she is involved in extracurricular activities, and typically she excels at anything she tries. Therefore, when she caused an accident her second day of driver's ed., her instructor was shocked. The instructor's disbelief is most probably a result of

(A) modeling
(B) accommodation
(C) a halo effect
(D) convergence
(E) behavioral dissonance

37. Which of the following transduces visual images?

(A) The cornea
(B) The pupils
(C) The cochlea
(D) The retina
(E) The ossicles

38. You enter a bakery and are delighted by the aroma. After a short time, however, you no longer notice the odors because of

(A) sensory perception
(B) sensory adaptation
(C) sensory transduction
(D) sensory detection
(E) sensory attrition

39. Carlotta is a well-adjusted, socially competent adolescent. Which of the following most likely represents her family's parenting style?

(A) Minimal supervision
(B) Permissive
(C) Authoritarian
(D) Authoritative
(E) Indulgent

40. The semicircular canals of the inner ear are important for helping a person to maintain

(A) tone quality
(B) melatonin
(C) balance
(D) olfaction
(E) transduction

41. The ability to perceive your front door as a rectangle even when it open and it casts a different retinal image is known as

(A) color constancy
(B) closure
(C) shape constancy
(D) size constancy
(E) sensory adaptation

42. Stimulation of norepinephrine receptors appears to produce

(A) euphoria
(B) increased motor activity
(C) alertness
(D) hunger
(E) hypertension

43. Research using the visual cliff suggests that human infants

(A) would go "over the cliff" if their mothers called them
(B) had learned by experience in crawling to perceive depth
(C) were not able to use any visual depth cues
(D) use monocular but not binocular cues for vision
(E) have innate depth perception at birth

GO ON TO THE NEXT PAGE.

44. All of the following are conditions sanctioned by the APA regarding the use of deception in a study EXCEPT

   (A) the research is of great importance and cannot be conducted without the use of deception
   (B) participants are expected to find the procedures reasonable upon being informed of them
   (C) participants must be allowed to withdraw from the experiment at any time
   (D) the research must be conducted as a double-blind study
   (E) experimenters must debrief the participants after the study is concluded

45. The belief that the mind and the body are separate and qualitatively different is referred to as

   (A) *tabula rasa*
   (B) the mind-body problem
   (C) nature vs. nurture
   (D) parallel processing
   (E) correlational conditioning

46. Which of the following best summarizes a view of classical behaviorism?

   (A) Behavior is under the control of external stimuli that either reinforce or punish actions, thereby affecting the likelihood of the occurrence of these behaviors.
   (B) Behavior can be controlled by introspection.
   (C) Behavior is the result of competing motives that result from mental events that occur outside of one's awareness.
   (D) Behavior influenced by internal drives and motivation.
   (E) Although behavior can be influenced by environmental factors, most actions and reactions occur as a result of genetic inference.

47. To which perspective are the roles of knowledge, information processing, and their interactions most central?

   (A) Psychoanalytic
   (B) Cognitive
   (C) Behaviorist
   (D) Evolutionary
   (E) Biopsychological

48. The study of cognitive, behavioral, and social changes across the lifespan are most directly studied by which of the following?

   (A) Psychometricians
   (B) Occupational psychologists
   (C) Developmental psychologists
   (D) Social psychologists
   (E) Cognitive behaviorists

49. One's ability to make inferences about the behavior of a population from the behavior of a sample of that population is referred to as

   (A) reliability
   (B) external validity
   (C) internal validity
   (D) inter-rater reliability
   (E) correlational statistical inference

50. A study designed to investigate the friendship patterns of abused children was conducted by videotaping the interactions of the children and later having three raters view the tapes and rate each child's pattern of behavior on a conflictual-behavior scale with values ranging from "constant conflict" to "minimal conflict." Which of the following kinds of reliability is most critical to this study, given the methodology used to measure the variables?

   (A) Coefficient-alpha reliability
   (B) Alternate-forms reliability
   (C) Inter-rater reliability
   (D) Test-retest reliability
   (E) Split-halves reliability

51. Hunger and eating are primarily regulated by the

   (A) somatosensory cortex
   (B) hypothalamus
   (C) medulla oblongata
   (D) occipital lobes
   (E) amygdala

52. The method of loci is a memory aid that employs which of the following?

   (A) Semantic encoding
   (B) Visual imagery
   (C) Auditory cues
   (D) Echoic memory
   (E) Read, recite, review

GO ON TO THE NEXT PAGE.

53. Which of the following are most directly designed to help determine whether the findings of a study reflect a truly replicable phenomenon rather than the outcomes of chance processes?

    (A) Inferential statistics
    (B) Descriptive statistics
    (C) Standard deviation
    (D) Extraneous variables
    (E) Correlation coefficients

54. In a sleep study, a researcher observes that the participant's eyes are beginning to dart as if he were watching a sporting event. The researcher notes that the participant has entered

    (A) stage 3 sleep
    (B) beta sleep
    (C) REM sleep
    (D) NREM sleep
    (E) delta-wave sleep

55. The gland, sometimes referred to as the "master gland," which regulates much of the action of the other endocrine glands, is called the

    (A) thyroid gland
    (B) pancreas
    (C) pituitary gland
    (D) adrenal gland
    (E) lymph system

56. The tendency of young children learning language to overuse the rules of syntax is referred to as

    (A) overconfidence
    (B) confirmation bias
    (C) overgeneralization
    (D) overjustification
    (E) the two-factor theory

57. To demonstrate causation, a researcher must

    (A) manipulate the way a participant responds to some aspect of a situation
    (B) operationalize dependent and independent variables
    (C) develop a hypothesis that predicts the relationship between variables
    (D) show that the manipulation of one variable invariably leads to predicted changes in another
    (E) demonstrate a positive rather than a negative correlation between variables

58. Learned helplessness is an example of the power of

    (A) expectation
    (B) positive reinforcement
    (C) negative reinforcement
    (D) classical conditioning
    (E) prepared learning

59. According to cognitive theorist Jean Piaget, children in which of the following stages of cognitive development are egocentric, or unable to understand another person's perspective?

    (A) sensorimotor stage
    (B) pre-operational
    (C) concrete operational
    (D) formal operational
    (E) pre-conventional stage

60. Georgia works in the local hospital because she wishes to help others, while Kathy works in the hospital strictly to make money. Their individual motivations demonstrate the difference between

    (A) primary and secondary drives
    (B) positive and negative loci of control
    (C) sympathetic and autonomic motivation
    (D) instinctive and derived drives
    (E) intrinsic and extrinsic motivation

61. People who struggle with depression often have trouble sleeping in part because of

    (A) elevated endorphin levels
    (B) decreased GABA levels
    (C) depleted epinephrine levels
    (D) increased dopamine levels
    (E) low serotonin levels

62. Tristan, a seven-year-old male, has an IQ of 128. Tristan's mental age is

    (A) seven
    (B) eight
    (C) nine
    (D) ten
    (E) eleven

GO ON TO THE NEXT PAGE.

63. Through reinforcement, pigeons are taught to peck at paintings by a particular artist. The fact that pigeons do not peck at the paintings of other artists represents

    (A) modeling response
    (B) reflexive response
    (C) distinctive stimulus
    (D) stimulus generalization
    (E) stimulus discrimination

64. While browsing in a bookstore, Vhamala is drawn to a particular book title. After a moment, she realizes that this book is one that a friend had been talking about at lunch the other day. The fact that Vhamala remembers that the book was mentioned at a recent lunch is an example of which of the following types of memory?

    (A) Phonemic
    (B) Systemic
    (C) Semantic
    (D) Structural
    (E) Episodic

65. The process of converting physical energy from the environment into neural impulses is known as

    (A) sensation
    (B) priming
    (C) transduction
    (D) encoding
    (E) detection

66. An experiment that presents participants with a stimulus and then, at a later interval, presents them with incomplete perceptual information related to the initial stimulus to see if they recognize the incomplete information more quickly is most likely studying the effects of

    (A) retroactivity
    (B) mnemonic devices
    (C) declarative memory
    (D) iconic memory
    (E) priming

67. Alfred Binet was primarily concerned with

    (A) discussing the role of genetics in levels of intelligence
    (B) measuring intelligence levels in children
    (C) measuring personality in children
    (D) measuring personality in adults
    (E) showing how adult personality can be modified

68. Hunter, a high school senior, excels at music, art, reading, problem solving, and soccer. Which of these strengths most clearly demonstrates his fluid intelligence?

    (A) Music
    (B) Art
    (C) Reading
    (D) Problem solving
    (E) Soccer

69. In psychoanalytic theory, which of the following statements most accurately explains the purpose of repression?

    (A) It allows individuals to indirectly express their anger toward others.
    (B) It encourages clients to shift difficult feelings about loved ones onto their therapists.
    (C) It is a means of dealing with thoughts that are very anxiety provoking.
    (D) It allows individuals to explain away acts to avoid uncomfortable feelings.
    (E) It is an unconscious model that allows people to describe the way things work.

70. If genetic factors play an important role in the development of intelligence as measured by an IQ test, then which of the following statements is most likely to be true?

    (A) The IQ scores of parents and their offspring will be more nearly alike than the IQ scores of fraternal twins.
    (B) The IQ scores of siblings reared together will be more nearly alike than the IQ scores of identical twins.
    (C) The IQ scores of fraternal twins reared together will be more nearly alike than the IQ scores of identical twins reared apart.
    (D) The IQ scores of fraternal twins will be equivalent in similarity to the IQ scores of identical twins.
    (E) The IQ scores of identical twins reared apart will be more nearly alike than the IQ scores of fraternal twins reared together.

GO ON TO THE NEXT PAGE.

71. Negative symptoms of schizophrenia include which of the following?

    (A) Visual hallucinations
    (B) Auditory hallucinations
    (C) Blunted emotional responses
    (D) Delusions
    (E) Excessive motor activity

72. A major contribution of Howard Gardner's theory of intelligence is that it

    (A) broadens the definition of intelligence
    (B) adds substantial support to the accuracy of the IQ test
    (C) relates the Gf-Gc theory of intelligence with environmental factors
    (D) simplifies the ways in which intelligence is measured
    (E) substantiates works such as *The Bell Curve*

73. Jim and Tim are identical (monozygotic) twins that were reared together. Scott and Michael are fraternal (dizygotic) twins that were reared together. Given the results of heritability studies of intelligence, which of the following outcomes are most likely to emerge

    (A) Jim and Tim will have very similar IQs.
    (B) Scott and Michael will have very similar IQs.
    (C) Both pairs will have very similar IQs.
    (D) Neither pair will have similar IQs.
    (E) Jim and Michael will have similar IQs.

74. Drive-reduction theories would provide a reasonable explanation for all of the following EXCEPT

    (A) In the middle of his five-mile race, Jerome grabs water from the water station to quench his thirst.
    (B) Ernest gobbles a few cookies on his way to class because he did not have time for lunch.
    (C) Tish decides to skip lunch because she is still full from eating a very large breakfast.
    (D) Cameron drives ten minutes out of her way to a fast-food place because she is hungry and only has two dollars.
    (E) Kezia is very full after eating dinner but decides to order the strawberry cheesecake anyway.

75. Abraham Maslow proposed the idea that some motives are more imperative to survival than others. Which of the following approaches expresses this?

    (A) Homeostatic regulation
    (B) Goal-setting
    (C) Expectancy-value
    (D) Cognitive dissonance
    (E) Hierarchy of needs

76. Which of the following is an example of a person who suffers from anterograde amnesia?

    (A) A six-year-old child who can't remember events related to her second birthday party.
    (B) A twenty-year-old woman who can't remember the details of a traumatic event that occurred six months ago.
    (C) A thirty-six-year-old man who experiences damage to his hippocampus and can't transfer information into his long-term memory.
    (D) A fifteen-year-old boy who fell off his bicycle without his helmet and can't remember the events right before his accident.
    (E) A forty-year-old woman who is recounting a story but can't remember where she first heard the story.

77. Which of the following responses was most likely acquired through classical conditioning?

    (A) The anxiety reaction of a woman who is driving on the highway for the first time after being involved in a major accident on that highway.
    (B) The frightened cry of a baby who is disoriented upon waking up from a nap.
    (C) The uncontrollable blinking of a contact lens wearer who has just gotten something in his eye.
    (D) The startled cry of a child who has just been awakened in the middle of the night by a loud clap of thunder.
    (E) The salivation of a laboratory rat who has begun to eat the treat that awaited her at the end of a T-maze.

GO ON TO THE NEXT PAGE.

78. Which of the following would be most useful in understanding a neighbor's interpretation of a certain family's recent crisis as being due to extreme financial distress?

    (A) Reinforcement theory
    (B) Classical behaviorism
    (C) Attribution theory
    (D) Hierarchy of needs
    (E) Cognitive dissonance

79. Children develop internal representational systems that allow them verbally to describe people, events, and feelings during which of Piaget's stages of cognitive development?

    (A) Sensorimotor
    (B) Preoperational
    (C) Symbolic
    (D) Concrete operational
    (E) Formal operational

80. According to Kohlberg, at the third (postconventional) level of moral development, individuals

    (A) follow rules in order to obtain reward
    (B) follow rules in order to avoid punishment
    (C) define what is right by what they have learned from others, especially authority figures
    (D) justify their moral action based on the need to maintain law and order
    (E) self-define principles that may or may not match the dominant morals of the times

81. Which of the following represents the correct order of auditory transmission from the time the sound is first heard to when it is processed in the brain?

    (A) oval window→ cochlea→ tympanic membrane→ auditory nerve→auditory canal
    (B) auditory canal→ auditory nerve→ cochlea→ tympanic membrane→ ossicles
    (C) tympanic membrane→ oval window→ cochlea→ auditory nerve→ auditory canal
    (D) auditory canal→ ossicles→ oval window→ cochlea→auditory nerve
    (E) cochlea→ ossicles→ oval window→ auditory canal→ auditory nerve

82. The Whorfian hypothesis of linguistic relativity helps explain why

    (A) Eskimos have many words relating to snow
    (B) parents use a high-pitched voice when speaking to infants
    (C) phonemes are not interchangeable with morphemes
    (D) cultures have developed different languages
    (E) some societies do not have written language

83. Many experts on parenting recommend different approaches to responding to an infant's needs. Some emphasize responding promptly to a newborn's cries to instill a sense of security, whereas others suggest letting the baby "cry it out." Which of the following accounts of development would be most relevant when weighing these different approaches?

    (A) Piaget's theory of cognitive development
    (B) The Whorfian hypothesis of linguistic relativity
    (C) Erikson's model of psychosocial stages
    (D) Descartes's theory of Cartesian dualism
    (E) Wilhelm Wundt's theory of structuralism

84. Which of the following clinicians most likely follows Carl Rogers's approach to psychotherapy?

    (A) Dr. Jones, who emphasizes the need for modification of undesirable behaviors in his patients.
    (B) Terence Springer, who counsels individuals to find their inner spirituality and develop their relationship with a supreme being.
    (C) Cathy Cooper, who is an empathic counselor who encourages clients through unconditional support to find their own path to better health and growth.
    (D) Utrese Leed, who creates a framework for her patients that defines ideal psychological growth and development and who supports their efforts toward professional achievement.
    (E) Ute Shrom, who takes a physiological approach to recovery through strenuous physical challenges that break down and subsequently build up one's character.

GO ON TO THE NEXT PAGE.

85. An obese individual with a breathing-related sleep disorder most likely suffers from which of the following?

   (A) Narcolepsy
   (B) Hypersomnia
   (C) Insomnia
   (D) Sleep apnea
   (E) Hypnotic susceptibility

86. Certain cross-cultural studies have suggested that six facial expressions are recognized by people of virtually every culture. Which of the following correctly lists these expressions?

   (A) Happiness, sadness, anger, loathing, lust, and surprise
   (B) Happiness, sadness, indifference, fright, surprise, and dislike
   (C) Happiness, sadness, desire, repulsion, fear, and surprise
   (D) Happiness, sadness, fight, flight, indifference, and anger
   (E) Happiness, sadness, fear, anger, surprise, and disgust

87. Which of the following is primarily a chemical sense?

   (A) touch
   (B) vision
   (C) taste
   (D) hearing
   (E) kinesthesis

88. Anorexia nervosa is a life-threatening illness that can lead to permanent physiological changes (such as brittle bones) and even death. Which of the following individuals would be the most likely to develop this illness?

   (A) Maria, a 16-year-old Caucasian female, who is an A student and talented musician, but who feels that her life is out of control.
   (B) Leticia, a 15-year-old African American female, who is an A student and exceptional athlete, plus an avid reader.
   (C) Rosa, a 26-year old Hispanic female, who has just received her law degree, is struggling with debt from school, and having difficulty finding employment.
   (D) Virginia, a 14-year-old Caucasian female, who is a C student, is sexually promiscuous, and is experimenting with drugs.
   (E) Jaeling, a 29-year-old Asian American female, who is a stay-at-home mother of two and has a very tight budget to maintain.

89. Individuals in which of the following occupations will be potentially LEAST likely to be susceptible to health problems as a result of disrupted circadian rhythms?

   (A) Shift nurse
   (B) Police officer
   (C) Flight attendant
   (D) Medical resident
   (E) College professor

90. Janice often has feelings of hostility and contempt for her husband of forty years. However, instead of expressing these feelings, Janice goes overboard to dote on her husband. Janice is using which of the following defense mechanisms?

   (A) Rational philosophy
   (B) Reaction formation
   (C) Repression
   (D) Sublimation
   (E) Passive aggression

GO ON TO THE NEXT PAGE.

91. While visiting a museum, you study a statue by walking around it and examining it from many different places in the room. The retinal images of the statue change, but you do not perceive these changes because of

    (A) convergence
    (B) motion parallax
    (C) perceptual constancy
    (D) interpositioning
    (E) perceptual acuity

92. REM sleep is considered to be paradoxical sleep because

    (A) brain patterns change from alpha waves to delta waves over the course of a night's sleep
    (B) people can always act out the content of their dreams
    (C) people will try to increase REM sleep if deprived of REM sleep for a period of time
    (D) sleep cycles may change with age
    (E) the mind is very active, but the body is in a state of paralysis

93. All of the following are stages in the development of language that children of virtually every culture go through EXCEPT

    (A) babbling
    (B) holophrastic speech
    (C) telegraphic speech
    (D) introductive speech
    (E) grammatical speech

94. Probabilistic reasoning from specific observations to general propositions is known as

    (A) deductive reasoning
    (B) inductive reasoning
    (C) intuitive reasoning
    (D) statistical reasoning
    (E) observational reasoning

95. Two "cognitive shortcuts" that can lead to errors in information processing are

    (A) the representativeness heuristic and the availability heuristic
    (B) inductive reasoning and deductive reasoning
    (C) morphemic processing and phonemic processing
    (D) prototypic development and fuzzy concept development
    (E) top-down processing and bottom-up processing

96. Which of the following accurately states the order of transmission of visual information?

    (A) Optic nerve; ganglion cells; bipolar cells; rods and cones
    (B) Bipolar cells; ganglion cells; fovea; optic nerve
    (C) Rods and cones; retina; optic nerve; ganglion cells
    (D) Bipolar cells; rods and cones; fovea; optic disk
    (E) Rods and cones; bipolar cells; ganglion cells; optic nerve

97. Which of the following best summarizes Carl Rogers' view of personality?

    (A) Personality traits such as inhibition, extroversion and conscientiousness are constant over time.
    (B) People's personality traits are overwhelmingly positive and goal-directed.
    (C) Personality is mainly formed by behavioral expectations.
    (D) Individual personalities vary based on differences in traits, emotions, and thought processes.
    (E) Situational variables are more important in determining the way a person will act than are broad personality dispositions.

98. Research has shown a possible connection between the neurotransmitter acetylcholine and which of the following mental disorders?

    (A) Parkinson's disease
    (B) Alzheimer's disease
    (C) Schizophrenia
    (D) Mania
    (E) Depression

GO ON TO THE NEXT PAGE.

99. Which of the following best explains why babies have poor vision for the first few weeks of life?

    (A) The nodes of Ranvier have not yet formed.

    (B) The neural connections to the primary visual cortex are not fully connected.

    (C) The axons are covered in tight coats of lipids, which impede neural firing.

    (D) The synaptic cleft of the neuron is filled with an aqueous humor.

    (E) The glial cells are absent at birth.

100. In a study of brain development, two groups of rats were reared in a laboratory setting. In Group I, each rat was raised in isolation with no toys, while in Group II, rats were divided into small groups and given toys to play with. Which of the following statements most accurately reflects the probable findings of this study?

    (A) The rats raised in Group I will have forebrains that weigh more than those of the rats raised in Group II.

    (B) The rats raised in Group I will have forebrains that weigh less than those of the rats raised in Group II.

    (C) The brains of the rats raised in Group I will not be noticeably different from the brains of the rats raised in Group II.

    (D) The brains of the rats raised in Group I will consist of more white matter while the brains of the rats raised in Group II will consist of more gray matter.

    (E) The brains of the rats raised in Group I will consist of more gray matter while the brains of the rats raised in Group II will consist of more white matter.

END OF SECTION I

PSYCHOLOGY
SECTION II
Time—50 minutes
Percent of total grade—33 $\frac{1}{3}$

Directions: You have 50 minutes to answer BOTH of the following questions. It is not enough to answer a question by merely listing facts. You should present a cogent argument based on your critical analysis of the question posed, using appropriate psychological terminology.

1. Psychology differs from other fields of science in that it does not have a single paradigm upon which most scientists agree.

    A.   Based on your knowledge of psychology, explain why the field of psychology has multiple perspectives rather than a single paradigm upon which most psychologists agree. Then, compare and contrast any TWO of the following perspectives in psychology to illustrate why multiple perspectives remain in psychology:

- Biological
- Humanistic
- Psychoanalytic
- Behaviorist
- Cognitive

    B.   How would psychologists of the two perspectives you chose work with Margot, a sixteen-year-old girl with anorexia nervosa?

2. Many people are concerned with the seeming inability of the prison system to rehabilitate criminals.

    A.   Based on your knowledge of learning, argue against the traditional prison system by explaining how each of the following could be used in a rehabilitation program:

- Operant conditioning
- Positive and negative reinforcement
- Shaping

    B.   Choose ONE of the above methods of learning and the explain how it could be used to reform a convicted thief.

STOP

END OF EXAM

20

Practice Test 1:
Answers and
Explanations

Section 1

1. **A** *Ask It Like It Is:* What are damaged areas of the brain called? *Answer Before You Answer:* Lesions. If you don't remember, use POE. (B) *hemispheres* and (C) *brain lobes* are areas of the brain. (D) *cortical adhesions* is made up, and (E) *corpus collosum* connects the left and right hemispheres of the brain.

2. **B** *Ask It Like It Is:* The study of mental processes is called... *Answer Before You Answer:* Hopefully you recognize the definition of *psychology*. If you draw a blank, use POE to determine the answer: Is (A) *biology* the study of *mental* processes? No, so cross it off. (C) *cognition* might throw you off, so keep it and check the others. Is (D) *scientific method* the study of *mental* processes? It may be involved in the study of mental processes, but that is not its defining feature so cross it off. The same is true of (E) *research*. While *cognition* definitely involves the mind, it should be clear that *psychology* is defined as the study of mental processes.

3. **E** *Ask It Like It Is:* Which kind of scientist emphasizes the importance of culture? *Answer Before You Answer:* Culture should mean *anthropology* to you. If not, get reviewing, and use POE. Are (B) *structuralists* the kind of scientists that emphasize culture? Even if you don't remember what structuralists are, the name does not imply culture. If you are completely unfamiliar with (B), leave it and move on. (C) *sociobiologist* may throw you, but (D) *behaviorists* should be one you can easily eliminate. When you plug in (E) *anthropologists*, it should jog your memory. Remember, this is question number three, so keep it simple and go for the easier choice.

4. **B** *Ask It Like It Is:* Culturally based versus psychologically based? *Answer Before You Answer:* Look for something that is not considered "innate." Is (A) *caring for one's children* cultural? It seems that most cultures do it in some form, but if you are unsure, leave it. (B) *arriving on time for work* is not something that is done in every culture so this looks good. (C) *having the desire to reproduce* and (D) *seeking food and water* are primary drives present in all cultures, and (E) *smiling* has also been found as a universal facial expression. Even if you are not sure about (A) or (E), this is question number four, and (B) is clearly something that occurs only in time-oriented cultures.

5. **C** *Ask It Like It Is:* Yellow Brick Road rewards you after a specific number of purchases. Which of the following means "reward after specific number of purchases?" *Answer Before You Answer:* Fixed-ratio. If you don't remember, anything like fixed number will get you to your answer using POE. Get rid of (A) *variable-ratio* and (B) *variable-interval* because they are *variable*, and (E) *continuous* because you are not being continuously rewarded. *Fixed-ratio* refers to *ratio* or *number*, whereas (D) *fixed-interval* refers to *interval* or *time*.

6. **D** *Ask It Like It Is:* Circle *neurotransmitters* and *pleasure*. *Answer Before You Answer:* Dopamine. If you don't remember, use POE to get rid of the ones you do recognize. Is (A) *GABA* associated with pleasure? No, so cross it off. Is (B) *acetylcholine* associated with pleasure? No, it has something to do with memory. (C) *serotonin* may throw you off, so leave it if you are unsure. (E) *adrenaline* is not a neurotransmitter so cross it off.

7. **B** *Ask It Like It Is:* Which research tool involves watching people without interacting with them? *Answer Before You Answer:* Naturalistic observation. If you remember only observation, you are still fine. POE will get rid of everything else: Is (A) *quasi-experimental* the same as observation? No, cross it off. Is (C) *correlational research* the same as *observation*? If you don't know, leave it. Is (D) *random sampling* the same as *observation*? No. Is (E) *case study* the same as *observation*? No.

8. **C** *Ask It Like It Is:* Confounding variable is something that may confound (render uninterpretable) the results. What is it in this study? *Answer Before You Answer:* She gives the test in the morning at one school, and in the afternoon at another. If you missed this point, use your definition of confounding variable to evaluate each answer choice. Is (A) the fact that the research is done at *two different schools* a potential problem with the study? No, that is part of what she is comparing. Is (B) the fact that she is comparing the *same grade* a potential problem? Definitely not. Is (C) the fact that the students are tested at different times a potential problem? Bingo. Is (D) the fact that she is testing the students *on the same day* a potential problem? No. Is (E) the fact that she is administering a basic skills exam a potential problem? No.

9. **B** *Ask It Like It Is:* Developmental psychologists do what kind of research? *Answer Before You Answer:* Cross-sectional research. If you don't know this, you better start reviewing. Use POE to eliminate the rest of the choices.

10. **A** *Ask It Like It Is:* How do narcotics work? *Answer Before You Answer:* They imitate endorphins. If you are not sure exactly how they work but know they imitate a chemical substance in the brain, use POE. Do narcotics imitate (A) endorphins? Endorphins are chemicals in the brain that have to do with pleasure, so this could be it. Do narcotics imitate (B) hormones? This is less likely because hormones are secreted throughout the body and for a wide variety of purposes. Cross it off. Do narcotics imitate (C) secretions? What secretions? Too broad, so cross it off. Do narcotics imitate (D) GABA? This is a specific neurotransmitter—too specific to be the thing that all narcotics imitate. Cross it off. Likewise for (E) acetylcholine. The answer must be (A).

11. **B** *Ask It Like It Is:* Someone will be more likely to recall a list of positive words if... *Answer Before You Answer:* S/he was in a positive frame of mind while hearing the words. Use POE: Does (A) the *researcher* exhibiting a positive mood mean the same thing as the participant being in a positive frame of mind? No, so cross it off. Does (B) the *participant* being in a positive mood mean the same thing as the participant being in a positive frame of mind? Yup. Does (C) the participant considering himself a positive person *regardless of his mood during the experience* mean the same thing as the participant being in a positive frame of mind during the experience? No. Does (D) the participant considering the *initial testing experience* positive mean the same thing as the participant having a positive frame of mind during the experience? Careful—it doesn't mean the same thing. Cross it off. Does (E) the participant perceiving the list of words as positive *regardless of the true meaning of the words* mean the same thing as the participant being in a positive frame of mind during the experience? No, plus you know that the words are positive. Cross it off. Your answer must be (B).

12. **C** *Ask It Like It Is:* Circle *minimum amount of physical energy. Answer Before You Answer:* Absolute threshold. If you don't remember, use POE. Would (A) *JND* (just noticeable difference) be the amount of energy needed to notice a stimulus? No, it somehow involves a change. Cross it off. The same is true of (B) *difference threshold.* (D) *median difference* is made up and sounds it, as does the made up (E) *hit threshold.*

13. **D** *Ask It Like It Is:* Circle *hippocampus.* What does the hippocampus do? *Answer Before You Answer:* It is important in memory. If you don't remember, use POE. Is the hippocampus involved in (A) *emotional regulation*? No, emotion is tied to the amygdala. Cross it off. Is the hippocampus involved in (B) *motor coordination*? No, the cerebellum and parts of the reticular formation control movement. Is the hippocampus involved in (C) *speech production*? No, speech production is a result of areas of the cerebral cortex. Is the hippocampus involved in (D) *learning*? Could be. Is the hippocampus involved in (E) *perception*? No, perception is a function carried out by the cerebral cortex. The answer must be (D).

14. **E** *Ask It Like It Is:* Circle *medulla oblongata.* The medulla oblongata is critical for basic life functions, such as respiration. *Answer Before You Answer:* If the medulla oblongata is destroyed, it's all over, baby. If you don't remember, you can probably still get rid of a few choices with POE. (C) and (D) involve speech and vision, which are clearly tied to other areas of the brain. Be sure to review the major components of the brain if you missed this item.

15. **D** *Ask It Like It Is:* Which system prepares the body for fight or flight? *Answer Before You Answer:* Sympathetic nervous system. If you have trouble remembering if it's the (D) *sympathetic* or (E) *parasympathetic*, try this mnemonic: The sympathetic nervous system is *sympathetic* to your problems, so it responds. POE should have gotten rid of (A) *the central nervous system*, (B) *the somatic nervous system*, and (C) *the sensorimotor nervous system*, even if you couldn't remember whether it was (D) or (E).

16. **A** *Ask It Like It Is:* Which aspect of this study is the independent variable? *Answer Before You Answer:* The placement of the bottle of milk. The milk is being moved back and forth to see if the monkeys attach to the food or to the mothers. In other words, the milk is being manipulated to see what response will occur—it is therefore the independent variable. If you don't remember, POE your way to the answer using your common sense. In (B), why would the independent variable be the wire mother over the cloth mother? (D) and (E) are essentially the same answer, so they can't be right, and (C), (D), and (E) all talk about preferences, meaning responses, meaning dependent variables. (A) has to be it.

17. **D** *Ask It Like It Is:* Cats that were only allowed to see through one eye at a time will have what kind of vision problems? *Answer Before You Answer:* Using both eyes together. Which answer choice means using both eyes together? Binocular vision. (D) is the only answer that mentions binocular cues. (A) interposition depth perception would be hard to evaluate in a cat, as would be (B) perceptual constancy. Be careful of (C)—just because it mentions left and right doesn't mean it contains the full answer. It is still talking about monocular cues. (E) would again be hard to evaluate because it involves perception.

18. **E** *Ask It Like It Is:* Circle the words *control group*, and then go to the experiment and label the control group. *Answer Before You Answer:* Because the study is about the effects of music on memory, the second group, which had no music, is the control group. Use POE to get rid of the other choices.

19. **A** Use the same process you did in number 18. *Ask It Like It Is:* Circle *dependent variable*, then go find it. *Answer Before You Answer:* The dependent variable is the thing being tested so the number of words recalled is the dependent variable. Use POE to get rid of the other choices.

20. **B** *Ask It Like It Is:* Who is most often diagnosed with ADHD? *Answer Before You Answer:* Boys. This is something you should know. Don't get sucked in by overly detailed answers such as (D) or (E).

21. **A** *Ask It Like It Is:* Circle *psychoanalytic*. *Answer Before You Answer:* Psychoanalytic = Freud = unconscious forces. Use POE: Does (A) *unconscious forces* mean unconscious forces? Yup. Does (B) *response to external reward and punishment* mean unconscious forces? No. Does (C) *product of genetic programming* mean unconscious forces? No. Does (D*) compilation of the ways in which people think and act* mean unconscious forces? Not really, so cross it off. Does (E) *each person's striving to reach full potential* mean unconscious forces? Not necessarily. The answer must be (A).

22. **D** *Ask It Like It Is:* Circle *categorical*. Categorical versus continuous. *Answer Before You Answer:* Something that is an either/or versus an ongoing kind of trait. Use POE. Is (A) *intelligence* an either/or? No, it is more of an ongoing trait. Cross it off. Is (B) *disposition* an either/or? No. Is (C) *optimism* an either/or? Careful, it is not true that you must be either optimistic or pessimistic. It is more of a continuum. Cross it off. Is (D) *gender* an either/or? Yes, in most cases you are either male or female. Is (E) *personality* an either/or? No.

23. **C** *Ask It Like It Is:* The fact that she didn't see alternative uses for the paper is known as… *Answer Before You Answer:* Functional fixedness. (B), (D), and (E) are made up and (A) *confirmation bias* refers to something else.

24. **D** *Ask It Like It Is:* What was Elise doing to remember the number? *Answer Before You Answer:* Rehearsing it over and over. Use POE. Because you know she is rehearsing, you can get rid of (A), (C), and (E). Does it seem like a rehearsal that is elaborative or maintenance? Your answer must be (D) *maintenance rehearsal.*

25. **E**   *Ask It Like It Is:* The serial position curve has something to do with the position of the words in regard to recall. Which of the words would the person be most likely to forget, given the position of the word in the list? *Answer Before You Answer:* The serial position phenomenon actually says people tend to forget items in the middle of a list, so the answer must be (E), license, because it is in the center of the list.

26. **D**   *Ask It Like It Is:* Circle *smallest unit. Answer Before You Answer:* Morphemes. If you don't remember, use POE to get rid of (B) *phenotypes* and (E) *syntactical rules.*

27. **E**   *Ask It Like It Is:* Circle *abnormally elevated or expansive mood.* Which disorder involves extreme happiness or "bigness"? *Answer Before You Answer:* Mania. If you don't remember, use POE. Does (A) *depression* manifest itself in extreme happiness? No. Does (B) *schizophrenia* manifest itself in extreme happiness? Extreme happiness is not a defining characteristic of schizophrenia. Does (C) *euphoria* manifest itself in extreme happiness? Yes, but is it a disorder? Be careful—this response is a trap. Does (D) *dysthymia* manifest itself in extreme happiness? If you don't know, leave it. Does (E) *mania* manifest itself in extreme happiness? Yes. Your answer is (E).

28. **D**   *Ask It Like It Is:* Which hormone is essential for sleep regulation? *Answer Before You Answer:* Melatonin. If you don't remember, use POE. Is (A) *estrogen* essential for sleep regulation? No. Cross it off. Is (B) *adrenaline* essential for sleep regulation? No. Is (C) *testosterone* essential for sleep regulation? No. Is (D) *melatonin* essential for sleep regulation? If you don't remember, leave it. Is (E) *dopamine* essential for sleep regulation? No, and it's not a hormone. The answer has to be (D).

29. **C**   *Ask It Like It Is:* How are Jacob's mother's actions influencing his behavior? *Answer Before You Answer:* She is giving into his demands, thereby negatively reinforcing his behavior. Even if you are unsure, you know that his behavior is somehow being reinforced, so use that information to get rid of (A), (D), and (E).

30. **B**   *Ask It Like It Is:* Circle the words *reinforcement* and *learning.* Both of these terms mean you want to modify behavior. *Answer Before You Answer:* B. F. Skinner is the only behaviorist in this list. If you don't remember his name, use POE to get rid of the ones you know are not behaviorists: (A) *Freud,* (C) *Rogers,* (D) *Ainsworth* and (E) *Darwin.*

31. **C**   *Ask It Like It Is:* Circle *97th percentile.* Which of the choices is a pretty high, but not the highest, IQ score? *Answer Before You Answer:* 130s. If you don't know, use your common sense and POE. (A) *85* and (B) *100* are definitely too low. (C) *130* is considered very high but not extreme. (D) *150* and (E) *170* are rare, more like the 99th percentile.

32. **B**   *Ask It Like It Is:* Circle *Pavlov.* What was Pavlov's big discovery? *Answer Before You Answer:* While experimenting with dogs, he discovered that they would salivate at the sight and sound of the person bringing their food, even before eating their food. This fact led Pavlov to discover classical conditioning. Because you know he experimented with dogs, get rid of (A), (C), and (D). (B) is the answer closest to yours.

33. **B** *Ask It Like It Is:* What type of parenting is most beneficial to children? *Answer Before You Answer:* Be careful of (A)—it's the trap answer. (C), (D), and (E) are all negative types of parenting.

34. **E** *Ask It Like It Is:* Why do people stay aroused after an emergency? *Answer Before You Answer:* Adrenaline is still in their blood. Use POE. Cross off both (A) and (B) because they deal with neurons. (A) is also a false statement—neurons do *not* remain graded after they fire. Watch out for (C): Adrenal glands do secrete epinephrine but they would not continue to do so after the crisis has passed. This is the trap answer. Be sure to read each choice completely. (D) is false because it is the sympathetic system that puts the body in a state of fight or flight. (E) is the closest to your answer.

35. **D** *Ask It Like It Is:* Which system returns the body to normal after an emergency? *Answer Before You Answer:* Parasympathetic nervous system. (B) *peripheral nervous system* and (E) *central nervous system* are not part of the autonomic system. Remember our mnemonic for distinguishing between (C) and (D): The *sympathetic* nervous system is *sympathetic* to your stress, so it responds.

36. **C** *Ask It Like It Is:* Tina's teacher is shocked at her bad driving because… *Answer Before You Answer:* Tina is always good—halo effect. If you don't remember the term, use POE. Does (A) *modeling* mean always being perceived as good? No, cross it off. Does (B) *accommodation* mean always being perceived as good? No. Does (C) *halo effect* mean always being perceived as good? Sounds like it. Does (D) *convergence* mean always being perceived as good? No. Does (E) *behavioral dissonance* mean always being perceived as good? No. The answer must be (C).

37. **D** *Ask It Like It Is:* Circle *transduces*. Transduce means to convert physical energy into neural impulses. *Answer Before You Answer:* The retina. If you are not sure, use POE. Does (A) the *cornea* convert physical energy into neural impulses? No, it refracts light. Cross it off. Do (B) the *pupils* convert physical energy into neural impulses? No, they control the amount of light that enters the eye. Does (C) the *cochlea* convert physical energy into neural impulses in vision? If you are unsure, leave it. Does (D) the *retina* convert physical energy into neural impulses? Yes, it contains the rods and cones that process visual sensations. Do (E) the *ossicles*—the bones of the middle ear—convert physical energy into neural impulses?

38. **B** *Ask It Like It Is:* Why don't you notice the bakery smells after a while? *Answer Before You Answer:* Adaptation. You get used to the smell, and your senses don't pay attention to it as much because it is constant and not a critical piece of information. Use POE to get rid of (A), (C), and (D) because they wouldn't explain why you would no longer notice the aroma. (E) is not a real psychological term.

39. **D**   *Ask It Like It Is:* If Carlotta is so well-adjusted, what's her family's parenting style? *Answer Before You Answer:* Authoritative. This parenting style seems generally to be the most effective. The parents set rules and expectations, but they are not completely domineering. Even if you don't remember the term, you know the style is structured but not overbearing. Use POE to get rid of (A), (B), and (E). Watch out for (C)—it is the trap. Authoritarian parents are domineering, which can be unhealthy for children.

40. **C**   *Ask It Like It Is:* Circle *semicircular canals*. What do they do? *Answer Before You Answer:* Help a person maintain his/her balance. If you don't remember, use POE. Could (A) the semicircular canals of the inner ear help maintain *tone quality*? Maybe. Leave and check the others. Could (B) the semicircular canals of the inner ear help maintain *melatonin*? No, melatonin involves sleep regulation. Cross it off. Could (B) the semicircular canals of the inner ear help maintain *balance*? Hopefully this answer reminds you of the connection between the ear and balance. Could (D) the semicircular canals of the inner ear help maintain *olfaction*? No, olfaction is smell. Could (E) the semicircular canals of the inner ear help maintain *transduction*? Although transduction occurs in the inner ear, that is not the purpose of the semicircular canals.

41. **C**   *Ask It Like It Is:* Why does the shape seem the same even though sensory information changes? *Answer Before You Answer:* You have to account for experience and expectation of constancy. Because we're talking about the door being rectangular, it's shape constancy and not color constancy (E) or size constancy (D).

42. **C**   *Ask It Like It Is:* Circle *norepinephrine receptors*. What happens when they are stimulated? *Answer Before You Answer:* A person experiences increased alertness. Does (A) *euphoria* mean increased alertness? No. Cross it off. Does (B) *increased motor activity* mean increased alertness? No. Does (C) *alertness* mean increased alertness? Yup. Does (D) *anxiety* mean increased alertness? Not exactly. Does (E) *hypertension* mean increased alertness? No.

43. **B**   *Ask It Like It Is:* Circle *visual-cliff studies*. They are studies in which infants are subjected to an optical illusion of a drop. *Answer Before You Answer:* The infants won't crawl into the area that looks like a drop. You need to read all the choices and compare them if you don't remember visual-cliff studies. POE should get rid of (C) and (D) as very unlikely. (B) is the most probable.

44. **D**   *Ask It Like It Is:* Which of the answers is NOT one of the conditions of the APA regarding deception? Be careful, because four of the five answer choices here are "right" while only one is "wrong." *Answer Before You Answer:* A study must be very important, unable to be done without deception, not objectionable to the participant when s/he is informed at the end of the study (must inform), and must allow a participant to stop at any time. Cross off any answer that matches these. The one remaining is your answer.

45. **B** *Ask It Like It Is:* What is the mind versus body problem called? *Answer Before You Answer:* Mind-body problem. Don't make it harder than it is. This is only a medium question.

46. **A** *Ask It Like It Is:* Circle *behaviorism. Answer Before You Answer:* Behaviorists believe that behavior is the result of learning and consequences. Find an answer that exemplifies this tenet and use POE. "Introspection" makes (B) wrong. (C) is psychodynamic, and (E) is way off.

47. **B** *Ask It Like It Is:* Circle *knowledge* and *information processing.* Who cares about how knowledge and information processing interact? *Answer Before You Answer:* Cognitive psychologists. Use your knowledge to get rid of the other four choices.

48. **C** *Ask It Like It Is:* Who studies psychological development through the *life span*? *Answer Before You Answer:* Developmental psychologists. If you don't remember, use what you know to POE. Do (A) *psychometricians* study people throughout the life span? No. Cross it off. Do (B) *occupational psychologists* study people throughout the life span? No, they study occupation stuff. Do (C) *developmental psychologists* study people throughout the life span? Yes, as the people *develop*. Do (D) *social psychologists* study people throughout the life span? Not necessarily. Do (E) *cognitive behaviorists* study people throughout the life span? No.

49. **B** *Ask It Like It Is:* If you can generalize from a sample it's called… *Answer Before You Answer:* Generalizability. Use your work to POE the other choices.

50. **C** *Ask It Like It Is:* What makes this study valid? The methodology used involves researchers evaluating various behavior patterns of children. Therefore, the evaluators need to do an unbiased, accurate job. *Answer Before You Answer:* Inter-rater reliability. Use POE if you don't remember the term. (A) and (B) are made-up terms. Does (C) *inter-rater reliability* address the accuracy of the evaluators? Yes. Does (D) *test-retest reliability* address the accuracy of the evaluators? No. Does (E) *correlational statistical inference* address the accuracy of the evaluators? No.

51. **B** *Ask It Like It Is:* What area of the brain regulates hunger and eating? *Answer Before You Answer:* Hypothalamus. If you don't remember, use POE. Does (A) the *somatosensory cortex* regulate hunger and eating? Probably not—it is a cortex, and somehow involves "sensory" stuff, and hunger is a primary drive. Cross this off. Does (C) the *medulla oblongata* regulate hunger and eating? Probably not because you know it is a part of vital organ functioning. Do (D) the *occipital lobes* regulate hunger and eating? No, they involve vision. Does (E) the *amygdala* regulate hunger and eating? No, it is involved in emotions. The answer must be (B).

52. **B** *Ask It Like It Is:* How does the method of loci memory aid work? *Answer Before You Answer:* Loci is plural for locus or locality, which implies visualization. Use POE. Does (A) *semantic encoding* mean visualization? No. Cross it off. Does (B) *visual imagery* mean visualization? Yes. Does (C) *auditory cues* mean visualization? No. Does (D) *echoic memory* mean visualization? No, it also means auditory (think *echo*). Does (E) *read, recite, review* mean visualization? No.

53. **A** *Ask It Like It Is:* Which helps determine if the findings of a study mean something or if they were a fluke? *Answer Before You Answer:* Inferential statistics. If you don't remember, use POE to evaluate the answer choices. Could (A) *inferential statistics* help determine if the findings of a study mean something? They help to infer stuff, so probably. Keep it and read the others. Could (B) *descriptive statistics* help determine if the findings of a study mean something? They only describe, so probably not. Cross it off. Could (C) *standard deviation* help determine if the findings of a study mean something? Cross it off. Same goes for (D) *extraneous variables*. Could (E) *correlation coefficients* help determine if the findings of a study mean something? No, so the answer must be (A).

54. **C** *Ask It Like It Is:* When there is rapid eye movement, what sleep cycle are you in? *Answer Before You Answer:* REM. Don't be confused by the other choices— this is a medium question, and you know you want REM.

55. **C** *Ask It Like It Is:* Which gland is called the master gland? *Answer Before You Answer:* Pituitary gland. If you don't remember, use POE to get rid of (B) and (E) because they are not glands. You also know that (D) adrenal gland is responsible for adrenaline, not a lot more, so cross it off, too.

56. **C** *Ask It Like It Is:* What types of mistakes do all children make when learning language? *Answer Before You Answer:* They learn to use the rules of grammar, but they apply them too generally. Use POE. It must be (C), *overgeneralization*.

57. **D** *Ask It Like It Is:* What does a researcher have to do to show that one thing causes another? *Answer Before You Answer:* Show that manipulating one variable consistently leads to changes in another variable. Use POE to find the answer that is closest to yours. (A) is unethical, (B) and (C) would do nothing to show causation. Don't get trapped by (E).

58. **A** *Ask It Like It Is:* Circle *learned helplessness*. What does it mean? It means being helpless because you believe you are helpless. *Answer Before You Answer:* It's a result of expectation. If you don't remember the term expectation, use POE. Could (A) *expectation* lead to being helpless simply because you believe you are helpless? Yes—your expectations determine your ability. Could (B) *positive reinforcement* lead to being helpless simply because you believe you are helpless? Doesn't make sense, and neither does (C) *negative reinforcement*. Could (D) *classical conditioning* lead to being helpless simply because you believe you are helpless? No—there is no classical conditioning involved. Could (E) *prepared learning* lead to being helpless simply because you believe you are? Doesn't make sense. The answer must be (A).

59. **B** *Ask It Like It Is:* At what stage of development is a child egocentric? *Answer Before You Answer:* Use POE. (A) object permanence develops in the *sensorimotor stage.* (C) conservation occurs in the *concrete operational* stage. Choices (D) and (E) refer to Kohlberg's stages of moral development, which is another topic entirely. The answer must be (B).

60. **E** *Ask It Like It Is:* Georgia is motivated by internal issues or emotions, while Kathy is motivated by money. How are these motivations different? *Answer Before You Answer:* Georgia is motivated intrinsically, that is, she is rewarded by the work itself and not by some external reward, while Kathy is motivated extrinsically, that is by an external reward—money. If you don't remember the terms, use POE. (A) *primary and secondary drives* doesn't make sense, so cross it off. (B) po*sitive and negative loci of control* also doesn't address the internal versus external motivations. (C) *sympathetic and autonomic motivation* are made-up terms, and (D) *instinctive and derived drives* refer to basic drives, not social motivations.

61. **E** *Ask It Like It Is:* Circle *depression.* What chemicals in the brain are involved in depression? *Answer Before You Answer:* Depression should make you think "serotonin." If it doesn't, use POE to get rid of a few choices. Get rid of (A) and (D) due to elevated levels (not likely with depression). Review disorders and their relationship to chemicals in the brain.

62. **C** *Ask It Like It Is:* Circle *mental age. Answer Before You Answer:* His IQ indicates a nine-year-old intelligence level, so that's his mental age. Don't get trapped by (A) *seven.*

63. **E** *Ask It Like It Is:* Why do the pigeons not peck at other artists? *Answer Before You Answer:* Stimulus discrimination. They peck at the one they have learned and can distinguish from the others. Use this information to POE (A) *modeling response* and (B) *reflexive response,* and (D) *stimulus generalization* because it is the opposite idea.

64. **E** *Ask It Like It Is:* She recalls the book by also recalling the lunch. What memory is she calling up? *Answer Before You Answer:* Episodic memory. She relates the memory to a recent episode. Use POE to get rid of the other four choices.

65. **C** *Ask It Like It Is:* Converting physical energy into neural impulses is called… *Answer Before You Answer:* Transduction. If you don't remember, use POE. (A) *sensation* is out since it only involves detection of energy, not conversion. The same is true of (E) *detection.* You can also eliminate (D) *encoding* because it is not involved in conversion.

66. **E** *Ask It Like It Is:* A person is shown something. Later, she is shown incomplete information related to the first thing she was shown. The experimenter watches to see if she recognizes the incomplete information more quickly than usual. In other words, does the fact that she saw related stuff make identifying the second set of stuff easier? *Answer Before You Answer:* The researcher is studying the effects of priming. If you don't remember the term, use POE. Cross off (B) because no mnemonic devices are used. (C) *declarative memory* is out because that is memory of retrieved and "declared" information. (D) *iconic memory* is out because we don't know if these are visual images or other types of information.

67. **B** *Ask It Like It Is:* What did Binet study? *Answer Before You Answer:* Binet = intelligence. He studied intellectual potential in children. Knowing he studied intelligence will help you cross off (C) through (E). Then take a smart guess. You know he developed some kind of test, and most intelligence testing is done on children. (B) is your smart guess.

68. **D** *Ask It Like It Is:* Circle *fluid intelligence*. Fluid, as in real-time, flexible information-processing intelligence, versus crystallized intelligence, as in acquired factual knowledge. Which of the subjects involves real-time, flexible intelligence? *Answer Before You Answer:* Problem solving. All the others require primarily crystallized intelligence.

69. **C** *Ask It Like It Is:* Circle *repression*. Repression means keeping stressful thoughts out of conscious awareness. *Answer Before You Answer:* Repression is a defense mechanism that keeps anxiety-producing information out of conscious awareness for our protection. Use POE to find the answer that is closest to yours. (A) is the definition of passive aggression, (B) is transference, and (D) is rationalization. (E) doesn't make any sense—people can't describe what is unconscious.

70. **E** *Ask It Like It Is:* Genetics over environment in intelligence. Which answer shows that? *Answer Before You Answer:* Find an answer that shows genes/biology as more important than environment. Use POE. (B) and (C) say the opposite. (D) also would not support genetics. In (A), fraternal twins are more genetically similar than parents and their offspring, so this answer does not support genetics. The answer must be (E).

71. **C** *Ask It Like It Is:* Circle *negative symptoms*. Remember *negative* means the absence of something. *Answer Before You Answer:* Lack of normal emotional responses. If you don't remember, POE will get rid of all the other choices because each describes the presence, not the absence, of something.

72. **A** *Ask It Like It Is:* Circle *Gardner*. His work involves the theory of multiple intelligences. *Answer Before You Answer:* His perspective helped redefine and expand the traditional definition of intelligence. Use POE to find the answer that is closest to yours. (B) and (E) are way off base, (C) is too specific, and (D) is not true because Gardner's approach actually makes measurement more complex.

73. **A** *Ask It Like It Is:* Circle *heritability*. In other words, inherited. Another question about genetics over environment. *Answer Before You Answer:* The monozygotic (identical) twins will be more similar than the dizygotic (fraternal) twins. If you don't know the terms, POE and common sense will get rid of (D) and (E).

74. **E**   *Ask It Like It Is:* Circle *drive-reduction theories* and *EXCEPT*. Four of the choices will show a reduction in a drive, whereas one will not. *Answer Before You Answer:* Cross off all the answers that show a response that reduces a drive. The remaining choice will be the answer. In (A), Jerome is thirsty and quenches his thirst, thus satisfying his drive. Cross off this response. In (B), Ernest didn't eat lunch, implying hunger, so he eats cookies, trying to reduce his hunger drive. Cross it off. In (C), Tish is not hungry so she doesn't eat. Although this is not drive *reduction*, it is not against natural drives. Leave it and see if there is a better choice. In (D), Cameron is hungry and needs food, so she goes out of her way to get it. This is drive reduction, so cross it off. In (E), Kezia orders more food even though she is very full. This desire goes against drive reduction, so this is your answer.

75. **E**   *Ask It Like It Is:* Circle *Maslow* and *motives*. *Answer Before You Answer:* Maslow theorized that needs are arranged hierarchically, from physiological needs to self-actualization needs. Use POE. Does (A) *homeostatic regulation* have to do with hierarchy? No. Cross it off. Does (B) *goal-setting* have to do with hierarchy? No. Do (C) *expectancy-value* or (D) *cognitive dissonance* have to do with hierarchy? No. (E) *hierarchy of needs* is it.

76. **C**   *Ask It Like It Is:* Circle *anterograde amnesia*. *Answer Before You Answer:* Look for an example of someone who can't form new memories. Get rid of (B) and (D) because they are clearly "after" memories. (A) involves infantile amnesia and (E) is an example of source amnesia.

77. **A**   *Ask It Like It Is:* Circle *classical conditioning*. *Answer Before You Answer:* Find a choice that demonstrates a conditioned response to a stimulus. (B), (C), and (D) are not conditioned responses. Beware of (E); it's a trap because it uses rats, but notice that the rats salivate once they begin to eat. (A) demonstrates a conditioned fear response after experiencing an accident on the highway.

78. **C**   *Ask It Like It Is:* Which will help you understand how a person or persons interpret the behavior of others? *Answer Before You Answer:* Attribution theory. Attribution theory addresses how one person or group attributes certain things to another person or group in order to understand the other person's or group's actions or behaviors. If you don't remember this, use POE. Could (A) *reinforcement theory* help explain how one group interprets the actions of another? Reinforcement has nothing to do with how groups interrelate. Cross it off. Could (B) *classical behaviorism* help explain how one group interprets the actions of another? No. Could (C) *attribution theory* help explain how one group interprets the actions of another? How they attribute things to others? Could be. Leave it. Could (D) *hierarchy of needs* help explain how one group interprets the actions of another? No. Could (E) *cognitive dissonance* help explain how one group interprets the actions of another? No. Your answer must be (C).

79. **B** *Ask It Like It Is:* During which of Piaget's stages of development do children develop symbolic and verbal representations? *Answer Before You Answer:* Preoperational. If you don't remember, think about the age at which this behavior occurs. You may recall the order of the stages and their approximate ages: sensorimotor, ages zero to two; preoperational, ages two to seven; concrete operational, ages seven to twelve; formal operational, ages twelve and up. The development of language and symbolic thinking occurs between the ages of two and seven. Use POE to get rid of (A) because *sensorimotor* definitely does not imply symbolic thought, and (C) because *symbolic* is not one of Piaget's stages.

80. **E** *Ask It Like It Is:* Circle *Kohlberg* and *third (postconventional) level. Answer Before You Answer:* As postconventional implies, this stage of morality centers on carefully weighed principles that may or may not be *conventional*—they are determined by the individual. You may remember that Kohlberg only asserted three stages, and this third one is the most advanced, so look for an answer that encompasses the most advanced form of moral thinking. (A) and (B) illustrate the first or preconventional stage of development. (C) and (D) represent the second or conventional stage of development.

81. **D** *Ask It Like It Is:* Circle *order of transmission. Answer Before You Answer:* Use POE to assess the correct order based on what you know about the process of transmission.

82. **A** *Ask It Like It Is:* Circle *Whorfian hypothesis of linguistic relativity*. What did Whorf say about language and its relation to behavior? *Answer Before You Answer:* Linguistic constructs of various cultures have an influence on behavior. Find an answer that illustrates this principle. If you don't remember Whorf, use your common sense and the clues in the question to evaluate each answer. "Linguistic relativity" means how language works relative to something. Once you start to read the answers, it becomes apparent that that something is culture. (A) is the only one that clearly shows how the language is a factor in regard to the behavior.

83. **C** *Ask It Like It Is:* Which theory relates to how children develop in relation to their primary care givers? *Answer Before You Answer:* Erikson's model of psychosocial development. If you don't remember, get rid of the choices that clearly do not relate to children's psychological development: (B), (D), and (E).

84. **C** *Ask It Like It Is:* Circle *Carl Rogers*. How did he approach psychotherapy? *Answer Before You Answer:* Rogers believed in empathy and unconditional support that would promote self-discovery. If you don't remember, you know that Rogers is a big name in psychology, so get rid of the clearly *un*-psychological answer choices—(B), (E), and (D) due to the "professional achievement" goal.

85. **D** *Ask It Like It Is:* Circle *breathing-related sleep disorder. Answer Before You Answer:* Apnea. Your clue is "breathing-related." If you don't remember, you can still cross off (B), (C), and (E) because they are not breathing-related.

86. **E** *Ask It Like It Is:* What facial expressions are found in all cultures? *Answer Before You Answer:* List the ones you can think of: happiness, sadness, anger, fear, surprise. Then use POE. You can also use POE to get rid of lists that have inappropriate choices: (A) is out because of "lust," (C) is out because of "desire," (D) is out because of both "fight" and "flight." "Indifference" is the problem with (B).

87. **C** *Ask It Like It Is:* Circle *chemical property*. *Answer Before You Answer:* Find something that is a result of chemical interaction. Even if you don't remember that taste is a chemical sense, use POE to get rid of the answers that are definitely physical properties: (A), (B), (D), and (E) are all physical or mechanical processes.

88. **A** *Ask It Like It Is:* Who is most likely to become anorexic? *Answer Before You Answer:* List what you know about the typical anorexic: white female, teenager, usually good student, need for control. Then use POE. Because she is more likely to be Caucasian, get rid of (B), (C), and (E). (D) is your trap answer—anorexia tends to afflict young women who seem confident and successful.

89. **E** *Ask It Like It Is:* Circle *circadian rhythms* and *LEAST*. Circadian rhythms involve sleep patterns. Four of the choices will show people who may work odd or night hours. *Answer Before You Answer:* Choose the profession that is a normal "day" job. That eliminates (A) through (D).

90. **B** *Ask It Like It Is:* Which means acting the opposite of how she feels? *Answer Before You Answer:* Reaction formation. If you don't remember, use POE: (A) is made up, (D) and (E) don't mean acting the opposite of how one feels. (C) is your trap answer—she is doing more than repressing.

91. **C** *Ask It Like It Is:* Why don't you notice the changes in the statue as you view it from different places? Why does the image remain constant? *Answer Before You Answer:* Perceptual constancy. If you don't remember the term, use POE and your common sense. (E) is definitely out. Could (A) *convergence* mean that the image remains constant? Convergence means coming together, so not really. Cross it off. The same is true of (D) *interpositioning*. You may not be sure about (B) *motion parallax*, but "perceptual constancy" makes the most sense because the image remains constant.

92. **E** *Ask It Like It Is:* Circle *paradoxical sleep*. *Answer Before You Answer:* A paradox is a statement that seems self-contradictory, but is actually true. (A), (B), (C), and (D) are properties of sleep, but no paradox is noted.

93. **D** *Ask It Like It Is:* Children of every culture go through certain stages of development of language. Four of the choices list those stages; pick the other one. *Answer Before You Answer:* Kids babble, use holophrastic speech (using one word to convey a full meaning), telegraphic speech (like a telegram—sentences made of the critical words only), and grammatical speech. If you don't remember all the stages, use POE to get rid of (A) and (E) because you know that all children go through these stages. (D) is not a stage of speech development so it is the answer.

94. **B** *Ask It Like It Is:* Inferring from an observation to a generalization is what kind of reasoning? *Answer Before You Answer:* Inductive reasoning. If you don't remember, POE what you can. Be careful on (A); deductive reasoning is something that can be clearly deduced, not inferred or probabilistic. (D) *statistical reasoning* is also out. (C) and (E) are not the correct psychological terms.

95. **A** *Ask It Like It Is:* What are two "thought shortcuts" that can lead to mistakes? *Answer Before You Answer:* The representative heuristic (making assumptions about what someone or something must be based on representative characteristics) and the availability heuristic (assuming that something that is readily accessible in one's memory is common to others). If you don't recall these terms, use POE. Can (B) *inductive reasoning and deductive reasoning* be thought shortcuts that might lead to errors? Deductive reasoning sure wouldn't. Cross this off. (C) uses two language terms as a means of confusing you so cross it off. You may not be sure about (D) so leave it as a choice. (E) *top-down processing and bottom-up processing* are not considered thought shortcuts but rather ways of processing information.

96. **E** *Ask It Like It Is:* What's the route visual information takes? *Answer Before You Answer:* Retina, bipolar cells, ganglion cells, and optic nerve. If you don't remember, you probably know that transduction starts in the retina, so rods and cones are first. Cross off (A), (B), and (D). Rods and cones are in the retina, so that takes care of (C).

97. **B** *Ask It Like It Is:* Circle *Rogers* and *view of personality*. What did Rogers say about personality? *Answer Before You Answer:* Rogers believed in the goodness of the individual. If you are not sure, use POE. Cross off (A) because it is extreme and untrue (is that *always* the case?), and (C) is a behavioral explanation of personality. (D) and (E) were not statements of Rogers.

98. **B** *Ask It Like It Is:* Circle *acetylcholine*. It's related to what disease? *Answer Before You Answer:* Alzheimer's. If you don't remember, you may remember that dopamine is somehow tied to Parkinson's, so you can cross off (A). If you have reviewed disorders enough, you will also know that it is not tied to (C), (D), or (E), so the answer must be (B).

99. **B** *Ask It Like It Is:* Why do babies lack clear vision shortly after birth? *Answer Before You Answer:* Not all neural connections are in place at birth. If you don't know, use POE to get rid of what you can. (E) is way off (aqueous humor is in the eye). Glial cells do not deflect messages so (C) is out, and myelination is a tight coat of lipids, so watch out for (D).

100. **B** *Ask It Like It Is:* The study is about brain development, and Group I had no stimulation whereas Group II did. What are the likely results? *Answer Before You Answer:* Group II will show greater brain development. Although this is the last question and it is quite long, it is not hard if you use your common sense and POE. Evaluate each answer choice to see which shows that Group II has greater brain development. Because Group I rats had no stimulation, will their brains be bigger? Will there be no difference? Get rid of (A) and (C). (D) and (E) are essentially the same answer, inserted to confuse you. The answer must be (B).

SECTION II

1. Essay number one is worth nine points. Two points are awarded for defining perspectives and explaining why there are many perspectives in the field of psychology. Two points are awarded for describing and giving an example of one of the perspectives, and another two points for doing the same for another perspective. One point is given for comparing/contrasting the two chosen perspectives. One point is given for accurately explaining how a psychologist of one of the perspectives would work with the example student, and one point is given for doing the same with the other chosen perspective.

This is what our "student" chose to do for her essays. She scored an eight out of nine on this essay. Use this as a sample of a high-scoring essay.

Sample Essay

The human psyche is complicated and, thus, the field that studies it is equally complicated. To have a single paradigm, you have to have something measurable and definable, such as the structure of the atom or the process of gestation. Fields such as chemistry and biology have objective elements with which to create a paradigm. The human psyche, however, cannot be measured or defined in that way, so while most scientific fields have a single accepted paradigm, psychology is comprised of a variety of perspectives, and psychologists typically align themselves with one of the perspectives.

For example, one of the first perspectives on psychology was the psychodynamic perspective forumlated by Sigmund Freud. Through his clinical work, Freud came to believe that a person's thoughts and behaviors were a product of motives competing for expression. Further, he felt that much of this struggle took place beneath the consciousness of the individual, similar to an "iceberg"— the tip of the iceberg is visible at the surface, but the bulk of it lies beneath the water. Today, the psychodynamic perspective is still popular among clinicians, and can often shed light on research findings through the use of the case study, its main method of research.

Another popular perspective on psychology is the behaviorist perspective. Behaviorism arose partly in opposition to the psychoanalytic approach. Behaviorists believe that you can't know anything about what you can't see, so they focus almost exclusively on behavior as it is observed through experimentation. They believe that all behavior is the result of consequences and conditioning. Ivan Pavlov was instrumental in the creation of the field through his accidental discovery of what is now known as classical conditioning—dogs learning to salivate at the anticipation of food even when no food is present. B. F. Skinner was also very instrumental in the development of behaviorism into a full-fledged perspective through his creation of the Skinner box—a box in which various animals were put and then conditioned to exhibit certain behaviors.

In addressing individuals, psychoanalysts and behaviorists take very different approaches. A psychoanalyst who was working with Margot, the anorexic sixteen-year-old, would spend a lot of time delving into her past to try to uncover unconscious motives for her behavior. A behaviorist, on the other hand, would not be concerned with the cause of the anorexia, but would instead work out a behavior modification program to help Margot over the problem. For example, the behaviorist might have Margot eat something small and then provide her with positive reinforcement. After a while, they would probably only provide the reinforcement if she ate something bigger. Although both methods might reach the same end, the two together would likely achieve the greatest long-term success.

2. Essay number two is worth seven points. Two points are awarded for defining classical conditioning and giving an example, plus explaining how it could be used to improve a prisoner's behavior. Two points are awarded for defining positive and negative reinforcement and giving an example of each, plus explaining how they could be used to improve a prisoner's behavior. Two points are awarded for defining shaping and giving an example, plus explaining how it could be used to improve a prisoner's behavior. One point is given for applying one of the learning techniques to modify a thief's behavior.

This is what our "student" chose to do for her essays. She scored a seven out of seven on this essay. Use this as a sample of a high-scoring essay.

Sample Essay

Although the concept sounds fine, prisons just don't seem to work. Instead of rehabilitating prisoners, they create a separate culture in which crime and criminal thinking are the norm. Instead of putting convicted criminals into a system that is destined to fail, a rehabilitation setting could be created using operant conditioning. Operant conditioning is the conditioning of behavior through the association of a desired behavior with some type of reward. For example, with animals, if a scientist wanted to teach a pigeon to peck only at selected artistic works, he could condition the pigeon to do so by rewarding him when he pecked at those works, and punishing him when he pecked at others. The same thing could be done with criminals. To get a criminal to not want to commit a crime again, a psychologist could condition an aversive response into the criminal whenever he saw—and eventually whenever he thought of—the crime.

Another option would be to use positive and negative reinforcement to shape a criminal's behavior. Positive reinforcement, giving a reward to someone for doing the right thing, could be used to provide criminals with needed or desired items for X period of time of good behavior. Similarly, negative reinforcement is the removal of something bad as a reward for good behavior. Therefore, a criminal, who would most likely start out under serious restrictions, would be granted more and more freedom, the longer he demonstrated the desired behavior.

Finally, shaping is a great way to mold someone's behavior. Shaping involves first praising actions that are remotely close to what you want to achieve, and then later praising actions only as they get closer and closer to the desired behavior. For example, at the beginning of the process, if a criminal does anything right, he is praised or rewarded. Then, after he begins to consistently demonstrate good behaviors, he is only praised or rewarded when he sustains that good behavior for longer and longer periods of time.

Shaping could be used to modify a thief's behavior so that he will never steal again. In the beginning, the thief is praised simply for using his own things. After he begins to consistently use his own things, the psychologist could begin to put him into more tempting situations, and then praise him when he doesn't take anything. Once the thief overcomes a low-level temptation—like the lunch room—he could be taken to a K-Mart, then a Macy's, then a jewelry store. Each time, he would be praised at first for lasting without taking anything for five minutes, then ten, and so on. Once the K-Mart didn't seem tempting anymore, he could be brought to the next level and again shaped into the right kind of behavior. This could not be accomplished in a prison setting because he would never be allowed out into the real world so he would never overcome his temptations.

21

Practice Test 2

AP® Psychology Exam

DO NOT OPEN THIS BOOKLET UNTIL YOU ARE TOLD TO DO SO.

At a Glance
Total Time
1 hour and ten minutes
Number of Questions
100
Percent of Total Grade
66 2/3%
Writing Instrument
Pen required

Instructions

Section I of this exam contains 100 multiple-choice questions. Fill in only the ovals for numbers 1 through 100 on your answer sheet.

Indicate all of your answers to the multiple-choice questions on the answer sheet. No credit will be given for anything written in this exam booklet, but you may use the booklet for notes or scratch work. After you have decided which of the suggested answers is best, completely fill in the corresponding oval on the answer sheet. Give only one answer to each question. If you change an answer, be sure that the previous mark is erased completely. Here is a sample question and answer.

<u>Sample Question</u>   <u>Sample Answer</u>

Omaha is a

(A) state
(B) city
(C) country
(D) continent
(E) village

Use your time effectively, working as quickly as you can without losing accuracy. Do not spend too much time on any one question. Go on to other questions and come back to the ones you have not answered if you have time. It is not expected that everyone will know the answers to all of the multiple-choice questions.

About Guessing

Many candidates wonder whether or not to guess the answers to questions about which they are not certain. Multiple-choice scores are based on the number of questions answered correctly. Points are not deducted for incorrect answers, and no points are awarded for unanswered questions. Because points are not deducted for incorrect answers, you are encouraged to answer all multiple-choice questions. On any questions you do not know the answer to, you should eliminate as many choices as you can, and then select the best answer among the remaining choices.

This page intentionally left blank.

PSYCHOLOGY
SECTION I
Time—1 hour and 10 minutes
100 Questions

Directions: Each of the questions or incomplete statements below is followed by five answer choices. Select the one that is best in each case and then completely fill in the corresponding oval on the answer sheet.

1. Substances that are toxic to humans often taste

    (A) sour
    (B) sweet
    (C) salty
    (D) bitter
    (E) bland

2. Sigmund Freud was the founder of which of the following perspectives in psychology?

    (A) Biological perspective
    (B) Behavioral perspective
    (C) Cognitive perspective
    (D) Psychoanalytic perspective
    (E) Humanistic perspective

3. A behavior that is elicited automatically by an environmental stimulus is called a(n)

    (A) conditioned response
    (B) condition
    (C) aversive stimulus
    (D) reflex
    (E) drive

4. Emotional, cognitive, and behavioral tendencies that constitute underlying personality dimensions on which individuals vary are referred to as

    (A) traits
    (B) moods
    (C) temperaments
    (D) tenets
    (E) personalities

5. The field of psychology arose out of which of the following?

    (A) Biochemistry
    (B) Physics
    (C) Philosophy
    (D) Cross-cultural anthropology
    (E) Statistics

6. Six-month-old Sasha loves to play "peek-a-boo" with her mother, an indication that she has developed a sense of

    (A) play versus learning
    (B) transitivity
    (C) metacognition
    (D) attachment anxiety
    (E) object permanence

7. Studying a few subjects in great depth to investigate a rare condition is known as

    (A) an experiment
    (B) a case study
    (C) naturalistic observation
    (D) correlational research
    (E) longitudinal research

8. Which of the following is the most accurate definition of learning?

    (A) The result of a variety of experiences that temporarily shape behavior
    (B) An enduring change in an organism's behavior based on experience
    (C) The sole result of classical and operant conditioning
    (D) The association of experiences due to their occurrence in close proximity
    (E) A change in behavior that is not susceptible to extinction

GO ON TO THE NEXT PAGE.

9. A group of participants in a sleep study are to be deprived of sleep for four days. After their second sleepless night, participants may begin reporting which of the following?

(A) Hunger
(B) Thirst
(C) Lack of coordination
(D) Hallucinations
(E) Increased respiration

10. Conflicting attitudes or behaviors that create tension within a person's mind are referred to as

(A) persuasion
(B) general adaptation syndrome
(C) serial position
(D) cognitive dissonance
(E) fluid intelligence

11. Endorphins are chemicals that

(A) elevate mood and reduce pain
(B) increase alertness and reduce drowsiness
(C) lower or raise the threshold for the firing of neurons
(D) cannot cross the blood-brain barrier
(E) always elicit an action potential from a neuron

12. Nell decides not to throw her stuffed animal in the toilet after she witnesses her brother Matthew being punished for putting his stuffed animal in the toilet. Nell's decision exemplifies

(A) prepared learning
(B) tutelage
(C) scheduled reinforcement
(D) shaping
(E) vicarious conditioning

13. A game show like *Jeopardy!* asks players to demonstrate which of the following types of intelligence?

(A) IQ
(B) Crystallized intelligence
(C) Fluid intelligence
(D) General intelligence
(E) Multiple intelligence

14. Which of the following is often true of memory recall?

(A) People are more likely to recall information that is congruent with their prior schemas.
(B) People will not recall information unless it is stored in working memory.
(C) People have no ability to recall information that has been extinguished.
(D) People will recall nonsense syllables more rapidly than they will sets of numbers.
(E) People will not recall information for which they did not create a mnemonic device.

15. Objects that absorb light appear

(A) black
(B) white
(C) dark
(D) bright
(E) ultraviolet

16. Chantal says that her mother is domineering and overbearing. All of Chantal's friends agree that she is the one that has these characteristics, not her mother. Freud would suggest that Chantal's behavior exemplifies which of the following defense mechanisms?

(A) Repression
(B) Regression
(C) Projection
(D) Displacement
(E) Denial

17. A psychologist who believes in the humanistic perspective would be most likely to agree with which of the following statements?

(A) All behavior can be traced to human biological functions.
(B) People's behavior is primarily a result of free will.
(C) Behavior results from conditioning.
(D) Human behavior is a result of conflicting unconscious motives.
(E) People are able to understand and analyze the behavior of humans.

GO ON TO THE NEXT PAGE.

18. Which of the following lobes of the brain is central to visual sensation and perception?

    (A) Occipital
    (B) Temporal
    (C) Parietal
    (D) Frontal
    (E) Cerebral

19. In order for the mean, mode and median of a data set to be equal, the distribution must be

    (A) positively skewed
    (B) asymmetrical
    (C) negatively skewed
    (D) normal
    (E) abnormal

20. The adaptive response of a six-month-old child who shows distress when an attachment figure leaves is known as

    (A) secure attachment
    (B) centration
    (C) object permanence
    (D) separation anxiety
    (E) detachment adaptation

21. B. F. Skinner was well known for his work involving the

    (A) biological perspective
    (B) behavioral perspective
    (C) cognitive perspective
    (D) psychodynamic perspective
    (E) humanistic perspective

22. A researcher has asked participants to complete a questionnaire that will assess how frequently in their lives they experience various emotions using a scale from 1 (never) to 5 (very often). The researcher is particularly interested in the relationship between guilt feelings and other emotions. This researcher is most likely conducting which of the following types of research?

    (A) Demographic
    (B) Observational
    (C) Correlational
    (D) Experimental
    (E) Statistical

23. Which of the following is the term used to describe a number of psychotic disorders that involve disturbances in nearly every dimension of human psychology including thought, perception, behavior, and communication?

    (A) Schizophrenia
    (B) Mental retardation
    (C) Dissociative disorder
    (D) Depression
    (E) Endorphisms

24. Which of the following most accurately describes the firing of a neuron?

    (A) It occurs gradually as the neuron reaches hyperpolarization.
    (B) It has an all-or-none quality: it either happens, or it does not.
    (C) Its strength diminishes as it travels along the soma.
    (D) It occurs only in the post-synaptic neuron.
    (E) Stronger stimulations make a neuron fire harder.

25. Xavier is beginning his first year of college. He is eager to find a few other freshmen to "hang out" with. Psychologists would say that Xavier is motivated by a(n)

    (A) fraternization need
    (B) assimilation need
    (C) attachment need
    (D) affiliation need
    (E) loneliness need

26. The fact that Will was better able to memorize his lines in the school play after finding out the meanings behind the words best illustrates the influence of

    (A) chunking
    (B) shaping
    (C) maintenance rehearsal
    (D) elaborative rehearsal
    (E) semantic memory

GO ON TO THE NEXT PAGE.

27. The role of the outer ear is to

   (A) transduce sound waves to stimulate the ossicles
   (B) conduct sound by exciting the cilia in the inner ear
   (C) protect the eardrum while it transduces sound
   (D) convey auditory messages to the temporal lobes
   (E) collect and focus sounds from the air

28. At the outset of a study on eating habits, a researcher asks participants a variety of questions, including whether they typically eat breakfast. Whether or not a person eats breakfast is a(n)

   (A) categorical variable
   (B) continuous variable
   (C) dependent variable
   (D) independent variable
   (E) conditioned variable

29. In most people, the left hemisphere of the brain is dominant for

   (A) language
   (B) logic
   (C) analytical reasoning
   (D) mathematical reasoning
   (E) spatial reasoning

30. A piano teacher is helping a student learn a new piece. At first, she praises the student for playing correct notes. After the student begins to show proficiency with the notes, the teacher only praises the student when he adds the proper dynamics and interpretation to the segments he plays. The teacher's method of instruction is an example of which of the following types of training techniques?

   (A) Negative reinforcement
   (B) Negative punishment
   (C) Shaping
   (D) Chaining
   (E) Discriminating

31. After discovering that she was at the early stages of an eating disorder, Maria's parents insisted Maria see a therapist. Although Maria attended the therapy sessions, she was late, uncooperative, and even hostile. After some time, her counselor began to explore Maria's feelings of hostility and found that they actually were feelings she held for her parents. Maria's uncooperativeness and hostility toward her counselor is an example of

   (A) suppression
   (B) conflicting motives
   (C) transference
   (D) countertransference
   (E) reaction formation

32. Tonya runs into an old schoolmate on the street. During their brief conversation, Tonya is unable to recall the schoolmate's name. Days later, she remembers the name out of the blue. To remember the name "out of the blue" is an example of

   (A) tip-of-the-tongue phenomenon
   (B) chunking
   (C) deductive reasoning
   (D) inductive reasoning
   (E) parallelism

33. Hypnosis has been used effectively to diminish

   (A) alcohol abuse
   (B) chronic pain
   (C) night terrors
   (D) kinesthetic abilities
   (E) Alzheimer's disease

34. Which of the following best explains why mnemonic devices such as the method of loci are typically effective at helping individuals remember information?

   (A) They encode information and store it in STM so that it is easy to retrieve.
   (B) They "file" information in a predictable order so that it is easy to retrieve.
   (C) They enhance memory capacity by augmenting representational fields.
   (D) They encourage individuals to write down everything they wish to remember.
   (E) They connect new information to information already stored in LTM.

GO ON TO THE NEXT PAGE.

35. Quinn awoke from a dream, shaking and covered with sweat. When his wife asked him what had happened, he said he had dreamed he was falling to his death. Quinn's experience is often categorized as a(n)

    (A) hallucination
    (B) phobia
    (C) narcoleptic event
    (D) night terror
    (E) nightmare

36. Which of the following terms describes the behavioral component of negative attitudes toward particular groups?

    (A) Bias
    (B) Conditioning
    (C) Catharsis
    (D) Passive aggression
    (E) Discrimination

37. Which of the following disorders is the result of an abnormality of the twenty-first chromosomal pair?

    (A) Bipolar disorder
    (B) Huntington's Chorea
    (C) Down's syndrome
    (D) Obsessive-compulsive disorder
    (E) Histrionic personality disorder

38. All of the following are examples of punishment EXCEPT

    (A) grounding a teenager for staying out past curfew
    (B) spanking a child for misbehavior
    (C) permanently revoking the driving privileges of a third-time DWI driver
    (D) refusing to return the boss' phone call after not getting the expected raise
    (E) placing a puppy that has shredded a chair in a confinement cage

39. Carl Jung's concept of a repository of ideas, feelings, and symbols shared by all humans and passed genetically from one generation to another is known as Jung's theory of the

    (A) cultural subconscious
    (B) general awareness
    (C) heritability coefficients
    (D) collective unconscious
    (E) integrated intelligence

40. According to Dr. William Sears, noted authority on infants and child-rearing, infant brain development is, in part, influenced by longer and more frequent periods of active sleeping and dreaming or

    (A) REM sleep
    (B) NREM sleep
    (C) Delta sleep
    (D) Stage 3 sleep
    (E) Stage 4 sleep

41. The rules that govern the placement of words and phrases in a sentence are called

    (A) semantics
    (B) grammar
    (C) syntax
    (D) phonemes
    (E) morphemes

42. An animal is not likely to associate a conditioned stimulus (CS) with an unconditioned stimulus (UCS) if the

    (A) delay between the CS and the UCS is too long
    (B) interval schedule between the two stimuli is variable
    (C) fixed rational schedule between the two stimuli is altered
    (D) interstimulus ratio is variable
    (E) CS and the UCS occur simultaneously

43. All of the following are examples of secondary drives EXCEPT

    (A) recreation
    (B) sex
    (C) approval
    (D) friendship
    (E) exercise

44. Which of the following is an example of a continuous variable?

    (A) Race
    (B) Species
    (C) Intelligence
    (D) Gender
    (E) Birth order

GO ON TO THE NEXT PAGE.

45. The staggering and slurred speech of a person who has consumed too much alcohol is most likely the result of altered functioning in the

    (A) limbic system
    (B) thalamus
    (C) sensorimotor cortex
    (D) amygdala
    (E) cerebellum

46. After a big Thanksgiving dinner replete with turkey, stuffing, and all, Karmina becomes violently ill. In the weeks that follow this event, Karmina feels an unexplainable aversion to chicken, one of her favorite dishes. Karmina's feeling about chicken reflects

    (A) response generalization
    (B) latent learning
    (C) prepared learning
    (D) unconditioned stimulus response
    (E) stimulus generalization

47. Perception refers to the process by which

    (A) receptors gather information from the environment
    (B) sense organs transmit information to the brain for initial processing
    (C) the brain organizes and interprets sensations
    (D) the brain minimizes responses to stimuli that do not change
    (E) individuals evaluate stimuli

48. The driver of a car that has pulled up next to you at a red light turns up the volume on her radio. The increase in perceived sound that you experience is primarily due to

    (A) neurons firing more intensely
    (B) increased secretions by the pituitary gland
    (C) changing frequency of soundwaves
    (D) more neurons firing more frequently
    (E) increased speed of sensations traveling down the "what" pathway

49. Which of the following illustrates why most people can detect the difference between Coke and Pepsi most of the time?

    (A) Subliminal perception
    (B) Absolute threshold
    (C) Signal detection theory
    (D) Difference threshold
    (E) Weber's law

50. Complete the following example using deductive reasoning: All students who attend the Peddie School study Latin. Some students who study Latin also study calculus. Jerome is a student at the Peddie School. It can therefore be determined that

    (A) Jerome studies calculus
    (B) Jerome studies Latin
    (C) Jerome studies both calculus and Latin
    (D) Jerome studies either calculus or Latin
    (E) Jerome studies neither Latin nor calculus

51. Lynda is a confident, capable woman who takes responsibility for her own actions. Lynda has a(n)

    (A) manic coping strategy
    (B) discriminative expectancy
    (C) internal locus of control
    (D) external locus of control
    (E) generalized expectancy

52. Which of the following refers to the benefit of having an emotional release to reduce aggressive tendencies?

    (A) James-Lange theory of emotion
    (B) Counterconditioning
    (C) Catharsis hypothesis
    (D) Transference
    (E) The two-factor theory

53. Which of the following terms refers to the body's tendency to maintain a relatively constant state that permits cells to live and function?

    (A) Perceptual constancy
    (B) Set-point
    (C) Homeostasis
    (D) Kinesthesia
    (E) Affect regulation

GO ON TO THE NEXT PAGE.

54. Periods of special sensitivity to specific types of learning that shape the capacity for future development are known as

   (A) maturation periods
   (B) critical periods
   (C) primary development periods
   (D) secondary development periods
   (E) shaping periods

55. According to researchers Darley and Latanne, bystander intervention occurs when a large number of people witness a crime. What social psychology concept could best explain this phenomenon?

   (A) Social loafing
   (B) Prejudice
   (C) Conformity
   (D) Obedience
   (E) Diffusion of responsibility

56. Lisa, determined to get away from her abusive father, leaves home and moves in with an abusive boyfriend. Lisa's choice of an abusive boyfriend is an example of Sigmund Freud's theory of

   (A) psychoanalytic conflict
   (B) opposing motives
   (C) id, ego, and superego
   (D) behavioral dysfunction
   (E) cognitive dissonance

57. Piaget proposed that children develop knowledge by

   (A) constructing reality out of their own experiences
   (B) participating in traditional learning environments
   (C) responding to physiological changes
   (D) modeling various cultural influences
   (E) drawing on genetically predisposed knowledge

58. A longitudinal study would be useful in assessing which of the following?

   (A) Age differences
   (B) Gender differences
   (C) Cultural environments
   (D) Changes in behavior over time
   (E) Sequential studies

59. Calvin's fear of dogs was so great that he could not even visit his friends who had dogs or who lived in a neighborhood that had a lot of dogs. Once he sought help, he worked to overcome this fear first by witnessing his counselor playing with a dog and then, after a while, by actually touching and petting a dog himself. The method used to help Calvin overcome his fears is known as

   (A) countertransference
   (B) peer-counselor alliance
   (C) rational-emotive therapy
   (D) flooding
   (E) systematic desensitization

60. A clinical psychologist who is working with an aggressive child seeks to understand the child's behavior in light of the dynamics of the entire family. Which of the following best identifies the approach the psychologist has chosen?

   (A) Cognitive social approach
   (B) Behavioral approach
   (C) Psychoanalytic approach
   (D) Paternal approach
   (E) Systems approach

61. The manual of clinical syndromes published by the American Psychiatric Association that is used for descriptive diagnosis is commonly called the

   (A) *ANOVA*
   (B) *DSM-IV-TR*
   (C) *APA Desk Reference*
   (D) *Diagnosis of Disorders Digest*
   (E) *Clinicians Reference Manual III*

GO ON TO THE NEXT PAGE.

62. Which of the following samples would be considered most representative of male college students?

   (A) A group of thirty fraternity brothers from Penn State.
   (B) A random sample taken between classes in the business wing of various universities.
   (C) Sixty male members of each class from Princeton, Yale, Harvard, Dartmouth, and Columbia.
   (D) Twenty male members of each class from a cross-section of colleges and universities.
   (E) One-thousand male college graduates from across the country.

63. The myelin sheath that covers the axons of most neurons serves to do which of the following?

   (A) Increase the number of messages a dendrite can receive.
   (B) Increase the speed with which messages can be transmitted.
   (C) Maintain the amount of neurotransmitter needed to create an action potential.
   (D) Decrease the amount of information a dendrite can convey in one firing.
   (E) Decrease the amount of time it takes for an axon to fire across the synaptic cleft.

Questions 64-65 refer to the situation described below.

The book *A Clockwork Orange* portrays a violent individual being forced to watch violent films while simultaneously being induced by medication to vomit as a means of "curing" him. During this "treatment," the music of Beethoven is played in the background. As a result, the violent individual becomes ill not only when he views physical violence, but also whenever he hears Beethoven.

64. In this experiment, Beethoven's music is the

   (A) conditioned response
   (B) unconditioned response
   (C) conditioned stimulus
   (D) unconditioned stimulus
   (E) neutral stimulus

65. In this experiment, the individual's illness in response to the medication is the

   (A) conditioned response
   (B) unconditioned response
   (C) conditioned stimulus
   (D) unconditioned stimulus
   (E) neutral stimulus

66. Which of the following questions best frames the nature-nurture controversy?

   (A) To what degree is human behavior a result of free will versus determinism?
   (B) To what degree do external conditioning stimuli override individual loci of focus in regard to human behavior?
   (C) To what degree does the human capacity to nurture its young parallel other species in nature?
   (D) To what degree do unconscious motives versus potential consequences shape human behavior?
   (E) To what degree do inborn biological processes versus environmental events determine human behavior?

GO ON TO THE NEXT PAGE.

67. After a neuron has fired,

(A) a resting potential returns
(B) a graded potential is formed
(C) an action potential occurs
(D) hyperpolarization results
(E) ionization decreases

68. Iconic memory refers to

(A) visual sensory registries
(B) olfactory sensory registries
(C) frontal sensory registries
(D) STM sensory registries
(E) LTM sensory registries

69. Aaron Beck's negative triad of beliefs, which explains the cycle of depression by examining negative thoughts about self and the world, exemplifies this type of therapy.

(A) Psychoanalytic
(B) Cognitive
(C) Humanistic
(D) Behavioral
(E) Medical

70. While swimming in the ocean, Ivan is frightened by a dark shadow in the water even before he has the chance to identify what the shadow is. The synaptic connections taking place during this incident of fright are best described by which of the following?

(A) Messages are sent from the thalamus directly to the amygdala.
(B) Messages are sent from the thalamus to the "what" and "where" pathways.
(C) Messages are sent from the parasympathetic nervous system to the cerebral cortex.
(D) Messages are sent from the frontal lobes to the pituitary gland.
(E) Messages are sent from the occipital lobes to the parietal lobes.

71. A listener-sponsored radio station wants to estimate the amount of money the typical supporter contributes during a fund-drive. In a sample of 30 supporters, it was discovered that 22 of them gave $60, six of them gave $1,000, and two of them gave $10,000. Based on this sample, which of the following measures of central tendency would provide the most useful information to the radio station?

(A) Median
(B) Mode
(C) Histogram
(D) ANOVA
(E) *P*-value

72. Marie and Bengt decide to go to their favorite restaurant for dinner. When they enter the restaurant, they both begin to salivate at the idea that they will soon be eating their favorite entrée. The fact that they are anticipating the taste of the food even before it gets to them is an example of

(A) bottom-up processing
(B) top-down processing
(C) retroactive interference
(D) proactive interference
(E) sensory restriction

73. The instrument that has traditionally been used in sleep research to assess activity in the brain is called the

(A) signal detection device
(B) computerized axial tomography (CAT)
(C) magnetic resonance imaging (MRI)
(D) positron emission tomography (PET)
(E) electroencephalograph (EEG)

74. Curtis stares at an image of a yellow star for a full minute. When he moves his gaze to a blank piece of white paper, he is likely to see an afterimage that is

(A) green
(B) yellow
(C) red
(D) blue
(E) black

GO ON TO THE NEXT PAGE.

75. The obsessive fear of being in places or situations from which escape might be difficult is known as

 (A) claustrophobia
 (B) arachnophobia
 (C) social phobia
 (D) agoraphobia
 (E) paranoia

76. When a person experiences a discrepancy between an attitude and a behavior, the person experiences

 (A) cognitive dissonance
 (B) dissociation
 (C) behavioral dysfunction
 (D) metacognition
 (E) countertransference

77. People who have previously not gotten along are often able to put aside their differences in the face of a mutual crisis. Their need to work together is often referred to as a(n)

 (A) communal goal
 (B) superordinate goal
 (C) subordinate goal
 (D) alliance formation
 (E) truce agreement

78. Which of the following accomplishments accurately reflects why Wilhelm Wundt is sometimes referred to as the "father of psychology?"

 (A) He founded the first psychological laboratory in the late nineteenth century.
 (B) He developed psychoanalytical theory through his work in clinical environments.
 (C) He conducted experiments throughout the nineteenth century that led to the belief that all behavior is learned.
 (D) His research demonstrated that psychology should be free from all philosophical questions.
 (E) He created a standard of measurement in the late nineteenth century that later came to be known as inferential statistics.

79. Although they disagreed with his personal infidelities, many Americans supported President Bill Clinton's position and policy decisions during his term in office. This change in behavior to resolve the cognitive conflict isdichotomy of opinion demonstrates a split in

 (A) external locus of control
 (B) internal validity
 (C) self-representation
 (D) attitudinal coherence
 (E) approval ratings

80. Sanja hears a sound that she recognizes as the front door being shut. In order for her to detect the sound and process it so that she knows what it is, Sanja's ear funnels the sound waves to the inner ear in order to stimulate the cilia of the inner ear. This is a critical step in the process of

 (A) auditory transduction
 (B) olfactory perception
 (C) sensory interaction
 (D) decibel cognition
 (E) kinesthetic transference

81. Which of the following most accurately explains why a pool with water temperature of 82 degrees may feel cool to a person who has been sunbathing yet warm to a person who has been inside in the air conditioning?

 (A) Sensory restriction
 (B) Perceptual constancy
 (C) Relative clarity
 (D) Absolute threshold
 (E) Sensory adaptation

82. According to the Gestalt theory of perception, being able to identify a three-sided object as being a triangle, even though it is partially blocked from view is an example of

 (A) proximity
 (B) similarity
 (C) closure
 (D) continuity
 (E) connectedness

GO ON TO THE NEXT PAGE.

83. Psychoactive substances are drugs that alter consciousness by

    (A) inducing the secretion of excitatory hormones into the bloodstream
    (B) imitating the behaviors of various pheromones
    (C) facilitating or inhibiting neural transmission at the synapse
    (D) increasing an individual's hypnotic susceptibility
    (E) flooding post-synaptic receptors with subliminal commands

84. A child is frightened by the sudden barking of a neighbor's dog. Once her mother picks her up, the child begins to calm down as which of the following biological processes occurs?

    (A) The parasympathetic nervous system resumes control and reverses the sympathetic responses.
    (B) The sympathetic nervous system resumes control and reverses the parasympathetic responses.
    (C) The autonomic nervous system resumes control and reverses the peripheral responses.
    (D) The peripheral nervous system resumes control and reverses the autonomic responses.
    (E) The endocrine system resumes control and reverses the responses brought on by neurotransmitters.

85. The relaying of sensory information to the cerebral cortex is the primary function of the

    (A) hypothalamus
    (B) cerebellum
    (C) reticular formation
    (D) thalamus
    (E) medulla oblongata

86. Which of the following is an example of a result of operant conditioning?

    (A) Milo starts at the sound of a buzzer because it sounds very similar to the alarm clock that wakes him every morning.
    (B) Paula is promoted to vice president of her company, and vows to not lose touch with her employees.
    (C) Rebecca cancels her credit card to avoid paying the annual fee but plans to reinstate it in the new year.
    (D) Ashmed speaks louder than usual when he talks to his mother on the phone because she is hard of hearing.
    (E) Pika avoids eating red meat after she hears several horror stories about mad cow disease.

87. Which of the following best states why the study of twins is significant to the field of behavioral genetics?

    (A) If a psychological attribute is genetically influenced, then fraternal twins are more likely to share this attribute than are identical twins or other siblings.
    (B) If a psychological attribute is genetically influenced, then siblings reared together are more likely to share it than are identical or fraternal twins who are reared apart.
    (C) The degree of relatedness in MZ twins can be determined through studying the behavioral genetics of related DZ twins.
    (D) If a psychological attribute is genetically influenced, then identical twins are more likely to share this attribute than are fraternal twins and other siblings.
    (E) Phenotypic variances in twins are more obvious than in other siblings because twins have a 1.0 degree of relatedness.

88. Detection of a just-noticeable difference (JND) depends on the

    (A) presence of a "no stimulus" control and the sensitivity of the signal-detection equipment
    (B) initial determination of the absolute threshold and the variation of the difference threshold
    (C) frequency of the existing stimulus and the presence of one or more sensory modalities
    (D) establishment of a 50 percent "hit" rate and a long enough series of trials
    (E) intensity of the new stimulus and that of the stimulus already present

GO ON TO THE NEXT PAGE.

89. Lizette and her family watch the sunset over the ocean. While walking home in the increasing darkness, Lizette notices that she can no longer distinguish the colors of objects. Which of the following best explains why Lizette cannot see color in dim light?

(A) Rods, which are specialized for color vision, require more light to be activated whereas cones, which produce images in black, white, and gray, allow for vision in dim light.

(B) Cones, which are specialized for color vision, require more light to be activated whereas rods, which produce images in black, white, and gray, allow for vision in dim light.

(C) Cones, which are specialized for black and white vision, require a small amount of light to be activated whereas rods, which produce images in color, require greater amounts of light for vision.

(D) The receptive fields in the retina respond to the loss of light through light adaptation, the process of rapidly adjusting to a diminution of light.

(E) In order to perceive aspects of color such as hue, brightness, and saturation, rods require a great deal of light, while cones can perceive images in black, white, and gray with little light.

90. In the "cocktail party phenomenon," an individual can focus on one conversation and filter out all the surrounding stimuli. This is an example of

(A) sensory adaptation
(B) selective attention
(C) just noticeable difference
(D) continuity
(E) motion parallax

91. Jay suffers from periods of amnesia and frequent loss of a sense of personal identity. It is likely Jay has a(n)

(A) schizophrenic disorder
(B) associative disorder
(C) antisocial personality disorder
(D) manic-depressive disorder
(E) dissociative disorder

92. Which of the following correctly categorizes the components of Ivan Pavlov's research on conditioning?

(A) The dogs (subjects) were presented with food (CS) while also being presented with the sights and sounds of the presenter (UCS). After a time, the dogs salivated in response to the presenter (UCR).

(B) The dogs (subjects) were presented with food (UCR) while also being presented with the sights and sounds of the presenter (CR). After a time, the dogs salivated in response to the presenter (CS).

(C) The dogs (subjects) were presented with food (UCS) while also being presented with the sights and sounds of the presenter (CS). After a time, the dogs salivated in response to the presenter (CR).

(D) The dogs (subjects) were presented with food (CR) while also being presented with the sights and sounds of the presenter (UCR). After a time, the dogs salivated in response to the presenter (UCS).

(E) The dogs (subjects) were presented with food (neutral stimulus) while also being presented with the sights and sounds of the presenter (UCS). After a time, the dogs salivated in response to the presenter (CR).

93. In Pavlov's conditioning of dogs, the point at which the dogs salivated at the sound of the tone without the food being present is referred to as

(A) an unconditioned stimulus
(B) acquisition
(C) discrimination
(D) generalization
(E) spontaneous recovery

94. In developmental research, studying the same subjects over time is known as

(A) cross-sectional research
(B) cross-cultural research
(C) in-cohort sequential research
(D) longitudinal research
(E) correlational research

GO ON TO THE NEXT PAGE.

95. The goal of projective personality tests such as the Rorschach and Thematic Apperception Test (TAT) is to

   (A) gain insight into potential biochemical abnormalities
   (B) uncover unconscious thoughts and feelings
   (C) assess basic personality traits
   (D) assess cultural influences on personality
   (E) predict how personality is suited to particular occupations

96. Which of the following accurately summarizes a depressed person's view according to Aaron Beck's negative triad theory?

   (A) Depressed individuals cope with the three primary stresses—change, death, and monetary instability—through withdrawal.
   (B) Depressed individuals believe that when they are in a group, at least three individuals will view them negatively.
   (C) Depressed individuals hold a negative view of themselves, the world, and their futures.
   (D) Depressed individuals view the world in three stages—separation anxiety, development of an external locus of control, and failure to achieve.
   (E) Depressed individuals tend to form friendships with other depressed individuals, usually in groups of three.

97. Which of the following is an example of imprinting?

   (A) A mother eagle will fly under her young while they are learning to fly in case they begin to fall.
   (B) A newborn gosling will "attach" to the first moving object it sees, usually its mother.
   (C) An infant who is left by its primary care givers for significant periods of time develops an indifference to their presence.
   (D) A mother cat teaches her kittens how to clean themselves.
   (E) A premature infant grows rapidly in part as a result of constantly being held by a primary caregiver.

98. Each of the following is a step taken by a therapist who is employing systematic desensitization EXCEPT

   (A) helping the client experience the desired state of relaxation through hypnosis
   (B) teaching the client to relax through techniques such as deep breathing
   (C) constructing a hierarchy of feared images
   (D) instructing the client to picture each fearful image while maintaining a relaxed state
   (E) encouraging the client to confront her fears in real life

99. Max was typically out of control whenever he attended preschool. Teachers tried time-outs and other punishments to no avail. His parents and the school decided to work with Max by giving him a sticker each time he behaved for a full hour. Once he accumulated ten stickers, he could present them to his parents who would give him a reward. The method the school and parents chose to employ is referred to as

   (A) negative reinforcement
   (B) a token economy
   (C) a point value system
   (D) negative punishment
   (E) classical conditioning

100. Which of the following best states a conclusion of Stanley Milgram's study of obedience?

   (A) When faced with a difficult decision, people are more likely to follow the opinions of the crowd than to diverge from those opinions.
   (B) When challenged to commit a crime, people will most often refuse if they are not coerced, but will agree if an authority figure coerces them.
   (C) When asked to inflict pain on others, people are likely to inflict mild amounts of pain without remorse.
   (D) When asked to participate in a study, people are more likely to agree if they are offered some sort of compensation.
   (E) When an authority figure is present, people are more likely to obey orders than to question the wisdom of the orders.

END OF SECTION I

PSYCHOLOGY
SECTION II
Time — 50 minutes
Percent of total grade — $33\frac{1}{3}$

Directions: You have 50 minutes to answer BOTH of the following questions. It is not enough to answer a question by merely listing facts. You should present a cogent argument based on your critical analysis of the question posed using appropriate psychological terminology.

1. Jack, a three-year-old boy, has been throwing many tantrums lately and has been ignoring his parents' directions. Jack's parents are growing increasingly frustrated by his oppositional behavior. They decide to consult a developmental expert to ask for advice in dealing with their child. The developmental expert suggests that they consider the following factors in understanding Jack's behavior:

- Egocentrism
- Pre-conventional morality
- Erikson's stage of Initiative vs. Guilt
- Observational learning

   A. Define and provide an example of the application of each of the concepts listed above to explaining Jack's behavior.

   B. Explain how Jack's parents should integrate the knowledge of his developmental stage in their plan to deal with his tantrum behavior.

2. A major tenet of psychology is research and experimentation.

   A. Design a study to ascertain the impact of eating breakfast on school performance. Begin with your hypothesis, then outline your methods of research, defining and illustrating each. Be sure to address each of the following:

   - Variables
   - Representative sampling
   - Control group

   B. A school board is interested in your findings because they are considering instituting a before-school meal program. Explain how you would use statistics to clearly present your findings to them.

STOP

END OF EXAM

22

Practice Test 2: Answers and Explanations

Section 1

1. **D** *Ask It Like It Is:* Circle *toxic* and *taste. Answer Before You Answer:* Bitter or nasty. Toxic substances won't be (B) *sweet* or (E) *bland*, and probably not (C) *salty*. (D) *Bitter* is the strongest choice.

2. **D** *Ask It Like It Is:* Circle *Freud* and *perspectives. Answer Before You Answer:* Psychoanalytic. If you missed this one, you better hit the books.

3. **D** *Ask It Like It Is:* An automatic reaction to something is called a… *Answer Before You Answer:* Reflex. Rephrasing the question makes the answer much more obvious. Now use POE to quickly scan the answers. Watch out for (C) *aversive stimulus* and (E) *drive*.

4. **A** *Ask It Like It Is:* These things make up your personality. They are known as personality… *Answer Before You Answer:* Traits. If you are unsure, use POE. Are emotional, cognitive, and behavioral tendencies (A) *traits* that make up personality? Sounds good. Keep it and check the others. Are emotional, cognitive, and behavioral tendencies (B) *moods* that make up personality? No. Cross it off. Are emotional, cognitive, and behavioral tendencies (C) *temperaments* that make up personality? If you are unsure, leave it, although temperaments are more like moods. Are emotional, cognitive, and behavioral tendencies (D) *tenets* that make up personality? No, beliefs don't make up personality. Are emotional, cognitive, and behavioral tendencies (E) *personalities* that make up personality? No. (A) is your best choice.

5. **C** *Ask It Like It Is:* Psychology came from what origin? *Answer Before You Answer:* Philosophy. If you aren't sure, use POE to get rid of choices that wouldn't make sense. You need something that is concerned with thought processes and relationships, and is older than psychology. Cross off (A) *biochemistry*, (B) *physics*, and (E) *statistics* because none of these answers is concerned with thought processes. Watch out for (D) *cross-cultural anthropology*.

6. **E** *Ask It Like It Is:* She plays peek-a-boo, which means what developmentally? *Answer Before You Answer:* She knows that the fact that she cannot see her mother does not mean her mother is gone. In other words, she has developed object permanence. If you don't remember the term, use POE. Would a sense of (A) *playing versus learning* mean she knows her mother is not gone? No. Cross it off. Would a sense of (B) *transitivity* mean she knows her mother is not gone? No, it is something to do with transience or changing. Would a sense of (C) *metacognition* mean she knows her mother is not gone? She is too young for this level of complex thought. Would a sense of (D) *attachment anxiety* mean she knows her mother is not gone? No, it would mean the opposite. Would a sense of (E) *object permanence* mean she knows her mother is not gone? Bingo.

7. **B** *Ask It Like It Is*: Psychologists who study a few subjects in great depth are using….*Answer Before You Answer*: A case study. *Experiments* (A) show and effect relationships. *Naturalistic observation* (C) is often used by anthropologists to study people and animals in their natural environment. *Correlational research* (D) is used to study the relationship between or among variables. *Longitudinal research* (E) is used by developmental psychologists to assess change over time.

8. **B** *Ask It Like It Is:* Circle *definition of learning. Answer Before You Answer:* A change in behavior based on experience. Use POE to get rid of (A) because of the word *temporarily*, and (C) and (E) because they use extreme language. Learning involves a permanent change, not a mere association, so the answer is (B).

9. **D** *Ask It Like It Is:* If you don't sleep for two days, you may begin to experience… *Answer Before You Answer:* Hallucinations. If you are unsure, use POE. Sleepless doesn't mean without food and water so get rid of (A) *hunger* and (B) *thirst.* (E) is also way off base.

10. **D** *Ask It Like It Is:* When you struggle between what you want to do and what you ought to do, you are experiencing… *Answer Before You Answer: cognitive dissonance.* Watch out for (B), which is a trap answer. None of the other answer choices comes close to cognitive dissonance.

11. **A** *Ask It Like It Is:* Circle *endorphins.* What do they do? *Answer Before You Answer:* Make you feel good. Now use POE to find an answer that is close to yours. If you don't remember what endorphins do, POE will get rid of (D) and (E) because of the extreme language.

12. **E** *Ask It Like It Is:* Nell doesn't want to get in trouble like her brother did, so she won't throw her stuffed animal in the toilet. What is this called? *Answer Before You Answer:* Nell is learning by watching her brother's experience (vicariously through her brother). This is called vicarious conditioning. If you are unsure, use POE. Would (A) *prepared learning* mean learning from watching her brother's experience? No, it implies more direct learning. Cross it off. Would (B) *tutelage* mean learning from watching her brother's experience? No. Would (C) *scheduled reinforcement* mean learning from watching her brother's experience? No, that is not taking place here. Would (D) *shaping* mean learning from watching her brother's experience? Again, shaping is more direct. Would (E) *vicarious conditioning* mean learning from watching her brother's experience? Yup.

13. **B** *Ask It Like It Is: Jeopardy!* requires which type of intelligence? *Answer Before You Answer:* Crystallized intelligence—knowledge of facts. If you are unsure, use POE. Does (A) *IQ* mean knowledge of facts and trivia? No, it is a score on a very specific test. Don't confuse IQ with intelligence. Does (B) *crystallized intelligence* mean knowledge of facts and trivia? It sounds good. Keep it and check the others. Does (C) *fluid intelligence* mean knowledge of facts and trivia? No, it involves thinking and problem-solving skills. Does (D) *general intelligence* mean knowledge of facts and trivia? It might. Keep it. Does (E) *multiple intelligence* mean knowledge of facts and trivia? No, it involves a theory of various intelligences. (B) *crystallized intelligence* is more clearly associated with factual knowledge than (D) *general intelligence.*

14. **A** *Ask It Like It Is:* Circle *true of memory recall. Answer Before You Answer:* Not sure what they want, so evaluate each answer based on what you know of memory. (A) sounds logical and is also true—people recall information that is in keeping with their personal schemas. (B) is wrong because of "working" memory. Is (C) true? No, so cross it off. Same goes for (E). And (D) doesn't sound true either. It must be (A).

15. **C** *Ask It Like It Is:* What do objects that absorb light look like? *Answer Before You Answer:* Dark. Dark objects absorb light while bright objects reflect light. Beware of (A) *black*. The question does *not* say "objects that absorb *all* color."

16. **C** *Ask It Like it Is:* Chantal is trying to push off her unwanted negative qualities onto her mother so that the qualities are less threatening. This is called… *Answer Before You Answer: Projection.* Use POE to get rid of (A) *repression* because that would mean that Chantal were trying to push these unwanted feelings back into her unconscious mind. *Regression* (B) would mean that she were trying to revert back to an earlier stage of psychosexual development. *Displacement* (D) would imply that she were taking out her frustrations with her mother on a more socially acceptable target. *Denial* (E) would mean that Chantal were failing to accept that something unwanted or frightening was happening to her.

17. **B** *Ask It Like It Is:* Circle *humanistic perspective. Answer Before You Answer:* Humanists believe that people can control their behavior and that they strive to reach their full potential. Use POE to find an answer that agrees with this statement. (A) is the biological perspective, (C) is the behaviorist perspective, (D) is the psychodynamic perspective, and (E) is the cognitive perspective.

18. **A** *Ask It Like It Is:* Circle *visual*. Which lobe is involved in vision? *Answer Before You Answer:* Occipital lobe. If you don't know, use POE to get rid of (D) *frontal* (you probably know that the frontal lobe is used for a variety of more complex tasks), and (E) *cerebral* because this isn't a lobe of the brain.

19. **D** *Ask It Like It Is:* When are mean, median, and mode equal to the same number? *Answer Before You Answer:* In a normal distribution. If you don't remember, POE what you can. (A) and (C) represent distributions where scores are overwhelmingly low or high, respectively. *Asymmetrical* (B) is a generic term for a skewed distribution. *Abnormal* (E) is not generally a term used to describe distributions.

20. **D** *Ask It Like It Is:* When a six-month-old gets upset when Mom leaves it's called… *Answer Before You Answer:* Separation anxiety. Watch out for (A) *attachment anxiety*. (C) *object permanence* and (E) *detachment adaptation* would require a different response from the child.

21. **B** *Ask It Like It Is:* Circle *B. F. Skinner. Answer Before You Answer:* Skinner = behaviorism. If you missed this question, hit the books.

22. **C** *Ask It Like It Is:* She is using a survey to try to correlate guilt with other emotions. This kind of study is called… *Answer Before You Answer:* Correlational study. If you don't remember the term, use POE. Would (A) a *demographic* study try to correlate two or more emotions? No. Would (B) an *observational* study try to correlate two or more emotions? No, and it wouldn't involve a survey. Would (C) a *correlational* study try to correlate two or more emotions? Sounds good. Would (D) an *experimental* study try to correlate two or more emotions? Maybe, but not by using a survey. Would (E) a *statistical* study try to correlate two or more emotions? Use of statistics usually comes after the study. The answer is (C).

23. **A** *Ask It Like It Is:* Which term is used to describe many psychotic disorders? *Answer Before You Answer:* Schizophrenia. If you are unsure, use POE to get rid of (C) *dissociative disorder* and (D) *depression* because they are specific disorders, and (E) because it is a made-up term.

24. **B** *Ask It Like It Is:* Circle *firing of a neuron. Answer Before You Answer:* All or nothing. Use POE to get rid of answers that don't make sense. Get rid of (A) because firing does not occur gradually, (C) because this is also a false statement, and (E) because a neuron cannot fire "harder." (D) is also a false statement.

25. **D** *Ask It Like It Is:* The fact that Xavier wants to hang out with some new friends is called a(n)... *Answer Before You Answer:* Affiliation need. (A) *fraternization need*, (B) *assimilation need*, and (E) *loneliness need* are not true psychological terms, and (C) is too strong.

26. **E** *Ask It Like It Is:* Learning the meaning of something in order to increase your ability to memorize it is called... *Answer Before You Answer:* Semantic memory. If you are unsure of the exact term, POE should get rid of (C) and (D), because applying meaning is not simply rehearsing.

27. **E** *Ask It Like It Is:* Circle *outer ear. Answer Before You Answer:* Collect and magnify sound. Even if you are not sure, don't give the outer ear too much credit. Get rid of (A), (B), and (D).

28. **A** *Ask It Like It Is:* What kind of variable is eating breakfast in this study? *Answer Before You Answer:* Eating breakfast is an either/or thing, so it is a categorical variable. Even if you are not sure, POE can get rid of (C) *dependent variable* because it is not being observed and measured, (D) *independent variable* because it is not being manipulated, and (E) *conditioned variable* because it is not conditioned.

29. **A** *Ask It Like It Is:* Circle *left hemisphere. Answer Before You Answer:* Language functions. Even if you don't remember, use POE. (B) *logic* and (C) *analytical reasoning* are the same, so neither can be right. (D) *mathematical reasoning* and (E) *spatial reasoning* are two right-hemisphere functions, so (A) *language* is your best guess.

30. **C** *Ask It Like It Is:* Molding behavior by first praising all attempts and later only praising improved attempts is called... *Answer Before You Answer:* Shaping. If you don't remember the term, use POE. Could (A) *negative reinforcement* mean to first praise all attempts and then only praise improvements? No. Cross it off. Could (B) *negative punishment* mean to first praise all attempts and then only praise improvements? No. Could (C) *shaping* mean to first praise all attempts and then only praise improvements? Sure. Keep it and check the others. Could (D) *chaining* mean to first praise all attempts and then only praise improvements? No, chaining is linking together skills someone already has. Could (E) *discriminating* mean to first praise all attempts and then only praise improvements? No. The answer must be (C).

31. **C**   *Ask It Like It Is:* When a client takes out on her counselor the feelings she has for her parents, it's called... *Answer Before You Answer:* Transference. If you don't remember the term, use POE. Could (A) *suppression* mean to take out on the counselor feelings you have for your parents? No, it would involve keeping the feelings in. Could (B) *conflicting motives* mean to take out on the counselor feelings you have for your parents? It has the right tone but is still too weak. Cross it off. Could (C) *transference* mean to take out on the counselor feelings you have for your parents? Yes. Could (D) *countertransference* mean to take out on the counselor feelings you have for your parents? No, that's when the counselor puts stuff on the client. *Reaction formation* (E) would mean that she was taking on the opposite opinion of what she really feels.

32. **A**   *Ask It Like It Is:* Circle the last phrase. What is it called when you remember something you were not consciously trying to remember? *Answer Before You Answer:* Tip-of-the-tongue phenomenon. If you don't remember the term, you know what to do: POE. Could (A) *tip-of-the-tongue phenomenon* mean to remember something you were not consciously trying to remember? Yes. Quickly check the others. Could (B) *chunking* mean to remember something you were not consciously trying to remember? No, it is a learning technique. Could (C) *deductive reasoning* mean to remember something your were not consciously trying to remember? No. Could (D) *inductive reasoning* mean to remember something you were not consciously trying to remember? Nope. Could (E) *parallelism* mean to remember something you were not consciously trying to remember? No. Your answer must be (A).

33. **B**   *Ask It Like It Is:* Circle *hypnosis* and *diminish*. *Answer Before You Answer:* Chronic pain. If you don't remember this, use common sense to POE (A) *alcohol abuse*, (D) *kinesthetic abilities*, and (E) *Alzheimer's disease*.

34. **E**   *Ask It Like It Is:* Why do mnemonic devices work? *Answer Before You Answer:* They link information to stuff you already know. POE should get rid of (A) because of "STM" and (D) because it is impractical and unrealistic. Don't be thrown by the technical language of (B). (E) is the closest to your answer.

35. **E**   *Ask It Like It Is:* What's it called when you wake up horribly scared by a bad dream? *Answer Before You Answer:* A nightmare. POE will help you get rid of (A) *hallucination*, (B) *phobia*, and (C) *narcoleptic event*. You might be fooled by (D) *night terror*, but generally night terrors occur in a deeper sleep state than the REM sleep state that is typical of dreams and so do not produce vividly memorable experiences.

36. **E**   *Ask It Like It Is:* What is the term used to describe when prejudices are acted upon? *Answer Before You Answer:* Discrimination. Your clue is "behavioral component." (A) *bias*, (B) *conditioning*, and (C) *catharsis* are not directly related to the question. (D) *passive aggression* is way off base, so (E) *discrimination* is the best answer.

37. **C**   *Ask It Like It Is:* What happens when there is a break in the twenty-first chromosome pair? *Answer Before You Answer:* Down's syndrome. (C) says this.

38. **D**   *Ask It Like It Is:* Circle *punishment* and EXCEPT. *Answer Before You Answer:* Remember that punishment is something that is intended to make an undesirable response less likely (whether it works or not). Does (A) intend this? Yes, so it is an example of punishment. Cross this off as you need something that isn't. Does (B) intend this? Yes, so cross it off. How about (C)? Yes again, so eliminate it. (E) also attempts to lessen an undesirable response on the part of the puppy. Answer (D), refusing to return the boss' call after not getting the expected raise, is not intended to lessen an undesirable behavior on the part of the boss, if one could even define what that undesirable behavior was (not giving a raise is not an undesirable response, but a lack of a desired response). Your answer is (D).

39. **D**   *Ask It Like It Is:* Jung's theory of all humans sharing a collective set of ideas, feelings, and symbols is called… *Answer Before You Answer:* Jung's theory of collective unconscious. Even if you don't remember the term, POE will help. (A) *cultural subconscious* is made up, (C) *heritability coefficients* refers to something completely different, and (E) *integrated intelligence* is made up. (B) *general awareness* is too wimpy. The answer must be (D).

40. **A**   *Ask It Like It Is:* What is active sleeping and dreaming called? *Answer Before You Answer:* REM sleep. All the other choices are deeper stages of sleep.

41. **C**   *Ask It Like It Is:* Circle *placement of words and phrases in a sentence. Answer Before You Answer:* Syntax. If you don't remember, use POE to get rid of at least (D) and (E). (B) is too broad.

42. **A**   *Ask It Like It Is:* Animals won't put together the conditioned stimulus and the unconditioned stimulus if… *Answer Before You Answer:* They occur too far apart. Find the choice that is closest to yours—(A) *the delay between the CS and UCS is too long* is the best answer.

43. **B**   *Ask It Like It Is:* Circle *secondary drives* and *EXCEPT. Answer Before You Answer:* Four of the choices are secondary drives. (B) *sex* is a primary drive.

44. **C**   *Ask It Like It Is:* Circle *continuous variable. Answer Before You Answer:* Find an example of something that is on a continuum, not a category. Is (A) *race* on a continuum? No, not really. Cross it off. Is (B) *species* on a continuum? No. Is (C) *intelligence* on a continuum? Yes—it is not true to say you are either intelligent or you are not. There are lots of degrees. Is (D) *gender* on a continuum? No, you are either male or female. Is (E) *birth order* on a continuum? No, you were born in a certain order. The answer must be (C).

45. **E**   *Ask It Like It Is:* Dysfunction in what part of the brain would cause staggering and slurred speech? *Answer Before You Answer:* The cerebellum. If you don't remember, you can probably use POE to get rid of (B) *thalamus*, (C) *sensorimotor cortex*, and (D) *amygdala*.

46. **E**   *Ask It Like It Is:* Turkey made her sick. Why would chicken also make her queasy? *Answer Before You Answer:* Turkey and chicken are similar—stimulus generalization. If you don't remember the term, use POE. (B) *latent learning* and (C) *prepared learning* are obviously out. Does (A) *response generalization* mean associating similar stimuli? Be careful—it says *response* generalization.

Does (D) *unconditioned stimulus response* mean associating similar stimuli? Again, this is talking about a *response*. The answer must be (E) *stimulus generalization*.

47. **C** *Ask It Like It Is:* Circle *perception*. *Answer Before You Answer:* The process by which the brain organizes and interprets sensations. Use POE. (A) is the definition of sensation, (B) doesn't go far enough because perception is more than initial processing, and (D) refers to sensory adaptation. (E) takes it too far.

48. **D** *Ask It Like It Is:* What happens in order for you to perceive an increase in sound? *Answer Before You Answer:* More neurons fire more frequently. If you are unsure, use POE. Would (A) *neurons firing more intensely* make you perceive an increase in sound? Can neurons fire more intensely? No, so cross this answer off. (B) is way out of the ballpark. Would (C) *changing frequency of soundwaves* make you perceive an increase in sound? This phenomenon is not responsible for your perception of sound. Would (D) *more neurons firing more frequently* make you perceive an increase in sound? Yes. (E) is way out because the "what" pathway is related to vision.

49. **D** *Ask It Like It Is:* What allows us to tell the difference between two similar stimuli? *Answer Before You Answer:* The difference threshold or *Just Noticeable Difference (JND)*. This may seem tricky because all of the other choices are also related to thresholds. *Subliminal perception* (A) suggests that stimuli below the threshold can still unconsciously influence behavior. *Absolute threshold* (B) refers to the ability to detect a stimulus 50 percent of the time. *Signal detection theory (C)* refers to the ability to lower a threshold based on experience or expectation. *Weber's law* (E) refers to the need for stimuli to vary by a constant proportion in order for us to detect differences among stimuli.

50. **B** *Ask It Like It Is:* Jerome is a student at the Peddie School and all students at the Peddie School study Latin. *Answer Before You Answer:* Jerome takes Latin. This is the only thing you know definitely.

51. **C** *Ask It Like It Is:* She is confident and self-directed. Therefore she has… *Answer Before You Answer:* An internal locus of control. If you don't remember the term, use POE. Would a confident, self-directed person have an (A) *manic coping strategy*? No, that strategy would be dysfunctional. Cross this answer off. Would a confident, self-directed person have a (B) *discriminative expectancy*? This term doesn't make sense. Cross it off. Would a confident, self-directed person have a (C) *internal locus of control*? Hopefully this answer jogs your memory. Even if you aren't sure, the term sounds possible, so keep it and check the others. Would a confident, self-directed person have a (D) *external locus of control*? No, that would involve looking to others for your own direction or self-worth. This answer is the opposite of what you want. Would a confident, self-directed person have an (E) *generalized expectancy*? No. (C) is it.

52. **C** *Ask It Like It Is:* How do we refer to an emotional release that reduces aggressive tendencies? *Answer Before You Answer:* The catharsis hypothesis. *James-Lange* (C) is a theory that posits that physiological arousal precedes emotional experience. *Counterconditioning* (B) is a behavioral term. *Transference* (D) is a term used in psychoanalysis. *The two factor theory* (E) discusses the physiological arousal and cognitive evaluation that precede the experience of emotion.

53. **C** *Ask It Like It Is:* Circle *constant state that permits cells to live and function*. The body is in a state of… *Answer Before You Answer:* Homeostasis. This is a term you need to know. Even if you don't remember the exact term, you should be able to get rid of (B) *set-point*, (D) *kinesthesia*, and (E) *affect regulation*. Watch out for (A) *perceptual constancy*—it is the trap answer.

54. **B** *Ask It Like It Is:* Circle *periods of special sensitivity*. The times in which one is primed for learning are called… *Answer Before You Answer:* Critical periods. If you are unsure of the term, use POE to get rid of (A) *maturation periods* and (D) *secondary development periods*. Watch out for (C) *primary development periods* and (E) *shaping periods*—they are trap answers.

55. **E** *Ask It Like It Is:* What causes people to act differently in a crowd than they would individually? *Answer Before You Answer:* diffusion of responsibility. Use POE to rile out the other choices. *Social loafing* (A) refers to people's tendency to exert less effort in a group than they would individually. Close, but not right. *Prejudice* (B), *Conformity* (C), and *Obedience* (D) all increase when more people are present.

56. **A** *Ask It Like It Is:* She leaves a bad thing and goes to the same bad thing. *Answer Before You Answer:* Freud's theory of psychoanalytic conflict. If you don't remember the name of the theory, use POE. Could leaving a bad thing for the same bad thing be an example of (A) *psychodynamic conflict*? It's definitely a conflict, and most likely one taking place in the unconscious. Keep this and check the others. Could leaving a bad thing for the same bad thing be an example of (B) *opposing motives*? She is not experiencing opposing motives— she is going to the same bad thing. Cross this answer off. Could leaving a bad thing for the same bad thing be an example of (C) *id, ego, and superego*? Not really. Could leaving a bad thing for the same bad thing be an example of (D) *behavioral dysfunction*? Her behavior is dysfunctional, but this was not a theory of Freud's. (E) is a concept from social psychology, not Freudian theory.

57. **A** *Ask It Like It Is:* Circle *Piaget*. How do children develop knowledge? *Answer Before You Answer:* From their own experiences. Use POE to find the answer closest to yours. (B) is out, as is (C) and (E). Don't get drawn in by (D).

58. **D** *Ask It Like It Is:* Which needs to be studied over a long period of time? *Answer Before You Answer:* Anything that is related to changes over time. Use POE to find an answer that is close to yours. Be careful on (A)—*age differences* could be measured by studying groups of people at different ages, not necessarily the same people at different ages. Look for an answer that is more clear. (D) *changes in behavior over time* is the closest to yours.

59. **E** *Ask It Like It Is:* He slowly got over his fear by gradual exposure and eventual participation. This is called… *Answer Before You Answer:* Systematic desensitization. If you don't remember the term, use POE. Could (A) *countertransference* mean gradual exposure and participation? No. Could (B) *peer-counselor alliance* mean gradual exposure and participation? No, so cross it off. Could (C) *rational-emotive therapy* mean gradual exposure and participation? Sounds possible. Keep it and check the rest. Could (D) *flooding* mean gradual exposure and participation? Doesn't sound very gradual.

Cross it off. Could (E) *systematic desensitization* mean gradual exposure and participation? Yes. This refers to a process of gradual exposure to a fear stimulus.

60. **E** *Ask It Like It Is:* She wants to understand the child's behavior in light of the child's family dynamics. This is known as a... *Answer Before You Answer:* Systems approach. Look at the systems the child is a part of to reveal information about the child's behavior. If you don't remember the term, use POE. You can get rid of (B) *behavioral approach* and (C) *psychoanalytic approach* because you are familiar with those approaches. (D) *paternal approach* is a made-up term. (A) *cognitive social approach* tends to focus more on the role of cognition in behavior.

61. **B** *Ask It Like It Is:* What's the APA diagnostic manual called? *Answer Before You Answer: DSM-IV-TR.* Use POE to get rid of (A) *ANOVA,* which is a measure of statistics, and (C) *APA Desk Reference,* (D) *Diagnosis of Disorders Digest,* and (E) *Clinicians Reference Manual III* because they are made-up titles.

62. **D** *Ask It Like It Is:* Circle *samples* and *male college students. Answer Before You Answer:* Find a group that represents males from a wide variety of colleges. Use POE. (A) and (C) would not represent all college males, nor would (B) because the sampling is done in the business wing. Be careful of (E)—*college graduates*—some of whom graduated a half-century ago—do not represent college students.

63. **B** *Ask It Like It Is:* What does the myelin sheath do? *Answer Before You Answer:* Covers the axons to speed transmission of messages. If you remember that myelination is not complete in children, which contributes to their lack of coordination, use that information to infer that myelination improves some aspect of neural communication. Eliminate (D) and (E). POE (A) because dendrites don't receive messages. (C) is also false.

64. **C** *Ask It Like It Is:* Circle *Beethoven's music,* then identify what role it plays in the scenario. *Answer Before You Answer:* Conditioned stimulus. At the least, you should be able to use POE for (A) *conditioned response* and (B) *unconditioned response* because the music is a stimulus, not a response.

65. **B** *Ask It Like It Is:* Circle *illness in response to the medication.* What is that in the scenario? *Answer Before You Answer:* An unconditioned response. At the least, you know that the illness is a response so eliminate (C) *conditioned stimulus,* (D) *unconditioned stimulus,* and (E) *neutral stimulus.* Is it conditioned? No, because the medicine is inducing the illness.

66. **E** *Ask It Like It Is:* Circle *nature-nurture controversy,* then jot down your understanding of the nature-nurture controversy. *Answer Before You Answer:* To what degree is behavior shaped by nature/genetics over nurture/environment? Use POE to find the answer that is closest to yours. Get rid of (A) and (B). (C) is stupid; it just throws in the terms *nurture* and *nature.* (D) is comparing psychodynamic and behaviorist perspectives.

67. **C**   *Ask It Like It Is:* When a neuron is fired, what happens? *Answer Before You Answer:* Depolarization causes an action potential. If you have no idea, you should still be able to eliminate at least (D) *hyperpolarization results* and possibly (A) *a resting potential returns* because the cumulative effect of something does not normally lead to the return of a resting state.

68. **A**   *Ask It Like It Is:* Circle *iconic memory.* What is an icon? A picture or representation. *Answer Before You Answer:* Visual memory. Even if you are not sure, you should be able to eliminate (C) *frontal sensory registry,* (D) *STM sensory registry,* and (E) *LTM sensory registry* as out of the ballpark.

69. **B**   *Ask It Like It Is*: What kind of therapy is Aaron Beck most closely associated with? *Answer Before You Answer*: Cognitive therapy. Tip: even if you don't remember Beck, there are other clues in the question that will lead you to the correct answer. Focus on the phrase negative thoughts and you can make the connection to cognitive theory.

70. **A**   *Ask It Like It Is:* He is frightened without even knowing what the object is. What is happening neurologically? *Answer Before You Answer:* There is some sort of immediate emotional response before the "thought centers" are consulted. In other words, messages must travel directly to the amygdala. Use POE to get rid of (E) because it sends visual information to another lobe and not to an emergency or emotive system. Get rid of (C) because it is the parasympathetic, not the sympathetic. Get rid of (D) because how would the message have gotten to the frontal lobes? (B) is referring to visual pathways.

71. **B**   *Ask It Like It Is:* They want to know what the typical listener gives. Based on their sample, it's $60. So they want to know the number that appears most frequently in the sample. *Answer Before You Answer:* Mode. You can use POE to get rid of (A) *median* because it is a trap answer. (C) *histogram* is a type of graph, and (D) *ANOVA* and (E) *p-value* involve statistical evaluation of results.

72. **B**   *Ask It Like It Is:* Bengt and Marie salivate in anticipation of their favorite meal. This indicates that… *Answer Before You Answer:* Motivation can have a top-down effect on perception. Get rid of (A) because this is not an example of bottom-up processing. (C) and (D) are not relevant because there is no interaction of old and new information and (E) *sensory restriction* is not indicated because there is no lack of sensory input.

73. **E**   *Ask It Like It Is:* What instrument, traditionally used in sleep research, assesses brain activity. *Answer Before You Answer:* EEG. (A) *signal detection device* has nothing to do with brain activity detection. (B) *CAT* and (C) *MRI* are used to locate brain lesions. (D) *PET* is a very recent technology, so it is not the one that has been traditionally used.

74. **D**   *Ask It Like It Is:* Circle *afterimage.* He is looking at something yellow. His afterimage will be… *Answer Before You Answer:* Blue. Even if you don't remember afterimages, you should remember the pairs of colors red-green and yellow-blue. If you don't, you will likely remember that red and green go together (red-green color blindness is a common thing). Eliminate (A) *green* and (C) *red.* Also, eliminate (B) *yellow*—this is too hard a question for the afterimage to be the same color. You can also guess that the opposite color image of black is white, so (D) *blue* is your best guess.

75. **D**   *Ask It Like It Is:* The fear of being in situations that are hard to escape from is called… *Answer Before You Answer:* Agoraphobia. Watch out for (A) *claustrophobia*, because it is a trap answer. This question doesn't say anything about small places. Common sense should also get rid of (E) *paranoia*.

76. **A**   *Ask It Like It Is:* Circle *discrepancy between an attitude and a behavior*. If someone thinks one thing but does something else, s/he may experience… *Answer Before You Answer:* Cognitive dissonance—mental conflict. If you don't remember the term, use POE. Could (A) *cognitive dissonance* mean mental conflict? Sure sounds it. Keep it and check the others. Could (B) *dissociation* mean mental conflict? No, cross it off. Could (C) *behavioral dysfunction* mean mental conflict? No, it's about behavior. Cross it off. Could (D) *metacognition* mean mental conflict? No, nothing about conflict here. Could (E) *contertransference* mean mental conflict? No. It must be (A).

77. **B**   *Ask It Like It Is:* A crisis can cause people to forget their differences and work together. This is called a(n)… *Answer Before You Answer:* Superordinate goal—their need to work together overrides their personal differences. Even if you don't remember the term, use POE. Get rid of (C) *subordinate goal* because it is *subordinate*. (E) *truce agreement* is stupid, and (A) *communal goal* and (C) *subordinate goal* are too wimpy.

78. **A**   *Ask It Like It Is:* Circle *Wilhelm Wundt* and *father of psychology*. *Answer Before You Answer:* He founded the first psych lab. Even if you don't remember Wilhelm, use the info in the question and your brain power to POE. (B) is out because it describes Freud. (C) is out because you know that Pavlov and Skinner are the big guys in behaviorism. (D) is extreme (*all* philosophical questions). Of the remaining choices, (A) sounds more impressive.

79. **D**   *Ask It Like It Is:* People disagreed with him and yet support him. This demonstrates a split in… *Answer Before You Answer:* Attitudinal coherence. If you don't remember the term, you know that people think both good and bad stuff about the guy, so it is a split in homogeneous ideas. (D) *attitudinal coherence* is the closest to "homogeneous ideas."

80. **A**   *Ask It Like It Is:* The sound waves stimulate the cilia of the inner ear. This is called… *Answer Before You Answer:* Transduction. If you don't recognize this as the description of transduction, POE what you can. Olfaction and kinesthesia have nothing to do with hearing so eliminate (B) *olfactory perception* and (E) *kinesthetic transference*. (D) *decibel cognition* is made up, and (C) *sensory interaction* is not the same as perception.

81. **E**   *Ask It Like It Is:* Why does the water feel cool at first but then eventually feel comfortable once you have been in it for a while? *Answer Before You Answer:* Sensory adaption. The water temperature is the same, but your body adapts to the coolness of the water.

82. **C**   *Ask It Like It Is:* What does it take to identify or recognize something, even when the object is obstructed? *Answer Before You Answer:* Matching it against something retained in LTM in Gestalt theory is known as *closure*. The other choices are also Gestalt principles but they do not fit the question asked. *Proximity* (A) refers to the nearness of objects. *Similarity*, (B) matches like items. *Continuity* (D) and *connectedness* (E) are too closely related.

83. **C** *Ask It Like It Is:* How do psychoactive drugs work? *Answer Before You Answer:* Kind of like neurotransmitters. (A) is out because of hormones, (B) is way out, and (D) and (E) are stupid.

84. **A** *Ask It Like It Is:* She begins to calm down as what system takes back over? *Answer Before You Answer:* Her emergency response systems are turned off, and her parasympathetic system takes back over. Don't confuse (B) with (A). Central and peripheral are not the right systems, so (C) and (D) are out. Get rid of (E)—the endocrine system does not control neurotransmitters.

85. **D** *Ask It Like It Is:* What part of the brain relays information to the cerebral cortex? *Answer Before You Answer:* The thalamus. If you don't remember, try to POE what you can. The (B) *cerebellum* plays a role in movement and balance, so cross it off. The (C) *reticular formation* is involved in maintaining consciousness and regulating activity throughout the central nervous system. You should know that (E) the *medulla oblongata* is responsible for regulating life-sustaining processes. The (A) *hypothalamus* regulates a lot of our primary drives.

86. **D** *Ask It Like It Is:* Circle *operant conditioning*. What does it mean? *Answer Before You Answer:* It has to do with "day-to-day operations" as opposed to classical conditioning. POE (B) and (C) because they have nothing to do with conditioning. (A) is an example of classical conditioning.

87. **D** *Ask It Like It Is:* Why are twins significant when studying the role of genetics in behavior? *Answer Before You Answer:* Because identical twins come from the same egg, so they are genetically identical. In (A), don't confuse fraternal with identical twins. (B) is emphasizing environmental factors. (C) doesn't make sense (MZ twins are identical twins, whereas DZ twins are fraternal twins). (E) is the "confuse the test-taker" answer—a statement with a lot of jargon that doesn't say anything important but does confuse you. Because you used smart strategies, you won't get trapped.

88. **E** *Ask It Like It Is:* Noticing a change in a stimulus depends on what? *Answer Before You Answer:* How intense the new stimulus is as compared to that of the existing stimulus. (A) and (D) try to confuse you with technology—get rid of them. (C) is stupid—if you are present, so are your sensory modalities. (B) is a "confuse the test taker" answer.

89. **B** *Ask It Like It Is:* Why can't she see color in dim light? *Answer Before You Answer:* Color transduction (cones) requires more light than does the transduction of black and white images (rods). If you know that cones are color and rods are black and white, you can get rid of (A), (C), and (E). You can tell (D) is wrong because of "rapidly adjusting" to light changes.

90. **B** *Ask It Like It Is:* Why can an individual attend to certain stimuli while filtering out other stimuli? *Answer Before You Answer*....selective attention. Use POE to rule out the other choices.

91. **E** *Ask It Like It Is:* Amnesia and loss of personal identity are characteristic of what? *Answer Before You Answer:* Dissociative disorder. You can use POE to get rid of (A) *schizophrenic disorder* and (D) *manic-depressive disorder* due to your knowledge of disorders. (B) is a trap. This behavior is not antisocial, so get rid of (C).

92. **C** *Ask It Like It Is:* Which correctly identifies Pavlov's research? *Answer Before You Answer:* Subject: *dogs;* UCS: *food;* CS: *sight/sound of presenter of food.* CR: *salivating in response to presenter.* Read each choice very carefully. This is not hard, but it is tricky and time-consuming. If pressed for time, skip and come back.

93. **B** *Ask It Like It Is:* In classical conditioning, what is it called when the learner first reacts to the conditioned stimulus when the unconditioned stimulus is not present? *Answer Before You Answer:* It is called acquisition. An *unconditioned stimulus* (A) prompts a response; it is not a reaction to a prompt. *Discrimination* (C) occurs when a learner responds only to the conditioned stimulus and nothing else. *Generalization* (D) occurs when the learner responds to the conditioned stimulus and to objects that are similar to the CS. *Spontaneous recovery* (E) occurs when a conditioned response suddenly reappears in the absence of additional conditioning.

94. **D** *Ask It Like It Is:* Circle *same objects over time.* Which type of study minimizes the effect of differences among age groups by studying these groups over long periods of time? *Answer Before You Answer:* Longitudinal research. (A), (B), and (C) offer a snapshot of a particular group at a particular time. *Correlational research* (E) is not relevant to the question being asked.

95. **B** *Ask It Like It Is:* What is the purpose of a projective personality test? *Answer Before You Answer:* To gain insight into unconscious motives. *Gaining insight into biochemical abnormalities* (A) would require medical intervention. *Assessing traits* (C) refers to objective personality tests such as the MMPI. (D) and (E) examine specific traits, but offer no causal explanations for why these traits occur.

96. **C** *Ask It Like It Is:* How does a depressed person see the world according to the negative triad theory? *Answer Before You Answer:* A depressed person has a negative view of himself, the world, and the future. Use the information in the question and your brain power if you don't know the study. (A) is too narrow in focus, (B) and (E) are kind of silly (*three* people to form a triad).

97. **B** *Ask It Like It Is:* Circle *imprinting.* What does it mean? *Answer Before You Answer:* An animal will attach to the first moving object it sees, presumably its mother. If you don't know imprinting, you can still guess the meaning and use POE. Get rid of (A) and (C) because they don't sound like imprinting. (E) is more of an example of a physiological response to positive attachment.

98. **A** *Ask It Like It Is:* Circle *systematic desensitization* and *EXCEPT.* Four of the choices will be a step in systematic desensitization—one will not. *Answer Before You Answer:* Systematic desensitization involves 1) learning to relax, 2) creating a hierarchy of images of one's fear, 3) picturing each fearful image while remaining relaxed, and 4) confronting one's fear in real life. Find these responses and cross them off. The remaining choice will be the answer. (A) mentions hypnosis, which seems out of the pattern of the rest of the choices.

99. **B** *Ask It Like It Is:* They used behavior modification that involved small rewards that can be traded in for bigger rewards. This is known as… *Answer Before You Answer:* Token economy. You should know that it is not (D) and (E) even if you are not sure what it is. It is also different from negative reinforcement, plus that is too easy an answer for item 99, so get rid of (A).

100. **E** *Ask It Like It Is:* Circle *Milgram* and *obedience*. What was the study and what were the conclusions? *Answer Before You Answer:* Big help if you know the study. Even if you didn't recognize his name, try to recall the most famous study on obedience ever done: This study is the one in which people were asked to punish a learner who was in the next room by administering electric shocks, beginning with mild shocks and ending with life-threatening shocks. The entire field was astounded that two-thirds of the participants actually administered the full-strength shocks, especially if an authority figure was in the room. So what is a conclusion of this study? If you only know a little of this information, you can still POE (A) *crowd mentality*, and (B) because the participants did not refuse.

Section II

1. Essay number one is worth 10 points. Two points are awarded for explaining each term and giving a relevant example of each term in Part A. Two points are awarded for explaining how his parents should treat his tantrum behavior in Part B.

   This is what our "student" chose to do for her essays. Use this as a sample of a decent essay.

Sample Essay

A. Age is key to understanding issues related to development. Jack is a three-year-old boy who is frustrating his parents with his constant tantrums and misbehavior. To understand how best to handle Jack's unwanted behavior, his parents must understand his cognitive and social stages of development if they are to effectively deal with his unwanted behaviors.

According to cognitive theorist Jean Piaget, Jack is in the pre-operational stage of cognitive development. During this stage of cognitive development, which lasts roughly from ages 2 to 6 years of age, children are egocentric. Egocentrism is different from self-centeredness, which is behavioral and not cognitive. Jack's parents try to reason with him when he misbehaves, but that is very ineffective because he doesn't understand what they are trying to say. Jack will continue to have tantrums until they find a better way to reach him, because he does not understand their point of view or their expectations.

Lawrence Kohlberg also studied cognitive development as it relates to moral development. As a three-year-old, Jack is most likely in the pre-conventional stage of moral development. Jack's morality is based on a system of rewards and punishments. He is not able to make moral decisions at his age based on what is best for his parents, his family, or his community. However, understanding this, his parents can modify his behavior by appealing to his desire to gain rewards and avoid punishments.

Jack's social stage of development is also crucial to understanding his tantrum behavior. According to Erik Erikson, a psychosocial theorist, Jack is in the Initiative versus Guilt Stage. During this stage, children begin to exert their independence and they become more assertive and sometimes aggressive. Jack is trying to exert his autonomy and he may do this in a very assertive way, such as by having tantrums in response to his parent's rules.

Although cognitive and social development are important factors to consider in evaluating Jack's behavior, we must also strongly consider environmental factors such as observational learning. Observational learning, or learning by imitation, may have a profound impact on Jack's behavior. For example, if Jack's parents model aggressive or assertive behaviors, Jack will learn to imitate these behaviors as he is in an impressionable stage in his development.

B. Now that Jack's parents fully understand his developmental processes and the influence of observational learning on his behavior, they can successfully eliminate his negative behaviors. For example, when Jack has a tantrum, they would be best advised to ignore his behaviors rather than to call attention to them. Trying to reason with him in the past had been unsuccessful due to his egocentrism. They should also set clear and consistent rules for him so that he can explore his autonomy while acting appropriately. They must also be mindful of their own behaviors and not get angry when frustrated because Jack will imitate their behaviors. The most important thing that Jack's parents must consider is that they must be consistent and they must keep in mind that his behaviors are typical of his stage of development and are not necessarily inappropriate.

2. Essay number two is worth eight points. One point is awarded for defining and creating a hypothesis, two points are awarded for including at least two methods of research, defining and explaining each. One point is given for each of the topics listed by defining and including it in the study. Two points are awarded for Part B, one for explaining the statistics used and the other for tying them into the hypothetical study.

This is what our "student" chose to do for her essays. Use this as a sample of a high-scoring essay.

Sample Essay

Does eating breakfast improve scholastic performance in high school? The study we are developing is designed to investigate just that. The hypothesis is that eating breakfast improves not only daily performance in school but overall scholastic achievement. Daily performance will be measured by performance on classroom activities plus class participation. Overall scholastic achievement will be measured by cumulative GPA.

To conduct this study, we first need to generate a representative sample of students. Random sampling is important to any study if there is to be generalizability—the information could be used to shed light on a larger population. To create a random sample, we will go to twenty high schools across the country. We will make sure there is an even distribution of urban, suburban, and rural schools. We will also make sure we have an equal number of boys and girls and a mixture of socioeconomic backgrounds.

In our study, our independent variable, the variable we plan to manipulate, is eating breakfast. Our dependent variable, the variable that will allegedly be influenced by our independent variable, is daily and overall scholastic performance. The second part of this study is a longitudinal study in that it needs to be conducted through at least one school year, and preferably throughout the four years of high school.

From our sample, we will create two groups: an experimental group and a control group. The control group will not eat breakfast in the morning, and their performance will be tracked. The experimental group will be served breakfast every day, and their performance will be tracked.

To present our findings to the school board, we would create a frequency distribution using a histogram. The frequency distribution is designed to show the number of times participants received each of the possible scores—in our case, to compare their eating breakfast with their daily performance. We would also analyze our findings to determine the p-value or probability that the results obtained were not a matter of chance.

The Princeton Review

1. YOUR NAME: _____
(Print)
Last   First   M.I.

SIGNATURE: _____ **DATE:** ____ / ____ / ____

HOME ADDRESS: _____
(Print)
Number and Street

_____ **E-MAIL:** _____
City   State   Zip

PHONE NO.: _____ **SCHOOL:** _____ **CLASS OF:** _____
(Print)

IMPORTANT: Please fill in these boxes exactly as shown on the back cover of your test book.

OpScan *i*NSIGHT™ forms by Pearson NCS EM-255325-1:654321
Printed in U.S.A.

© The Princeton Review, Inc.

5. YOUR NAME

First 4 letters of last name				FIRST INIT	MID INIT
Ⓐ	Ⓐ	Ⓐ	Ⓐ	Ⓐ	Ⓐ
Ⓑ	Ⓑ	Ⓑ	Ⓑ	Ⓑ	Ⓑ
Ⓒ	Ⓒ	Ⓒ	Ⓒ	Ⓒ	Ⓒ
Ⓓ	Ⓓ	Ⓓ	Ⓓ	Ⓓ	Ⓓ
Ⓔ	Ⓔ	Ⓔ	Ⓔ	Ⓔ	Ⓔ
Ⓕ	Ⓕ	Ⓕ	Ⓕ	Ⓕ	Ⓕ
Ⓖ	Ⓖ	Ⓖ	Ⓖ	Ⓖ	Ⓖ
Ⓗ	Ⓗ	Ⓗ	Ⓗ	Ⓗ	Ⓗ
Ⓘ	Ⓘ	Ⓘ	Ⓘ	Ⓘ	Ⓘ
Ⓙ	Ⓙ	Ⓙ	Ⓙ	Ⓙ	Ⓙ
Ⓚ	Ⓚ	Ⓚ	Ⓚ	Ⓚ	Ⓚ
Ⓛ	Ⓛ	Ⓛ	Ⓛ	Ⓛ	Ⓛ
Ⓜ	Ⓜ	Ⓜ	Ⓜ	Ⓜ	Ⓜ
Ⓝ	Ⓝ	Ⓝ	Ⓝ	Ⓝ	Ⓝ
Ⓞ	Ⓞ	Ⓞ	Ⓞ	Ⓞ	Ⓞ
Ⓟ	Ⓟ	Ⓟ	Ⓟ	Ⓟ	Ⓟ
Ⓠ	Ⓠ	Ⓠ	Ⓠ	Ⓠ	Ⓠ
Ⓡ	Ⓡ	Ⓡ	Ⓡ	Ⓡ	Ⓡ
Ⓢ	Ⓢ	Ⓢ	Ⓢ	Ⓢ	Ⓢ
Ⓣ	Ⓣ	Ⓣ	Ⓣ	Ⓣ	Ⓣ
Ⓤ	Ⓤ	Ⓤ	Ⓤ	Ⓤ	Ⓤ
Ⓥ	Ⓥ	Ⓥ	Ⓥ	Ⓥ	Ⓥ
Ⓦ	Ⓦ	Ⓦ	Ⓦ	Ⓦ	Ⓦ
Ⓧ	Ⓧ	Ⓧ	Ⓧ	Ⓧ	Ⓧ
Ⓨ	Ⓨ	Ⓨ	Ⓨ	Ⓨ	Ⓨ
Ⓩ	Ⓩ	Ⓩ	Ⓩ	Ⓩ	Ⓩ

2. TEST FORM

_____

3. TEST CODE

⓪	⓪	⓪	⓪
①	①	①	①
②	②	②	②
③	③	③	③
④	④	④	④
⑤	⑤	⑤	⑤
⑥	⑥	⑥	⑥
⑦	⑦	⑦	⑦
⑧	⑧	⑧	⑧
⑨	⑨	⑨	⑨

4. PHONE NUMBER

⓪	⓪	⓪	⓪	⓪	⓪	⓪
①	①	①	①	①	①	①
②	②	②	②	②	②	②
③	③	③	③	③	③	③
④	④	④	④	④	④	④
⑤	⑤	⑤	⑤	⑤	⑤	⑤
⑥	⑥	⑥	⑥	⑥	⑥	⑥
⑦	⑦	⑦	⑦	⑦	⑦	⑦
⑧	⑧	⑧	⑧	⑧	⑧	⑧
⑨	⑨	⑨	⑨	⑨	⑨	⑨

6. DATE OF BIRTH

MONTH	DAY		YEAR	
○ JAN				
○ FEB				
○ MAR	Ⓞ	Ⓞ	Ⓞ	Ⓞ
○ APR	①	①	①	①
○ MAY	②	②	②	②
○ JUN	③	③	③	③
○ JUL		④	④	④
○ AUG		⑤	⑤	⑤
○ SEP		⑥	⑥	⑥
○ OCT		⑦	⑦	⑦
○ NOV		⑧	⑧	⑧
○ DEC		⑨	⑨	⑨

7. SEX
○ MALE
○ FEMALE

8. OTHER
1 Ⓐ Ⓑ Ⓒ Ⓓ Ⓔ
2 Ⓐ Ⓑ Ⓒ Ⓓ Ⓔ
3 Ⓐ Ⓑ Ⓒ Ⓓ Ⓔ

Begin with number 1 for each new section of the test. Leave blank any extra answer spaces.

SECTION 1

1 Ⓐ Ⓑ Ⓒ Ⓓ Ⓔ	26 Ⓐ Ⓑ Ⓒ Ⓓ Ⓔ	51 Ⓐ Ⓑ Ⓒ Ⓓ Ⓔ	76 Ⓐ Ⓑ Ⓒ Ⓓ Ⓔ
2 Ⓐ Ⓑ Ⓒ Ⓓ Ⓔ	27 Ⓐ Ⓑ Ⓒ Ⓓ Ⓔ	52 Ⓐ Ⓑ Ⓒ Ⓓ Ⓔ	77 Ⓐ Ⓑ Ⓒ Ⓓ Ⓔ
3 Ⓐ Ⓑ Ⓒ Ⓓ Ⓔ	28 Ⓐ Ⓑ Ⓒ Ⓓ Ⓔ	53 Ⓐ Ⓑ Ⓒ Ⓓ Ⓔ	78 Ⓐ Ⓑ Ⓒ Ⓓ Ⓔ
4 Ⓐ Ⓑ Ⓒ Ⓓ Ⓔ	29 Ⓐ Ⓑ Ⓒ Ⓓ Ⓔ	54 Ⓐ Ⓑ Ⓒ Ⓓ Ⓔ	79 Ⓐ Ⓑ Ⓒ Ⓓ Ⓔ
5 Ⓐ Ⓑ Ⓒ Ⓓ Ⓔ	30 Ⓐ Ⓑ Ⓒ Ⓓ Ⓔ	55 Ⓐ Ⓑ Ⓒ Ⓓ Ⓔ	80 Ⓐ Ⓑ Ⓒ Ⓓ Ⓔ
6 Ⓐ Ⓑ Ⓒ Ⓓ Ⓔ	31 Ⓐ Ⓑ Ⓒ Ⓓ Ⓔ	56 Ⓐ Ⓑ Ⓒ Ⓓ Ⓔ	81 Ⓐ Ⓑ Ⓒ Ⓓ Ⓔ
7 Ⓐ Ⓑ Ⓒ Ⓓ Ⓔ	32 Ⓐ Ⓑ Ⓒ Ⓓ Ⓔ	57 Ⓐ Ⓑ Ⓒ Ⓓ Ⓔ	82 Ⓐ Ⓑ Ⓒ Ⓓ Ⓔ
8 Ⓐ Ⓑ Ⓒ Ⓓ Ⓔ	33 Ⓐ Ⓑ Ⓒ Ⓓ Ⓔ	58 Ⓐ Ⓑ Ⓒ Ⓓ Ⓔ	83 Ⓐ Ⓑ Ⓒ Ⓓ Ⓔ
9 Ⓐ Ⓑ Ⓒ Ⓓ Ⓔ	34 Ⓐ Ⓑ Ⓒ Ⓓ Ⓔ	59 Ⓐ Ⓑ Ⓒ Ⓓ Ⓔ	84 Ⓐ Ⓑ Ⓒ Ⓓ Ⓔ
10 Ⓐ Ⓑ Ⓒ Ⓓ Ⓔ	35 Ⓐ Ⓑ Ⓒ Ⓓ Ⓔ	60 Ⓐ Ⓑ Ⓒ Ⓓ Ⓔ	85 Ⓐ Ⓑ Ⓒ Ⓓ Ⓔ
11 Ⓐ Ⓑ Ⓒ Ⓓ Ⓔ	36 Ⓐ Ⓑ Ⓒ Ⓓ Ⓔ	61 Ⓐ Ⓑ Ⓒ Ⓓ Ⓔ	86 Ⓐ Ⓑ Ⓒ Ⓓ Ⓔ
12 Ⓐ Ⓑ Ⓒ Ⓓ Ⓔ	37 Ⓐ Ⓑ Ⓒ Ⓓ Ⓔ	62 Ⓐ Ⓑ Ⓒ Ⓓ Ⓔ	87 Ⓐ Ⓑ Ⓒ Ⓓ Ⓔ
13 Ⓐ Ⓑ Ⓒ Ⓓ Ⓔ	38 Ⓐ Ⓑ Ⓒ Ⓓ Ⓔ	63 Ⓐ Ⓑ Ⓒ Ⓓ Ⓔ	88 Ⓐ Ⓑ Ⓒ Ⓓ Ⓔ
14 Ⓐ Ⓑ Ⓒ Ⓓ Ⓔ	39 Ⓐ Ⓑ Ⓒ Ⓓ Ⓔ	64 Ⓐ Ⓑ Ⓒ Ⓓ Ⓔ	89 Ⓐ Ⓑ Ⓒ Ⓓ Ⓔ
15 Ⓐ Ⓑ Ⓒ Ⓓ Ⓔ	40 Ⓐ Ⓑ Ⓒ Ⓓ Ⓔ	65 Ⓐ Ⓑ Ⓒ Ⓓ Ⓔ	90 Ⓐ Ⓑ Ⓒ Ⓓ Ⓔ
16 Ⓐ Ⓑ Ⓒ Ⓓ Ⓔ	41 Ⓐ Ⓑ Ⓒ Ⓓ Ⓔ	66 Ⓐ Ⓑ Ⓒ Ⓓ Ⓔ	91 Ⓐ Ⓑ Ⓒ Ⓓ Ⓔ
17 Ⓐ Ⓑ Ⓒ Ⓓ Ⓔ	42 Ⓐ Ⓑ Ⓒ Ⓓ Ⓔ	67 Ⓐ Ⓑ Ⓒ Ⓓ Ⓔ	92 Ⓐ Ⓑ Ⓒ Ⓓ Ⓔ
18 Ⓐ Ⓑ Ⓒ Ⓓ Ⓔ	43 Ⓐ Ⓑ Ⓒ Ⓓ Ⓔ	68 Ⓐ Ⓑ Ⓒ Ⓓ Ⓔ	93 Ⓐ Ⓑ Ⓒ Ⓓ Ⓔ
19 Ⓐ Ⓑ Ⓒ Ⓓ Ⓔ	44 Ⓐ Ⓑ Ⓒ Ⓓ Ⓔ	69 Ⓐ Ⓑ Ⓒ Ⓓ Ⓔ	94 Ⓐ Ⓑ Ⓒ Ⓓ Ⓔ
20 Ⓐ Ⓑ Ⓒ Ⓓ Ⓔ	45 Ⓐ Ⓑ Ⓒ Ⓓ Ⓔ	70 Ⓐ Ⓑ Ⓒ Ⓓ Ⓔ	95 Ⓐ Ⓑ Ⓒ Ⓓ Ⓔ
21 Ⓐ Ⓑ Ⓒ Ⓓ Ⓔ	46 Ⓐ Ⓑ Ⓒ Ⓓ Ⓔ	71 Ⓐ Ⓑ Ⓒ Ⓓ Ⓔ	96 Ⓐ Ⓑ Ⓒ Ⓓ Ⓔ
22 Ⓐ Ⓑ Ⓒ Ⓓ Ⓔ	47 Ⓐ Ⓑ Ⓒ Ⓓ Ⓔ	72 Ⓐ Ⓑ Ⓒ Ⓓ Ⓔ	97 Ⓐ Ⓑ Ⓒ Ⓓ Ⓔ
23 Ⓐ Ⓑ Ⓒ Ⓓ Ⓔ	48 Ⓐ Ⓑ Ⓒ Ⓓ Ⓔ	73 Ⓐ Ⓑ Ⓒ Ⓓ Ⓔ	98 Ⓐ Ⓑ Ⓒ Ⓓ Ⓔ
24 Ⓐ Ⓑ Ⓒ Ⓓ Ⓔ	49 Ⓐ Ⓑ Ⓒ Ⓓ Ⓔ	74 Ⓐ Ⓑ Ⓒ Ⓓ Ⓔ	99 Ⓐ Ⓑ Ⓒ Ⓓ Ⓔ
25 Ⓐ Ⓑ Ⓒ Ⓓ Ⓔ	50 Ⓐ Ⓑ Ⓒ Ⓓ Ⓔ	75 Ⓐ Ⓑ Ⓒ Ⓓ Ⓔ	100 Ⓐ Ⓑ Ⓒ Ⓓ Ⓔ

The Princeton Review

1. YOUR NAME: _____
(Print)   Last   First   M.I.

SIGNATURE: _____   **DATE:** _____ / _____ / _____

HOME ADDRESS: _____
(Print)   Number and Street

_____   **E-MAIL:** _____
City   State   Zip

PHONE NO.: _____   **SCHOOL:** _____   **CLASS OF:** _____
(Print)

IMPORTANT: Please fill in these boxes exactly as shown on the back cover of your test book. ▼

OpScan *i*NSIGHT™ forms by Pearson NCS EM-255325-1:654321
Printed in U.S.A.

© The Princeton Review, Inc.

5. YOUR NAME

First 4 letters of last name				FIRST INIT	MID INIT
Ⓐ	Ⓐ	Ⓐ	Ⓐ	Ⓐ	Ⓐ
Ⓑ	Ⓑ	Ⓑ	Ⓑ	Ⓑ	Ⓑ
Ⓒ	Ⓒ	Ⓒ	Ⓒ	Ⓒ	Ⓒ
Ⓓ	Ⓓ	Ⓓ	Ⓓ	Ⓓ	Ⓓ
Ⓔ	Ⓔ	Ⓔ	Ⓔ	Ⓔ	Ⓔ
Ⓕ	Ⓕ	Ⓕ	Ⓕ	Ⓕ	Ⓕ
Ⓖ	Ⓖ	Ⓖ	Ⓖ	Ⓖ	Ⓖ
Ⓗ	Ⓗ	Ⓗ	Ⓗ	Ⓗ	Ⓗ
Ⓘ	Ⓘ	Ⓘ	Ⓘ	Ⓘ	Ⓘ
Ⓙ	Ⓙ	Ⓙ	Ⓙ	Ⓙ	Ⓙ
Ⓚ	Ⓚ	Ⓚ	Ⓚ	Ⓚ	Ⓚ
Ⓛ	Ⓛ	Ⓛ	Ⓛ	Ⓛ	Ⓛ
Ⓜ	Ⓜ	Ⓜ	Ⓜ	Ⓜ	Ⓜ
Ⓝ	Ⓝ	Ⓝ	Ⓝ	Ⓝ	Ⓝ
Ⓞ	Ⓞ	Ⓞ	Ⓞ	Ⓞ	Ⓞ
Ⓟ	Ⓟ	Ⓟ	Ⓟ	Ⓟ	Ⓟ
Ⓠ	Ⓠ	Ⓠ	Ⓠ	Ⓠ	Ⓠ
Ⓡ	Ⓡ	Ⓡ	Ⓡ	Ⓡ	Ⓡ
Ⓢ	Ⓢ	Ⓢ	Ⓢ	Ⓢ	Ⓢ
Ⓣ	Ⓣ	Ⓣ	Ⓣ	Ⓣ	Ⓣ
Ⓤ	Ⓤ	Ⓤ	Ⓤ	Ⓤ	Ⓤ
Ⓥ	Ⓥ	Ⓥ	Ⓥ	Ⓥ	Ⓥ
Ⓦ	Ⓦ	Ⓦ	Ⓦ	Ⓦ	Ⓦ
Ⓧ	Ⓧ	Ⓧ	Ⓧ	Ⓧ	Ⓧ
Ⓨ	Ⓨ	Ⓨ	Ⓨ	Ⓨ	Ⓨ
Ⓩ	Ⓩ	Ⓩ	Ⓩ	Ⓩ	Ⓩ

2. TEST FORM

_____

3. TEST CODE

⓪ ⓪ ⓪ ⓪	⓪ ⓪ ⓪ ⓪ ⓪ ⓪ ⓪

(bubbles 0–9 columns)

4. PHONE NUMBER

(bubbles 0–9 columns)

6. DATE OF BIRTH

MONTH	DAY		YEAR	
○ JAN				
○ FEB				
○ MAR	⓪	⓪	⓪	⓪
○ APR	①	①	①	①
○ MAY	②	②	②	②
○ JUN	③	③	③	③
○ JUL		④	④	④
○ AUG		⑤	⑤	⑤
○ SEP		⑥	⑥	⑥
○ OCT		⑦	⑦	⑦
○ NOV		⑧	⑧	⑧
○ DEC		⑨	⑨	⑨

7. SEX

○ MALE
○ FEMALE

8. OTHER

1	Ⓐ	Ⓑ	Ⓒ	Ⓓ	Ⓔ
2	Ⓐ	Ⓑ	Ⓒ	Ⓓ	Ⓔ
3	Ⓐ	Ⓑ	Ⓒ	Ⓓ	Ⓔ

Begin with number 1 for each new section of the test. Leave blank any extra answer spaces.

SECTION 1

1 Ⓐ Ⓑ Ⓒ Ⓓ Ⓔ	26 Ⓐ Ⓑ Ⓒ Ⓓ Ⓔ	51 Ⓐ Ⓑ Ⓒ Ⓓ Ⓔ	76 Ⓐ Ⓑ Ⓒ Ⓓ Ⓔ
2 Ⓐ Ⓑ Ⓒ Ⓓ Ⓔ	27 Ⓐ Ⓑ Ⓒ Ⓓ Ⓔ	52 Ⓐ Ⓑ Ⓒ Ⓓ Ⓔ	77 Ⓐ Ⓑ Ⓒ Ⓓ Ⓔ
3 Ⓐ Ⓑ Ⓒ Ⓓ Ⓔ	28 Ⓐ Ⓑ Ⓒ Ⓓ Ⓔ	53 Ⓐ Ⓑ Ⓒ Ⓓ Ⓔ	78 Ⓐ Ⓑ Ⓒ Ⓓ Ⓔ
4 Ⓐ Ⓑ Ⓒ Ⓓ Ⓔ	29 Ⓐ Ⓑ Ⓒ Ⓓ Ⓔ	54 Ⓐ Ⓑ Ⓒ Ⓓ Ⓔ	79 Ⓐ Ⓑ Ⓒ Ⓓ Ⓔ
5 Ⓐ Ⓑ Ⓒ Ⓓ Ⓔ	30 Ⓐ Ⓑ Ⓒ Ⓓ Ⓔ	55 Ⓐ Ⓑ Ⓒ Ⓓ Ⓔ	80 Ⓐ Ⓑ Ⓒ Ⓓ Ⓔ
6 Ⓐ Ⓑ Ⓒ Ⓓ Ⓔ	31 Ⓐ Ⓑ Ⓒ Ⓓ Ⓔ	56 Ⓐ Ⓑ Ⓒ Ⓓ Ⓔ	81 Ⓐ Ⓑ Ⓒ Ⓓ Ⓔ
7 Ⓐ Ⓑ Ⓒ Ⓓ Ⓔ	32 Ⓐ Ⓑ Ⓒ Ⓓ Ⓔ	57 Ⓐ Ⓑ Ⓒ Ⓓ Ⓔ	82 Ⓐ Ⓑ Ⓒ Ⓓ Ⓔ
8 Ⓐ Ⓑ Ⓒ Ⓓ Ⓔ	33 Ⓐ Ⓑ Ⓒ Ⓓ Ⓔ	58 Ⓐ Ⓑ Ⓒ Ⓓ Ⓔ	83 Ⓐ Ⓑ Ⓒ Ⓓ Ⓔ
9 Ⓐ Ⓑ Ⓒ Ⓓ Ⓔ	34 Ⓐ Ⓑ Ⓒ Ⓓ Ⓔ	59 Ⓐ Ⓑ Ⓒ Ⓓ Ⓔ	84 Ⓐ Ⓑ Ⓒ Ⓓ Ⓔ
10 Ⓐ Ⓑ Ⓒ Ⓓ Ⓔ	35 Ⓐ Ⓑ Ⓒ Ⓓ Ⓔ	60 Ⓐ Ⓑ Ⓒ Ⓓ Ⓔ	85 Ⓐ Ⓑ Ⓒ Ⓓ Ⓔ
11 Ⓐ Ⓑ Ⓒ Ⓓ Ⓔ	36 Ⓐ Ⓑ Ⓒ Ⓓ Ⓔ	61 Ⓐ Ⓑ Ⓒ Ⓓ Ⓔ	86 Ⓐ Ⓑ Ⓒ Ⓓ Ⓔ
12 Ⓐ Ⓑ Ⓒ Ⓓ Ⓔ	37 Ⓐ Ⓑ Ⓒ Ⓓ Ⓔ	62 Ⓐ Ⓑ Ⓒ Ⓓ Ⓔ	87 Ⓐ Ⓑ Ⓒ Ⓓ Ⓔ
13 Ⓐ Ⓑ Ⓒ Ⓓ Ⓔ	38 Ⓐ Ⓑ Ⓒ Ⓓ Ⓔ	63 Ⓐ Ⓑ Ⓒ Ⓓ Ⓔ	88 Ⓐ Ⓑ Ⓒ Ⓓ Ⓔ
14 Ⓐ Ⓑ Ⓒ Ⓓ Ⓔ	39 Ⓐ Ⓑ Ⓒ Ⓓ Ⓔ	64 Ⓐ Ⓑ Ⓒ Ⓓ Ⓔ	89 Ⓐ Ⓑ Ⓒ Ⓓ Ⓔ
15 Ⓐ Ⓑ Ⓒ Ⓓ Ⓔ	40 Ⓐ Ⓑ Ⓒ Ⓓ Ⓔ	65 Ⓐ Ⓑ Ⓒ Ⓓ Ⓔ	90 Ⓐ Ⓑ Ⓒ Ⓓ Ⓔ
16 Ⓐ Ⓑ Ⓒ Ⓓ Ⓔ	41 Ⓐ Ⓑ Ⓒ Ⓓ Ⓔ	66 Ⓐ Ⓑ Ⓒ Ⓓ Ⓔ	91 Ⓐ Ⓑ Ⓒ Ⓓ Ⓔ
17 Ⓐ Ⓑ Ⓒ Ⓓ Ⓔ	42 Ⓐ Ⓑ Ⓒ Ⓓ Ⓔ	67 Ⓐ Ⓑ Ⓒ Ⓓ Ⓔ	92 Ⓐ Ⓑ Ⓒ Ⓓ Ⓔ
18 Ⓐ Ⓑ Ⓒ Ⓓ Ⓔ	43 Ⓐ Ⓑ Ⓒ Ⓓ Ⓔ	68 Ⓐ Ⓑ Ⓒ Ⓓ Ⓔ	93 Ⓐ Ⓑ Ⓒ Ⓓ Ⓔ
19 Ⓐ Ⓑ Ⓒ Ⓓ Ⓔ	44 Ⓐ Ⓑ Ⓒ Ⓓ Ⓔ	69 Ⓐ Ⓑ Ⓒ Ⓓ Ⓔ	94 Ⓐ Ⓑ Ⓒ Ⓓ Ⓔ
20 Ⓐ Ⓑ Ⓒ Ⓓ Ⓔ	45 Ⓐ Ⓑ Ⓒ Ⓓ Ⓔ	70 Ⓐ Ⓑ Ⓒ Ⓓ Ⓔ	95 Ⓐ Ⓑ Ⓒ Ⓓ Ⓔ
21 Ⓐ Ⓑ Ⓒ Ⓓ Ⓔ	46 Ⓐ Ⓑ Ⓒ Ⓓ Ⓔ	71 Ⓐ Ⓑ Ⓒ Ⓓ Ⓔ	96 Ⓐ Ⓑ Ⓒ Ⓓ Ⓔ
22 Ⓐ Ⓑ Ⓒ Ⓓ Ⓔ	47 Ⓐ Ⓑ Ⓒ Ⓓ Ⓔ	72 Ⓐ Ⓑ Ⓒ Ⓓ Ⓔ	97 Ⓐ Ⓑ Ⓒ Ⓓ Ⓔ
23 Ⓐ Ⓑ Ⓒ Ⓓ Ⓔ	48 Ⓐ Ⓑ Ⓒ Ⓓ Ⓔ	73 Ⓐ Ⓑ Ⓒ Ⓓ Ⓔ	98 Ⓐ Ⓑ Ⓒ Ⓓ Ⓔ
24 Ⓐ Ⓑ Ⓒ Ⓓ Ⓔ	49 Ⓐ Ⓑ Ⓒ Ⓓ Ⓔ	74 Ⓐ Ⓑ Ⓒ Ⓓ Ⓔ	99 Ⓐ Ⓑ Ⓒ Ⓓ Ⓔ
25 Ⓐ Ⓑ Ⓒ Ⓓ Ⓔ	50 Ⓐ Ⓑ Ⓒ Ⓓ Ⓔ	75 Ⓐ Ⓑ Ⓒ Ⓓ Ⓔ	100 Ⓐ Ⓑ Ⓒ Ⓓ Ⓔ

NOTES

Navigate the admissions process with more guidance from the experts.

Ace the APs:

Cracking the AP Biology Exam, 2013 Edition
978-0-307-94508-2 • $18.99/$21.99 Can.
Ebook: 978-0-307-94580-8

Cracking the AP Calculus AB & BC Exams, 2013 Edition
978-0-307-94486-3 • $19.99/$23.99 Can.
Ebook: 978-0-307-94451-1

Cracking the AP Chemistry Exam, 2013 Edition
978-0-307-94488-7 • $18.99/$21.99 Can.
Ebook: 978-0-307-94452-8

Cracking the AP Economics Macro & Micro Exams, 2013 Edition
978-0-307-94509-9 • $18.00/$21.00 Can.
Ebook: 978-0-307-94581-5

Cracking the AP English Language & Composition Exam, 2013 Edition
978-0-307-94511-2 • $18.00/$21.00 Can.
Ebook: 978-0-307-94582-2

Cracking the AP English Literature & Composition Exam, 2013 Edition
978-0-307-94512-9 • $18.00/$21.00 Can.
Ebook: 978-0-307-94583-9

Cracking the AP Environmental Science Exam, 2013 Edition
978-0-307-94513-6 • $18.99/$21.99 Can.
Ebook: 978-0-307-94584-6

Cracking the AP European History Exam, 2013 Edition
978-0-307-94489-4 • $18.99/$21.99 Can.
Ebook: 978-0-307-94453-5

Cracking the AP Human Geography Exam, 2013 Edition
978-0-307-94514-3 • $18.00/$21.00 Can.

Cracking the AP Physics B Exam, 2013 Edition
978-0-307-94515-0 • $18.99/$21.99 Can.
Ebook: 978-0-307-94585-3

Cracking the AP Physics C Exam, 2013 Edition
978-0-307-94516-7 • $18.99/$21.99 Can.

Cracking the AP Psychology Exam, 2013 Edition
978-0-307-94517-4 • $18.00/$21.00 Can.
Ebook: 978-0-307-94586-0

Cracking the AP Spanish Exam with Audio CD, 2013 Edition
978-0-307-94518-1 • $24.99/$28.99 Can.

Cracking the AP Statistics Exam, 2013 Edition
978-0-307-94519-8 • $19.99/$23.99 Can.

Cracking the AP U.S. Government & Politics Exam, 2013 Edition
978-0-307-94520-4 • $18.99/$21.99 Can.
Ebook: 978-0-307-94587-7

Cracking the AP U.S. History Exam, 2013 Edition
978-0-307-94490-7 • $18.99/$21.99 Can.
Ebook: 978-0-307-94447-4

Cracking the AP World History Exam, 2013 Edition
978-0-307-94491-7 • $18.99/$21.99 Can.
Ebook: 978-0-307-94445-0

Essential AP Biology (flashcards)
978-0-375-42803-6 • $18.99/$20.99 Can.

Essential AP Psychology (flashcards)
978-0-375-42801-2 • $18.99/$20.99 Can.

Essential AP U.S. Government & Politics (flashcards)
978-0-375-42804-3 • $18.99/$20.99 Can.

Essential AP U.S. History (flashcards)
978-0-375-42800-5 • $18.99/$20.99 Can.

Essential AP World History (flashcards)
978-0-375-42802-9 • $18.99/$20.99 Can.